"I consider myself to be pretty emotionally intelligent. I've been part of a weekly men's group tending to our emotional lives and working to get more in touch with our deeper selves. We explore the deeply entrenched patterns we each have that keep us from being as happy and effective as possible. Over the last 17 years, we've supported each other in this work by bringing techniques we've learned in meditation practice, reevaluation counseling, and other strategies and techniques out there.

"Throughout this time, I've developed a deep knowledge of myself and am now routinely able to make connections between very old patterns and places where I feel stuck today. I've also become very facile with my emotions – I know what's going on inside, can let my feelings flow and express them with relative ease. Despite all of this, I have noticed just how difficult it is to really change. Feeling my feelings and knowing my patterns is one thing; crafting the life that I want and know that I'm capable of is another.

"This is where Joe's articulation of the Feeling Path comes in. The tremendous contribution Joe has made in developing the Feeling Path is to help us transform these stuck patterns into healing and wholeness. Each stuck pattern, each feeling of failure, each sense of shame literally becomes a part of us that has a positive manifestation and a tangible role in our joy. Joe's method brings to life a sense of lightness, relief, humor and possibility rather than the heaviness that can come with more traditional therapies. It is the most basic and most revolutionary kind of "self-help." I recommend the Feeling Path as a great supplement to any other mental health practice, any healing practice, any spiritual practice."

– Paul Fischburg, Seattle

"One of the first things I learned from Joe is that the universe tends toward wholeness. That might sound like a nice sentiment until you recognize that you are a part of this universe and given the right guidance you will recognize that wholeness is your natural tendency and your body is capable of showing you the way. For me, Joe was and continues to be the right guidance.

"In many ways he has demystified and made accessible to all people the power to literally map their consciousness and realign their inner geography. There are pathways to inner-knowing that the intellect cannot walk, and Joe has created a method that allows the deeper levels of consciousness to reveal and transform themselves. His work has certainly been powerful and transformative for me."

— David Robinson, The Circle Project

I was in the middle of a tough time where I was starting to identify past abuses in my life. I had many areas where I couldn't feel. Or when I did feel, I couldn't turn off the negative emotions. Thus, I was spiraling downward.

The Feeling Path helped me not only identify my feelings within my body, but the process then allowed me to convert them into something wonderful and beautiful that I could build upon. It really changed my path and helped me to see a better life. Thanks to Joe for his patience, his wisdom and insight.

— Carrie Bogner, Seattle

We give thanks

We give thanks for places of simplicity and peace.

Let us find such a place within ourselves.

We give thanks for places of refuge and beauty.

Let us find such a place within ourselves.

We give thanks for places of nature's truth and freedom of joy,

inspiration and renewal, places where all creatures may find

acceptance and belonging. Let us search for these places in

the world, in ourselves, and in others.

Let us restore them. Let us strengthen and protect them

and let us create them.

May we mend this outer world

according to the truth of our inner life

and may our souls be shaped and nourished

by nature's eternal wisdom.

– Michael Leunig

The Feeling Path

Restoring the Natural Wisdom of the Feeling Mind

A practical guide

PREVIEW EDITION
Limited Release

Joe Shirley

Published by Joe Shirley
Port Townsend, WA 98368

Printed by CreateSpace

Preview Edition, Limited Release, October 2011

Available for a limited time at:
CreateSpace.com/3637635 and Amazon.com

Front cover image courtesy of iStockPhoto.com/azpworldwide

Back cover images are composite Feeling Path maps by Joe Shirley

ISBN-13: 978-1463632823
ISBN-10: 1463632827

Contents

Preface to the Preview Edition

Dear friends,

This book holds wisdom. Not so much in the words I've written, but in what they can do for you. The discoveries I share here give you direct access to the deep wisdom within yourself. As you access that wisdom you will rediscover for yourself, through relevant and meaningful inner experience, many of the teachings from the great wisdom traditions. You will find your "inner guru."

At the same time, these discoveries fly in the face of many conventional beliefs about the mind, feeling, and human nature, beliefs that even you are likely to hold today. The most entrenched of these conventional beliefs – ideas that people are flawed, sinful, or animal in nature, and must rely on mechanisms of "command and control" to achieve any kind of peace or happiness – these beliefs are responsible for ever-more-disastrous rifts in our society and a steady march toward environmental crisis.

We must find alternate beliefs to guide us. I contend these new beliefs will have to meet a few criteria for them to have any hope to one day become the new standard.

1. These beliefs must emerge naturally from the inner experience of wholeness with presence.

2. Encountering these beliefs for the first time must compellingly invite and facilitate the experience of wholeness with presence, even among those for whom this experience is foreign or forgotten.

3. These beliefs must be easy to articulate and easy to understand.

4. Finally, these beliefs must support a new way of living together in which peace, happiness, and sustainability come easily and spontaneously.

I believe the discoveries in this book give us a simple practice for cultivating the experience of wholeness with presence, meeting the conditions for the first criterion. I also believe that if many of us engage in this practice and share our experiences with one another, the beliefs that emerge from our collective meaning-making will naturally evolve over time to meet criteria two through four.

This can't happen without you. It has taken me 17 years to wrap my head around these discoveries, to try to fully understand their implications and applications in our lives, and to develop easy ways to communicate them. With this book, I feel I've done the rough hewing. But I'm not finished yet, not by a long shot, and I can't do the work that remains by myself.

That's why I need your help. I'm putting out this Preview Edition as an invitation. I invite you to read the book, use what you learn, and join with others in offering your feedback and further developing the ideas and practices. To help you do this, I am creating a learning and collaboration community at FeelingPath.com. You'll be able to ask for help, take part in community conversations both online and over the phone, participate in learning activities, and offer your feedback. Please join me there.

My vision is that this book sees frequent updates as the knowledge advances through our continued exploration and application of this exciting new work. Please help me bring that vision into being right from the beginning. Let's work together to make the official First Edition of The Feeling Path as useful and provocative as possible.

With sincere wishes for your highest well-being,

Joe Shirley
Port Townsend
October 2011

Part 1:
Welcome to
The Feeling Path.

My Discovery

When I first discovered how to instantly shift a negative feeling to positive, I was stunned. I was lying in bed on a sunny afternoon, depressed. I focused on the actual, felt experience of the depression: a heavy, downward pull in my chest. I wondered what would happen if the direction reversed, if it were pulling upward instead. And I tried it out.

Not only was I able to imagine the pull going upward, but the feeling followed it. In seconds my mood lifted. I felt downright cheerful.

According to conventional models of psychology, we're not supposed to be able to do this. But I did. And you can too.

WARNING: The technique you are about to learn goes against many common beliefs about the mind. Using it may lead to strong feelings of shock and disbelief. You may find yourself thinking, "I can't believe this. It's so simple. Why didn't somebody show me this years ago?" You may ask yourself, "Why did I have to suffer through all that therapy / medication / seminars / mood swings / depression / anxiety / etc.??" These are good questions. I've asked them myself.

A year after I first discovered the technique, I worked with myself for a full day, mapping and moving seven different feeling states to bring a permanent end to my bipolar disorder. At the end of that day I felt like I was no longer the person I had come to know as myself. At the same time, I felt more authentically "myself" than I had ever felt in my entire life.

I cried, both out of gratitude for discovering this person who had lain hidden for so long, and out of grief. I had lost 15 years of my life which had been ruled by mood swings and all manner of disruption they had caused. And I would never get back my young adult life. It was gone forever. I dedicate this book to all those people who are losing the best years of their lives to emotional suffering, in hope that what I share may help bring that suffering to an end and liberate many bright and beautiful people to enjoy the sweet juice of life and share their gifts with the rest of us.

Bipolar disorder is supposed to be a life sentence. The experts say it is caused by a broken brain, and that it requires life-long management by strong medications, coping skills, and therapy.

But I am no longer bipolar. Period. And I ended my intense mood swings using the disarmingly simple technique I'm going to show you here. No therapy. No medications. No coping or management necessary.

You may have similar results. Your results may be different. I can't say for sure. I do know that I've guided hundreds of people through this technique for a wide range of issues. (The benefits of The Feeling Path are very definitely NOT limited to those with bipolar disorder, and are available to people with almost any kind of emotional distress or discomfort.) Most people I've worked with have experienced similarly extraordinary benefits. I hope you will too.

I've written this book with the intention of sharing as much as I can right now with people who can use what I've discovered. Some of you are people who want relief, now. Others are professionals whose job it is to help those who seek relief. Still others are those with an interest in discovering new ways to both alleviate suffering and promote the highest human flourishing. All of you will find something of value in these pages.

Now, let's get started.

Your Journey Starts Here

Seventeen years ago I walked through a doorway into a new territory I call the feeling mind. Ever since then I've been exploring this territory, getting to know my way around, making sense of its features, learning how to get from here to there.

I want to invite you through that doorway. In some ways, the doorway I want to show you is no big deal. It is in your own mind, and it's familiar – you walk by it all day long. It's as if your mind is a house, and this door is one of those secret panels behind a bookshelf on the wall.

It's always there, but you don't notice it. None of us do. But when you discover which book to pull from the shelf, the doorway gently opens to reveal a passage to wondrous new vistas.

Normally in clichéd stories about a secret doorway, the bookshelf is in a mansion, and it leads to a secret room behind the library or something. This situation is the other way around. It's more like you are living in a closet, and the secret doorway opens into the mansion.

The feeling mind is magnificent, elegant, and beautifully structured. It is far more interesting to explore than the endless circles of cogitation or wrinkles of perception. And with the discovery of the doorway I'm about to show you, you can actually explore it in great detail and with amazing depth.

So you may be wondering where this so-called doorway could be. You might think you know pretty much all there is to know about your own mind. Maybe you've spent decades pursuing personal growth and therapy. You might even be a professional in one of the fields specializing in psychology or neuroscience.

But I can assure you, no matter how extensive your experience, you've walked right by this secret passage just like everyone else. Just like everyone else, you've noticed nothing remarkable. Nothing to call your attention to this particular spot in the wall, this particular section of bookshelf. Nothing to suggest that behind this innocuous facade lies treasure.

Let me be clear, here. The entire fields of psychology, psychopharmacology, neuroscience, and psychiatry have missed this territory. And the consequences are dreadful. Without understanding the feeling mind, modern mental health treatment is floundering.

In order to fully understand something in the natural world, you must first observe it. Science progresses through rigorous observation. You must have a method of observation which allows you to make clear, precise distinctions: this, not that. And your method must be reliable, providing the same observational results each time you use them to observe something which is not, itself, changing. We have excellent models of this in the physical sciences, where prosthetic devices for our senses like microscopes and telescopes have allowed us to reliably see things at very small or very large scales.

But at the moment, in the current state of affairs in psychology we have no such observational method with which to observe the actual, felt experience of feeling, mood, or emotion. We do have tools by which to derive images of the brain in action, but these are limited in their usefulness by our inability to correlate what we observe with precise descriptions of the actual, conscious experience that accompanies these images. We have no way of comparing the experience of one feeling state to another in the same person, let alone between one person and another.

This rudimentary state of affairs affects many millions of people. Without a way to rigorously observe feeling states, we have no way to fully understand how they work. We can only speculate. And so when people suffer with feeling states that disrupt their lives, they are at the mercy of professionals who have no clear understanding of feeling, professionals who are making do with whatever theory or practice is in vogue in their particular professional community.

At the moment, the treatment you receive for your suffering will depend on which type of professional you visit. A psychiatrist or family doctor will subscribe to the theory that your suffering is caused by imbalances in brain chemistry, the treatment for which is medication. A psychotherapist will most likely believe that your suffering arises from your history, and releasing it requires adequate processing, healing, forgiveness, analysis, or whatever flavor of terminology they have studied. Others, more pragmatic, will draw from a grab bag of tools, intuitively applying the one they feel matches your situation best.

Now any one of these professionals may provide you positive benefit, but that benefit is likely to be from one of five sources:

1) Your faith in the professional's ability to help you, supported by their effectiveness in conveying authority and confidence in their ability to help you, may confer a placebo effect.

2) Side effects of your medications may indicate to you that your medication is "working," and strengthen the placebo effect.

2) Your positive relationship with the therapist may add a new resilience and perspective to your life.

3) You may bring to your meetings an intuitive way of inviting your own feeling states to shift in a positive direction.

4) Your chosen professional may demonstrate an inner balance and vitality that inspires and serves as a model for you.

Any or all of these are likely to improve your suffering. However, let's not fool ourselves. None of these rely on an actual understanding of feeling, of what it is, or how it works.

And so in addition to the many people who improve by seeking professional help, we have many more who do not improve, or who unfortunately experience an increase in suffering. For many people, this state of affairs puts them in an untenable position.

I was one of those people. Twenty-five years ago, my life was a shambles. I went to see a psychiatrist after reading a book that suggested a reason for my crisis. He confirmed that I met all the diagnostic criteria for bipolar disorder, and treatment required that I start medication immediately. I took the lithium for 10 days before hurling it into the trash basket, knowing that the choice I was making was a serious one. On the one hand, the medications available to help me would lead to side effects that would diminish my capacity for a quality life. On the other hand, my prognosis without medication was a likelihood of escalating disruption, with a high risk of ending in suicide.

This is the same untenable position many millions of people are placed in every year. Damned if you do, and damned if you don't. Uncertain benefits combined with high financial costs and potentially devastating side effects on the one hand, uncertain progress and the specter of continued, intractable suffering on the other. Without an understanding of what we're actually working with, we are left driving a high mountain highway with no guard rails and no brakes. There are casualties all along the way.

I would like to digress a bit, and take this argument one step farther, because I see it as one of the most important issues of our times. Because much of the professional community does not understand feeling, it places more and more emphasis on non-feeling solutions to suffering, medication being one of the most strongly promoted, with cognitive-behavioral approaches close behind. The more these other solutions are pushed as the answer to people's suffering, the more people divest themselves of the wisdom of feeling. Over time, individuals who have come to rely on a) chemistry and b) thoughts/behavior to attempt to manage their inner lives lose touch with the full richness of feeling. They become essentially feeling-disabled.

What are the consequences of this? For one, feeling-disabled parents tend to raise feeling-disabled children. The subtle, elegant dance between parent and young child becomes crippled, and the child is cut off from the rich, nuanced feedback she needs to learn about her world, and more importantly about herself.

A related consequence is that people's relationships, from their intimate relationships to their professional ones, become crippled as well. Feeling-disabled people interact more from the intellect, from rules and ideology, from scripted memory or expectation. Lost is the beautiful dance of humanity, and with its loss, others who are not directly disabled find their own feeling compromised. We can see this happening on a grand scale in our public conversations, where high-profile people have lost the ability to connect with both their allies and their adversaries, and these public conversations have devolved into the lowest of debates and attacks. Feeling-disabled people jump into the fray and advance its damaging effects. Feeling-intact people find themselves at a loss for how to engage, and withdraw.

These influences are feeding back into the system. The more we divest ourselves of the wisdom of feeling, the more crazy and difficult becomes our experience of life among other people. And the more crazy and difficult life seems, the more strongly we cling to the solutions offered us: stronger medication and stronger ideology, which feed back into further disabling of feeling. It is no wonder our nation is experiencing a pandemic of mental health issues, with rates of diagnosis and medication escalating year by year. Where is this going? Unless we succeed at reclaiming the wisdom of the feeling mind, and placing it at the center of our mental health policy as well as our public life, I fear for our future.

Fortunately, I believe this perilous trend can now be reversed. What I am sharing with you here is the missing method for precise observation through which we can advance the science of feeling. It is also the most elegant of methods by which any one of us can re-access the wisdom of feeling, and open ourselves again to the full richness of our human, feeling nature.

Whether you are a researcher or therapist, suffering or simply curious, I'm going to give you an introduction to this method and tell you how to use it for your own purposes. The method is simple enough for any non-professional to apply themselves, powerful enough to yield extraordinary results in the hands of someone with training. (I'll be offering training for professionals very soon. If you are interested, get involved at FeelingPath.com.)

For now, come with me. Let me show you how to pull the lever and open the passage to the wondrous mansion of the feeling mind.

What can you expect?

This method will require a bit of effort on your part. You won't "get it" without actually experiencing the results for yourself. So you deserve to know your efforts will be rewarded in great enough measure for you to take time out of the other important things in your life. Here's what you can expect to gain by reading the rest of this book, (and participating in the FeelingPath.com community).

1. For the average person experiencing inner distress, the opportunity for swift, permanent relief from almost any recurring pattern of dysfunctional mood, thought, or behavior.

2. For therapists, the opportunity to greatly improve your success in helping clients permanently transform recurring dysfunctional patterns.

3. For researchers, the opportunity to greatly enhance your ability to precisely identify inner feeling states of your research subjects, and to correlate those states with whatever your focus of research might be.

4. For those interested in philosophy, the opportunity for greater understanding of what makes us human: feeling, sentiment, inspiration, intuition – all those things considered soft or

difficult to define reveal themselves explicitly in the rigorous exploration of the feeling mind.

5.   For spiritual seekers, the opportunity for a more direct path to transcendent experience and greater access to the experience of mystery – the world of spirit is laid open to us in the structure of the feeling mind.

6.   For the adventurous, the opportunity to be a pioneer in one of the few frontiers remaining to the human project: the exploration of consciousness. Feeling Path Mapping opens exciting, uncharted territory for exploration.

7.   For the ambitious, the opportunity to lead the way in applying the new science of the feeling mind to getting breakthrough results in therapy, medicine, pharmacology, sports, performing arts, public speaking, personal growth, yoga, and who knows what else.

8.   For everyone, the opportunity to amplify and deepen the sweetness, fulfillment, enjoyment and meaning in your life.

If any of these areas are energizing to you, I can guarantee you will not be disappointed. I intend to lay it all out for you, as much as I can in this first book.

The discovery of the feeling mind opens a new field with unlimited promise. If you're a reasonably active, take charge kind of person, you should have no trouble at all extracting many hundreds of times the value of the time you spend absorbing this book. Please join us at FeelingPath.com for support in pursuing your passion through applying The Feeling Path.

So… are you in? Yes? Let's go!

A note about working alone

I highly encourage you to do this work with a facilitator. (See the facilitator's guide to mapping and moving in Part 3.) However, many of you will be quite comfortable working on your own using only the guidance of this book.

If this is your choice, let me alert you to the primary challenge of working with yourself, and suggest how to address this challenge. As you might expect having developed this process, I have worked almost exclusively as a solo explorer. I've had a great deal of success working alone, so I can't very well tell you not to do it. But it has been difficult at times, and I can tell you that things go much faster and more smoothly for those people who have the benefit of my facilitation than it does for those working independently.

The most significant challenge in working alone is when you choose to explore a feeling state that is un-resourceful such as sadness, lethargy, confusion or mental fog, you must first access this feeling – you must feel it in order to engage your sensory imagery.

Accessing this type of feeling can make continuing the work difficult. When you are feeling confusion, for example, anything you do can seem confusing to you. When you access sadness or lethargy, it can be hard to keep up your motivation and stick to a plan. When you are in touch with mental fog, it can be challenging to be clear about your experience.

An attentive facilitator will enable you to enter into these feelings while holding the container of the process. The facilitator can stay with the process, manage the details of mapping, take all the notes, and keep the explorer moving forward to the next step. But when you are exploring alone, it is easy to spin out, get lost in the feeling, and fail to follow through the process to its end. You can easily wind up wallowing in your emotions.

My advice is to externalize the process in whatever way works best for you. The first time I took myself through an extended mapping and transforming process with very intense feelings, I used my word processor and engaged in a dialogue between myself as explorer and myself as guide. I would ask the next question in the series as the facilitator by typing it on the screen. Then I would read the question as the explorer, and answer it, typing my answer on the screen for the facilitator role to read.

Nowadays, I often glance at the printed questions or ask the questions out loud in order to externalize them. It makes a big difference in my ability to follow through and complete what I begin no matter how heavy or challenging the feelings are. I find that when I remind myself to trust the process and follow it through, I can stay on track and complete the work. For many of you, simply having this section of the book will do the job.

Another technique you might consider is to use your mp3 player to record yourself asking the sequence of questions. You can play the questions back through headphones as you go into your exploration, pausing when necessary to take your notes. I haven't tried this method myself, but I imagine it could work very well for some people. If you'd like a recording of my voice leading you through the questions, contact me and I'll make that available.

When to use Feeling Path Mapping

The natural function of feeling is to provide accurate feedback about the state of balance in our life. When things are out of balance, our feelings appropriately signal us. We may feel fear, sadness, hurt, anger, and other feelings of distress.

These feelings call attention to themselves. When we have healthy feelings, they highlight what is out of balance, exaggerating it in our perception, and they motivate us to take action to restore balance. We move away from what threatens us, move toward what we've lost, appease what hurts us , confront what violates us, and in many other ways address the sources of our experiences of imbalance.

But when we are prevented from either feeling a signal or acting on its message, that signal can get locked into place. Distressing feeling states which originally signaled a state of imbalance become disconnected from the original situation and persist far into the future.

Many times these locked feeling signals remain largely out of our awareness, operating behind the scenes to shape our choices, perception, beliefs and behaviors. Often the ways these underground feeling states shape our lives lead us to recreate situations parallel to the one which stimulated the feelings in the first place. We find ourselves drawn to partners, workplaces, and communities which recreate the original dynamics of our family, for example. It's almost as if the feeling states are begging for an opportunity to complete their mission by giving us a chance to feel the signal and act to restore the balance in our lives.

I'm guessing you know what I'm talking about. You find yourself repeating certain patterns in your life, whether in your relationships, your profession, or your social life. In these patterns you experience over and over again the same sets of feelings and strong emotions. They happen seemingly of their own accord, almost as if directed by an unseen hand, ridiculously predictable. We sometimes feel we are at the mercy of these patterns, that we are powerless to prevent their recurrence.

These are the situations in which The Feeling Path is most useful. Mapping allows you to tease apart the various feeling states that drive your pattern. Moving reconnects each feeling to the experience of wholeness it was originally trying to achieve. Once feelings have been shifted, they are able to function once again as accurate feedback about the state of balance in your life.

When you systematically run the entire set of feeling states which drive any challenging pattern through the three steps of The Feeling Path, you will experience a wonderful liberation. The pattern will no longer own you. You will be free, and you will find yourself spontaneously making new choices, taking new paths, closing some old doors and opening new ones.

Three steps

The first step in The Feeling Path is to map it. Using the questions later in this section, you will put your attention on the actual, felt experience of one specific feeling, mood, or emotion you choose. You will identify its location, the qualities of substance it seems to have, its temperature, color, movement and sound.

These questions will help you create a tangible image of the feeling. This image gives you clarity about the feeling, and helps give you a little distance from it as well. So it's perfectly safe to dive into just about any emotion you might have using this mapping process.

Step two is to move it. You're going to use that image almost like a handle to shift the image towards what feels better. You'll shift the temperature, a little cooler, a little warmer, seeking just the right temperature. You'll shift the substance, a little harder or softer, a little heavier or lighter, all the way to discover just what qualities of substance feel best for that part of you. You'll do the same for the other aspects of the image, until you have completely transformed the image, and with it, the feeling itself.

Following the image toward what feels best is like following a compass. It points your way home; points to true north for you. And that feeling, that emotion, no matter how dark or difficult it might have been, will transform in a matter of just a couple of minutes into something that can be surprising to you how positive and powerful it is.

Step three is to live it. In this third and final step, you're going to take that new, positive feeling state and invite it back into the actual shape of your life, the actual situations that you inhabit. You'll see where it wants to lead you; what natural actions come from that new place.

Knowing where to look

Feeling is what makes us most human, yet it remains the most mysterious aspect of our consciousness. It is not emotion, which simply prepares our bodies for threats and opportunities. Feeling is complex, nuanced, profound. It inspires great works of art and heinous acts of destruction. It liberates our spirit and holds us prisoner. We are immersed in feeling every waking moment, yet we can hardly talk about it. (How many times has language failed you when you tried to share what you felt with someone you cared about?)

So what is feeling, exactly? Let's take on this question, right here, right now, you and I. Well... where do we start?

In science, when we want to know about something we start with precise observation. But how can we observe the inner experience of feeling with any kind of precision? I can't see what you feel, can't measure it, can't observe it in any objective sense. And as we've already noticed, your trying to tell me in ordinary language about what you feel is going to be imprecise and inadequate.

But if we listen carefully to your language, we can find a clue. What are some typical statements you might make about feeling?

When describing how they feel, people say things like,

- My heart is heavy.

- My stomach is in knots.

- My head is foggy.

- I'm so mad I could spit fire.

- I'm full of energy.

- I feel cold and empty inside.

There are two things to notice about this language. First, there is often a location, as if each feeling experience occupies a specific region in space, relative to the body. And second, there are often qualities that can be compared to qualities of materials we find in the physical world.

Location and material

Feeling is such an ongoing part of our day to day existence that it fades into the background most of the time. Even when we're overrun by strong emotions, we tend to focus more on the contents of our thoughts and perceptions, and less on the actual, felt experience of feeling itself.

The doorway I'm going to share with you is the actual, felt experience of feeling as revealed through a series of questions relating it to location and material qualities. I'm going to turn your attention to that palpable, felt sense. We'll use a series of questions that elicit very specific, precise, tangible images of the actual, interior experience of a feeling state.

These questions link the powerful imagery centers of our brain with the somatosensory experiences of feeling.

The images they create form a kind of visceral handle we can use to manipulate a feeling, instantly and directly. The first time I did a rudimentary form of this Feeling Path Mapping was with a feeling of hopelessness, (part of a recurring and familiar depression). I noticed a palpable, downward "pull" in the middle of my chest. I wondered what would happen if the downward pull reversed direction, and I imagined it doing so.

The effect startled me. My mood lifted instantly and I felt strangely cheerful. What the hell? Today that simple beginning has evolved into a handful of questions that elicit the experiential location, temperature, substance quality, color, movement, and sound of a feeling state, then allow us to interact with that state to change it.

As a tool for exploring the experience of feeling, these questions are unparalleled. First, the image they elicit provides greater precision, vividness, and objectivity to the experience of feeling, mood, and emotion than any other method. Second, the image enables us to directly interact with any feeling, moving it this way and that, and in so doing to discover even more about its nature.

The importance of actual experience

Any time we use a tool to enhance our perception, our universe expands. When Anton Leeuwenhoek first peered through a hand made microscope into a few drops of pond water and discovered bacteria noodling around, our universe expanded. When Galileo pointed a telescope at Jupiter and described its moons, our universe expanded. When Wilhelm Röntgen exposed his wife's hand to X-rays over a photographic plate and created the first visual image of the living skeleton, our universe expanded.

When our universe expands, it is very difficult for those who have not directly experienced that expansion to make sense of it. Try describing bacteria to tribal people of New Guinea. They'll laugh at you. Try explaining the orbits of Saturn's moons to a pre-Copernican theologian; he would disdain you.

It's no different here. This Feeling Path Mapping tool greatly expands our capacity to perceive feeling. It reveals patterns and structures that were previously invisible to all of us. The universe within us, the universe of our feeling mind, has expanded.

So I ask you: please be willing to play. Don't simply read this book without participating. If you are to understand this new territory it describes, you must roll up your sleeves. You must actually use the questions I share, you must explore your own feeling states. It may also help for you to share your explorations with others who are similarly exploring. Sit down with a friend or loved one and ask these questions of one another. Walk into this new territory together, point at the strange new sights and whisper "Ooh" and "Aah" and "Wow" to one another. You'll never have a second first time, so you might as well share it with someone you care about.

Step One: Map It.

To get started, think about what it is in your life that you would like to change. Where do you feel a gap between what you believe is possible in your life and what you're actually living? Start to explore your experience of that. Reflect on the last time you got caught in that loop or found yourself reacting in that old way that isn't the way you want to be in the world.

Choosing one feeling to work with

What is the pattern you would like to work with? Give it a name, and make a few notes on the following page or on a separate piece of paper, about your experience of this pattern in your life. Then reflect on the different feeling states that are typically part of this pattern for you. Make a list of these, giving the different feelings whatever names seem useful to you. (No need to restrict yourself to the standard vocabulary of emotion.)

BRIEFLY DESCRIBE YOUR PATTERN:

LIST YOUR FEELING STATES:

Choose one feeling state. How would you describe to a friend what it's like to have that feeling?

Choose one of those feelings, the feeling that seems like the biggest obstacle to having the life you want. What feeling, if it could cease to be part of your experience, would enable you to have a much easier time? Or even better, what if you could flip it upside down, turn it inside out, and have the feeling become its opposite? Which one of the feelings you listed would give you the greatest benefit if it were replaced by its opposite?

First impression

Circle that feeling on your list. And start to sink into the actual feeling of that, the actual way it feels to you in and around your body. Imagine how you would describe this to a friend. How would you tell your friend what it's like to have this feeling? What happens in your body? What happens in your mind? What kinds of things does it make you do? And jot down some of those things under the first impressions part of the page.

So now we're ready to actually do the mapping. On the following pages, you'll find a half dozen questions that help you elicit a very tangible image that brings the feeling to life. At the same time this image gives you a bit of distance. To create the image, you have to step away from the feeling. In being one step removed, you create a safety about the feeling, so that you can use this process to map even the most difficult emotions in a way that you're not going to get hijacked, you're not going to fall into it. (As mentioned earlier, you'll definitely find it easier to maintain this distance when you have someone else to hold the container of the process for you, asking the questions, taking the notes.

Making it up

These questions about imagery are different from normal conversation about feelings, emotions, memories or thoughts. And as you go through the questions, you might feel at first like you're making up the answers. That's OK. You're right. You are making up the answers.

What we're doing here is using a part of the brain that is very skilled with imagery and we're applying it. We're directing its attention towards the feeling part of your brain that is more amorphous and harder to clearly and objectively perceive.

We're using this imagery part of the brain almost like you would use an X-ray to get a very clear image of what's going on beneath the surface of the body, out of sight. As you answer these questions go with the first thing that comes to mind and then check it out. Does that actually feel right? Is it green versus blue? Is it a hard solid versus a liquid? You'll know. There's going to be an image that fits, that just feels right. Something different from that will feel like it doesn't fit.

Trust the feeling. Trust the image that comes to you. And try to set your logical mind aside as you do, because its expectations may not apply here. There is a strong logic to the feeling mind, but it is not necessarily the same logic we are accustomed to applying to mental and emotional experiences.

The mapping questions

So go ahead and put your attention on the feeling you've chosen to map. Let's get started. Take notes on a separate sheet of paper or use the worksheet pages immediately following these questions. Make a copy of the worksheet if that is convenient.

Location

The first question is about location.

> **If you were to say that the actual felt experience of this feeling was located somewhere in or around your body, where would you say that is?**

And I say "in or around" because feelings are not necessarily confined to the body. They can extend outside the body. Pay attention to that. Occasionally you'll even find a feeling state that exists completely outside the body. Probably not this first time around for you, but it can happen. So pay attention to where is the actual feeling relative to the physical structure of your body.

Just to be clear: we are paying attention to the felt sense, to feeling, which is not the same as monitoring body sensations. Feeling exists with reference to the body and to material experience, but it is not confined to the space of the body, or the physical sensations of breathing, heartbeat, digestion, muscle tension, etc.

You may find it helpful to close your eyes, and to eliminate the various sensory channels from your attention, one at a time. Release visual images. Release sounds. Release kinesthetic and tactile sensations. Notice that without those primary senses, and even without thought, you are still conscious. What is left is feeling. This is what you are mapping.

You may also find it helpful to scan the space of your body progressively. Start at your feet. Ask, "Does any part of the actual, felt experience of this [*feeling state*] exist in your legs? Does any part of this [*feeling state*] exist in your hips or pelvis?" Continue up through the body until you locate the feeling.

Substance

The second question has to do with substance.

> **Within the region of that feeling space you just identified, if you were to say that the actual felt experience of this feeling had qualities of substance, would you say that it seems more like a solid, a liquid, a gas, some kind of light or energy, or something else?**

And take a little bit of time to refine that. If it is a solid, does it seem **hard or soft**? Is it **heavy or light**? If it's a liquid or a gas or an energy, does it seem **thick or thin**? How easy would it be to move your hand through it for example? Make a note of the qualities of substances that you discover there.

Temperature

The next question is about temperature.

> **If you were to say that this feeling substance had a temperature, what temperature would you say it is?**

Does the feeling substance seem warmer or cooler than body temperature? Or is it more of a neutral body or room temperature? Or is it more extreme? Make a note of the temperature.

Color

Now, let's look at color appearance.

> **If you were to say that this feeling substance
> had color, what color would you say it is?**

And again, go with the first thing that comes to mind and then check it out. You might get a very specific, vivid shade of color. You might get more of a range of grays.

What color does it seem to be? And does this feeling substance seem more transparent, in a way that you can see through like glass? Is it more translucent, that light comes through it more like a lamp shade? Or is it opaque, more like a rock, where there's no way you could see through it? And are there other visual qualities that you notice? Make a note of those.

Movement

Now, let's turn our attention to movement.

> **Does this feeling substance seem to be
> moving in any way? Is there a flow, or a
> pulse, or a vibration? Is there any kind of a
> rotation? Or is there a force or a pressure?**

Make a note of the qualities of the movement. Is it steady, or intermittent, or random? If there's pressure or force, is it inward or outward or in some other particular direction? Pay attention to the details and make a note of those.

Sound

The next question is about sound.

If you listen internally, do you notice any kind of inner sound or voice that naturally accompanies this feeling?

In that space inside do you notice perhaps your voice or someone else's? One voice or more than one? Some sound, whether a natural sound, or a mechanical sound, or a hum, or something like that? Perhaps something musical? Make a note of what kind of sound you notice, including the possibility that either there is no sound, or that you notice the presence of silence.

Anything else?

Now scan over everything that you've written, through those questions. Is there anything you want to change, any adjustments? Anything you've discovered in some of the later questions about some of the earlier qualities? Go through and make those adjustments.

Drawing

For the next step, you can choose to either draw first or write about the beliefs first. On the worksheet I've provided an androgynous figure. If you were working with me we'd have a specifically male or female image that could be more fitting for you, but this works perfectly well. Draw the feeling as if you were standing outside of yourself, and you could actually see it. What would it look like, the way you've described it? Be open to discovering new aspects of the feeling as you draw.

For some feelings you only need either the side view or the straight on view. And consider these outlines as transparent bodies. It's like you can see all the way through, so it's neither front nor back, but one view. It's both. So draw what that would look like. Use color. Colored pencils work really great or any kind of markers or other media. Sometimes you'll draw the view from outside, other times it may be a cross section. Do whatever works for you. If you're using a separate sheet of paper, trace the outline and draw on that.

Beliefs

Each feeling state is an anchor for unique beliefs attached to that specific state. Inviting those beliefs into your awareness is an excellent way for you to track the effect of the feeling state in your life before and after you move it.

To access the beliefs, how would you capture in words what seems real, or true, or important from the perspective of this feeling? You may find it helpful to complete a sentence fragment like one of these:

- "I am…" or "I'm not…"
- "I have…" or "I don't have…"
- "I need…" or "I don't need…"
- "I can…" or "I can't…"

How would you complete one of those sentences as a way of expressing what this feeling seems to be about?

For some feelings it will feel more appropriate to say "You are…" or "You should…" for example, where there's some element of almost as if the feeling is engaging with you or against you in some way. So write whatever comes naturally to capture the embedded belief that is anchored by this feeling.

Summary

We've just finished up going through Step One: Map It, creating the tangible image which derives from the feeling state. By now you should have a clearer sense of what the experience of this feeling is for you. And you should also have the experience of connecting with your witness self. A lot of times when we have difficult emotions, feelings, we fall into them and we experience ourselves as if that anger or that sadness was us.

With the mapping, though, in order to answer these questions you have to step outside of the feeling. You have to place the origin of your attention outside the feeling in order to notice what color or substance it is, and that's a wonderful thing. We are made of many parts and some of those parts function as witnesses. And the more that we can access our witness self and the stronger we can make that part of ourselves; the easier it is for us to navigate emotionally challenging waters.

So this process of mapping, all by itself, can be very helpful for you in a variety of different situations. I encourage you to use it often.

Use the worksheet on the following pages to record your notes. Make copies, use separate sheets of paper or a journal, or download a template from FeelingPath.com to print as many as you need.

STEP 1: MAP IT.   **Date:**

Feeling Name:

Location:

Substance:

Temperature:

Color:

Movement:

Sound:

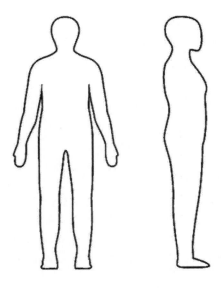

Beliefs:

Other Notes:

Reflecting and confirming

So how was that experience for you? What did you notice? Most people find that running through these questions seems frivolous at first, like they're just "making up" the answers. But then they find there's something more tangible about the image than they expected. Here are two ways to test that out.

First, select one of the image properties you're not sure about. "Try on" a different, random value for that property. For example, if the feeling you mapped seems green, test out whether it could possibly be red. If your feeling is hot, try out cold to see if it fits. Most likely, you will get a clear "No" to your substitutions. You may even be surprised at the level of specificity you get, finding it very clear that the temperature is 72 degrees, not 75, or this particular shade of turquoise, not that shade of green.

Mapping is a bit like sitting down with a police sketch artist to draw the bank robber's face. The artist may have a wide selection of face shapes, noses, eyes, mouths, and hair for you to select from. You may look through an array of noses, for example, and quickly discard those which are too sharp or too long, scanning to find the squat, rounded nose that looks "just right" to you. You do that with the other features of the face, and when you put it all together you experience an instant of recognition. "That's him, officer," you say. "That's the guy who done the deed." You'll have that same sense of rightness when you put all the elements of your feeling map together.

The second way to test out the credibility of your map is to choose a quality of your feeling state which seems more intense. Maybe yours is really cold, or really heavy for example. Now amplify that quality. If it's cold, imagine it getting colder. If heavy, imagine it getting heavier. What happens?

For most people, amplifying an extreme quality intensifies the feeling itself. Did that happen for you? It's pretty convincing, isn't it? Go ahead and reverse direction for that quality to return it to its original state.

[An important note: For a few people with certain brain-based dysfunctions such as psychosis or schizophrenia, and for others taking anti-psychotic or mood stabilizing medication like lithium or risperdal, the Feeling Path Mapping practice may not work very well. These conditions and medications seem to compromise the brain's ability to maintain and regulate the feeling mind. Every situation is different, though, and this is a new field, so it's certainly worth giving it a try no matter what your challenges might be. Ordinary mood disorders (including bipolar disorder) and standard SSRI anti-depressants do not seem to impede one's ability to experience the benefits of this work in any way.]

A few examples

To give you a point of reference, I'd like to share a few examples of another person's maps. Olivia has been working with me recently in exchange for writing about her experience. She began her work with the intention of clearing a problematic hesitation and resistance to writing itself, something that has made it difficult for her to pursue her dream of becoming a world-travelling journalist. Frankly, even though she is quite talented, this pattern of hesitation has made it difficult for her to earn more than a subsistence income from her writing for quite some time.

At this point in the narrative, I just want to present these states as examples. I think it will help you to have a general sense of how these Feeling Path Maps tend to show up.

Crumbling

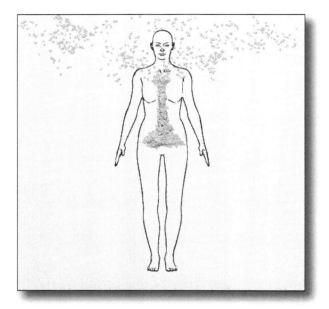

Feeling description: A falling in on myself. Sinking feeling, from chest into abdomen, kind of falling; like sand; cooler than body temp, lukewarm, not quite neutral; yellow, opaque; it falls and settles, and then I just kind of resign into it, with Folding In. Sound of a heavy sigh, air deflating.

A few thoughts/beliefs that come with this feeling: I shouldn't have put my work out there. I should have kept it closer.

This Crumbling was the first feeling state Olivia mapped. We chose to zoom in on this one after talking about her pattern of hesitation, and listing several other feeling states that were part of the pattern. Among them were feelings of Disappointment, Rejection, Fear, and others. The general pattern was of the sort, "If I put something out into the world that I've created, I'm inviting rejection, and if I'm rejected, I'll feel this inner collapse, this Crumbling."

The Crumbling is the anticipated result of putting something out there. So the best strategy in this case is to avoid putting things out there. Olivia used to fight this battle every single time she attempted to write a brief, few-hundred word article for the internet.

As you might imagine, this Crumbling feeling was quite uncomfortable for Olivia. At the same time, mapping it provided a measure of relief. It was as if she had gotten a little distance from the feeling, and was able to be a little more objective about her experience of it.

In creating the image, Olivia wasn't entirely sure the image was "right." She said the experience of mapping felt a little weird, like he was just making it up. I affirmed her experience, explaining that most people have a sense of unfamiliarity the first few times they do the mapping.

"It's like you've just discovered a new instrument," I told her. "Imagine looking through an electron microscope for the first time at a single hair from your head. What you see is weird and strange, and wonderful. But before long you'll become accustomed to peering into this new world."

Olivia accepted my invitation to confirm her image by exploring a couple of its qualities. I asked whether, if the Crumbling had qualities of being blue, or a liquid, or very cold, it would be the same feeling. She said very emphatically that Crumbling had none of those qualities. I asked her what would happen if the feeling became cooler and heavier, falling with greater force. She shook her head and told me no thank you, that's too uncomfortable. She was now convinced that this image was an accurate representation of her feeling state.

At this point, Olivia had passed through the doorway into the mysterious world of the feeling mind. She had successfully applied the tool of mapping to enhancing her awareness of a specific feeling state, and had been surprised at the richness and detail it revealed. By testing what it felt like to alter the image qualities of the feeling, Olivia had also taken the first steps to applying the mapping process to directly interacting with her feeling state. This would become more important as we continued the journey of discovery.

So what can we make of this first experience? There's something rather startling and unexpected about the tangibility, specificity, and detail of the image. Have you had a similar experience in mapping your first feeling state? What do you make of it?

Before rushing to interpret this first experience, let's explore a bit further to see what else comes to light. In talking through her pattern, Olivia mentioned a few other states that seemed important. We followed up on those the next time we met. I'll share a couple with you on the next page.

Isolated Outside

I'm standing back from the feeling. It's out in front, spherical, four feet in diameter; like a dense, foggy cloud, charcoal dark gray, wispy on the edges, dense in the middle, but you can run your hand through it, not solid. Kind of cold and damp. Just floating, pretty still. Total silence. Dense feeling at my heart, very dense but moisturey and gray and very

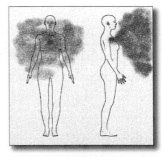

cold. It's like the cloud is coming out from my center, cold, and then it forms this cloud and gets cool and damp and less intense and bigger, like moisture particles.

I can see what's coming from here. So I'm safer back here. I can see what might come at me, so that I'm ready. It's safer here.

Longing

Deep inside, small, extends out of me, kind of elastic, way out there; soft, like many silk threads, close, not woven together; gray-blue, opaque; a gentle tug; a whisper, my voice, a part of me but completely outside of myself, from another space of existence, an older me, very gentle. A very steady pull.

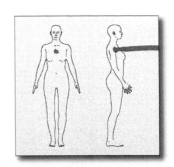

Knowing what's possible but not having it feels, not empty but less than full. Kind of the difference between feeling like I'm in the shadows looking at things that are possible and standing in the world. I remember feeling this when I was six or seven, a sense of longing, knowing something was possible but not knowing what it was.

Multiple states, multiple maps

This is the kind of thing you can expect as you begin to delve into the territory of the feeling mind. Each feeling state reveals itself to be specific, to have a distinct presence and identity. And the mapping questions provide a level of precision that is unprecedented in any other work with feeling, mood, or emotion. The depth of awareness Olivia achieved above could easily take many hours longer with any other method.

Notice how the states are interrelated. The silk threads of the Longing reach from the center of the heart, where Isolated Outside originates, and reach directly through that cloud. The cloud of Isolated Outside forms a barrier, protecting her, keeping her safely at a distance so she can "see what's coming." Yet the barrier also prevents her moving toward the source of the Longing. And all around them both we find the inner experience of the Crumbling, a loss of vitality at being kept from what is important.

This kind of dynamic interaction between feeling states is normal. Any pattern you map will have multiple states engaged in relationships that preserve the pattern. These configurations have always been there, driving your patterns the way my own configuration drove my bipolar disorder. And now, with Feeling Path Mapping, you can illuminate these configurations, clearly, vividly, precisely. It's a simple matter of bringing your felt sense of each feeling state to awareness through the imagery.

If you've noticed one or more other feeling states which seem closely connected to the one you already mapped, consider going through the mapping process again with each one. Do two or three before going forward to the moving phase of the work, to give yourself the experience of seeing just how the different parts fit together for you.

As you gain more experience with mapping, you will learn to trust your inner experience. Allow the method, the questions, to bring your inner experience of feeling to the surface, and rely on the actual, inner experiences of your feeling states to reveal what's really there for you. The more you do the mapping, the greater your skill and awareness in mapping further feeling states.

These tools will allow you to explore any aspect of your experience whatsoever. All consciousness is grounded in feeling, so any state of being you wish to explore can be elucidated with efficiency and precision using the Feeling Path Mapping questions. As you get more comfortable with the questions, you'll be able to map the feeling states underlying experiences like confusion, numbness, judgment, withdrawal, and others which have conventionally been considered to exist outside the realm of feeling, mood, or emotion.

Making sense of somatosensory imagery

Let's take a step back here for a moment. In mapping a feeling state, you had an experience which falls outside most conventional frameworks of explanation. What are we to make of this imagery having such a strong relationship with feeling? After 17 years mapping thousands of feelings for myself and others, I interpret it this way.

We arrive in this world as material beings embedded in a material world. From the time of our first awakening into infancy, (and even before we are born), we find ourselves immersed in stuff and qualities of stuff. As we learn about the world and about our bodies-in-the-world, our senses are saturated with experiences of solids, liquids, gases, light and energy with all their myriad properties. We experience ourselves as these substances, and we experience our environments as these substances. It is this world of substance that our embodied consciousness must first make sense of, navigate, and master in order for us to take on all of our higher functions and awareness.

So it should be no surprise that the fundamental substrate of consciousness is the felt experience of the stuff of our lives. Try this little thought experiment as a demonstration of the ubiquity of the extended felt sense:

1. Close your eyes. Imagine picking up a hammer, and lightly swinging it. Or choose some other tool more familiar to you. Can you sense the extension to your body, its heft, its rigidity? Can you sense just how you would move your body with this extension in order to accomplish a goal – driving a nail or prying a board?

2. Put the hammer down. Imagine dipping your hand in a pool of warm water, and swirling it around. Can you sense the weight, the fluidity, the texture of the water as you move your hand through it? Can you sense how you would push the water to create a small current?

Now, how did you do that? I contend that you were able to extend the felt experience of your body into your environment. I believe we are doing this all the time, constantly taking on the objects and materials of our surroundings as extensions of our sense of physical being. We are continually forming a multi-sensory, virtual material representation of our body-in-the-world.

One of my physical practices is a dance discipline called contact improvisation. Contact improv is a practice of taking on the weight and dynamics of another person as an extension of your own body in dance. You move together, communicating through touch and gravity and motion, becoming one expression through opening to one another's embodied physicality.

Contact improv is one discipline among many which draws upon and refines this power of somatosensory projection. Others include various sports, wilderness pursuits, expressive arts, crafts of all kinds, and many more. In fact, you will see shortly that even the most abstract and sublime of human pursuits, those we deem spiritual or mathematical for example, rely strongly on this capacity for somatosensory projection.

But why is this central capacity of our consciousness so unacknowledged? I believe it is a case of fish in water. We are immersed in it, so stepping outside the phenomenon to examine it can be difficult. And when you almost always have real, physical things to point to as origins of your somatosensory experience, you attribute the experiences to the things. Counterexamples, as when you experience strong somatosensory images with no physical referents in dream or fantasy, or when you engaged in exercises like the two above, are dismissed as irrelevant, "just in your head."

What I am saying here is that underlying all of our directly physical experience is a duplicate or shadow representation of our body and its physical environment, generated by the felt sense. The more accurately it represents actual properties of our material surroundings, the more effectively we are able to navigate and manipulate those surroundings. I believe this virtual physical world may be an essential component of the consciousness of all embodied, mobile creatures.

And for humans at least, that felt sense has a creative capacity as well, able to generate somatosensory images having no material origin. Our capacity to both perceive and create somatosensory imagery is profound. And I believe it is that capacity which gives rise to the endlessly diverse profusion of actual feeling state experiences we encounter in the course of our living. The diversity is far greater than our current language of feeling accounts for. And because feeling is highly subjective, available to no one but ourselves, it is difficult for us to talk about feeling in ways that accurately communicate to one another about our actual, felt experiences. We have no way to objectively corroborate our descriptions in the way we find so easy to do with visual, auditory, or even kinesthetic/tactile experiences.

The explicit questioning technique of Feeling Path Mapping fills in this gap and reveals astonishing elegance, complexity, and intelligence in the realm of feeling. I anticipate that these questions will also provide the means to scientifically verify the assertions I am making, and to connect them to current theories about embodied cognition and body schema. (For those readers who come to this work through its connection to your research, can you design a way to test this hypothesis? Contact me for assistance.)

Getting ready to move

Mapping existing feeling states is fascinating and therapeutic. But even more exciting is engaging with the map images in such a way as to directly transform the feeling state itself.

Previously, we were forced to use circuitous means to achieve a significant shift in feeling. We could attempt to analyze our thoughts and change them, hoping the new thoughts would feel better. We could engage with our physiology through various physical or meditative practices to overwhelm our feeling states and force ourselves toward more desirable inner experiences. We could hack the machinery of feeling in the brain using various chemical means including food, prescription medications, legal substances like nicotine or alcohol, and illegal drugs. We could turn our attention away from the undesired feelings by manipulating our internal or external environment through distractions such as entertainment, social activities, or outdoor pursuits.

Now we have the ability to go directly to any feeling state and move it directly, as if it were an object we could slide this way and that. Seventeen years ago, I imagined this was the holy grail of growth and healing. I thought there was nothing else I could ever need, that if I ever found myself in a funk that I could just map and move and be done with it. Choose your own feeling state! Live in joy forever!

But I want to quickly dissuade you of such blue sky visions. As I was to learn, the feeling mind is far more complex than to operate on a simple slider mechanism. I'd like to give you a few important pointers about this new territory, to save you wasting your time as you get started.

To understand what I'm about to share with you, it'll be important for you to have the experience of moving a feeling state you've mapped. If you have completed the mapping process earlier with a feeling state you'd like to move, great. If not, please go back to the preceding questions and complete the mapping before proceeding.

Step Two: Move It.

Now we're going to take the feeling that you mapped in Step One and alter the image as a way to transform the feeling itself. Return to your notes and drawing of the feeling you previously mapped. Read through your notes and refresh your experience of the feeling state. If needed, intensify one or more of the parameters of the image in order to feel the visceral twinge of the tangible link between the image and your state.

Moving a state is pretty straightforward but incredibly powerful. So before we start, make yourself comfortable. I want to talk about three frames that we need to set before we move forward.

Setting the frame

First of all, I want to acknowledge that this feeling you mapped is a part of you that has been expressing itself in a particular way. It took that form at some point in your life where that was necessary to signal that something was out of balance for you. At that time, it might have been that you weren't allowed to feel that, and you had to push it aside. Or it might have been that you weren't allowed to act on it, you didn't have the power to make the changes necessary. Or perhaps you weren't supported in the way you needed, to become aware of what that feeling was trying to tell you and take the action necessary to restore balance and harmony and wholeness in your life. So it had a function, that feeling. But that function was interrupted.

In this process, we want to restore this part's natural functioning so it can signal you, in an ongoing way, about the state of balance in your life. And the way that we're going to do that is we're going to reconnect this part of you with its original or ideal state. This part has a particular feeling state that is what it will feel in an optimal situation, in a perfect world. We want to reconnect with that. We're going to expand its horizons and reconnect it to the full range of expression that is available to it.

Safe to move

As we begin, we want to set three frames. First, as we go through the questions, we're going to be inviting specific properties of the feeling, specific qualities of that image you mapped, to shift. As those qualities shift, the feeling itself is going to shift along with them. By mapping, we've created this tangible image that serves almost like a visual handle, and we can take that handle and we can move it, and the feeling will move along with it. It's an amazing process.

> **I want to reassure this part of you that this process is safe. We're going to be shifting it – the feeling will become something new – but you can always put it back.**

We're not taking away the option for this part of you to signal you in exactly the same way, if for any reason that would be most appropriate. We are adding to its repertoire. We're adding a range of motion, but we're not taking away the possibility for this part of you to feel exactly what it has been feeling, if that is ever necessary.

In a perfect world...

The second frame is, because it's safe, I want to invite you to go for it. In this process, we're going to move the feeling. I want to invite you to allow this part of you to move as far as it can go.

> **What could this part of you experience
> in a perfect world, a world in which all of
> your needs are met, fully and completely,
> exactly the way you want them to be, and
> you know how to keep them that way?**

So, shifting this feeling, what could it become in a perfect world?

All parts of you

The third frame I want to set is to acknowledge that this feeling is not alone. There are other parts of you, other feeling states, that have an intimate relationship with this particular feeling. And sometimes that relationship seems to be one of dependence or control, in some way. Shifting this feeling might make another part come to the foreground and say, "Hey, wait a second. I'm not sure I want that shift to happen." For example, a feeling of shame might feel exposed if a protective feeling of anger transforms into something else.

Recognize, first of all, that this feeling we are moving can always go back the way it was, if that's necessary or desirable. Second, these other parts can learn that this process is available for every part of you.

> **I want to invite any other parts of you, any other feelings, to participate in this process as passive witnesses, learning from this process what is possible for every part of you.**

With that out of the way, let's move forward into the actual moving questions. We're going to go through the different properties of the image, starting with temperature. Keep notes on the template pages at the end of these questions, or make a copy of the template, or use a blank sheet of paper.

The moving questions

Place your attention on the feeling you mapped previously. You might have the image in front of you to help. I'm going to refer to this feeling as "this part of you," because as soon as we start moving it, it will no longer be that original feeling. The first image is specific to the feeling you mapped, and as we shift the image, the feeling itself is going to become something different. The old name for it will no longer be relevant.

Temperature

We're going to start with temperature. As we begin, temperature is often the easiest image parameter to shift and feel an instant, tangible result.

> **In this moment, in the spirit of exploration of what's possible, if this part of you were free to become warmer or cooler, what would feel better? What would this part**

> **of you prefer? And in becoming warmer**
> **or cooler, if this part of you were free**
> **to take on any temperature at all, what**
> **temperature would it most want to be?**

Write down the new temperature in your notes.

Substance

Let's move to substance quality.

> **So, in taking on that new temperature,**
> **if this part of you were free to become**
> **harder or softer, heavier or lighter, more**
> **or less dense, what would feel better? And**
> **in moving in that direction, if this part**
> **of you were free to take on qualities of**
> **any substance at all, would it prefer to be**
> **more like a solid… or a liquid… or a gas…**
> **or some kind of pure light or energy… or**
> **something else?**

If this part of you were free to choose from any substance at all, what kind of substance would it most want to be? And going into the finer qualities of that, in becoming that substance, does it want to be hard or soft, heavy or light, thick or thin? What other qualities do you want to notice about what substance this part of you most wants to be? Write these in your notes

Color

Next we'll look at color and other qualities of appearance.

> **So in taking on these new qualities of substance and temperature, if this part of you were free to become darker or brighter, what would it prefer? And in shifting in that direction, if this part of you could take on any color or colors of the rainbow, what color would it most want to be? And would it want to be transparent, translucent or opaque? And would it want to have any qualities of being luminous, iridescent, shimmering or sparkling?**

What other color or visual qualities do you notice this part of you wants to be?

Location

The next property we'll explore is location.

> **In taking on these new qualities of color, substance and temperature, if this part of you were free to locate itself anywhere in or around your body, or in <u>and</u> around your body, where would it want to be located?**

And then I invite you to expand that, as much as possible. Find the size and shape that would be optimal. If it wants to spread through your chest, for example, would it feel good to go up into your head? Down into your belly? All the way down into your legs? If it extends outside your body, how far? (Some feeling states will expand infinitely in all directions.) What is the optimal extent of this feeling? Where does it want to be located?

Movement

After exploring location, we naturally move on to movement.

> **In locating itself in this new location, how does this part of you want to be moving? Does it want to be flowing, or pulsing, or vibrating? Does there want to be any sense of a wave or a ripple? Does it want to be radiating in some way? What directions or other qualities of movement does this part of you most want to have?**

Explore qualities of movement in time as well, noticing pattern, rhythm, and randomness.

Sound

Finally, we dig into the quality of sound.

> **In taking on all these new qualities of movement, of substance, of location and temperature and color, if this part of you were free to generate an inner sound or voice, as a way of more fully expressing its true nature, what would that want to be?**

Would it want to be some kind of music or a natural sound? Some kind of voice? One voice or many? Male or female? What age? What would be the optimal inner sound to express this part of you?

Anything else?

And now, let's review. Going back through the different parameters, are there any other adjustments you want to make? Is there anything else you want to notice about what this part of you wants to be? Make those changes in your notes.

Beliefs

And now, turn your attention to the thoughts that naturally want to arise from this place.

> **If this part of you were free to express in words what seems most true or real or important, how would it do that? What does this part of you most want you to know?**

How might this part of you complete the sentence "I am…" or "I have…" or "I can…"? What else do you notice? Take some time with this.

New name?

And, finally, what name would you like to give this new feeling? What would it like to be called? You might find some ideas for the new name in the notes that you've taken already.

Drawing

And now, take some time with the template, the outline, and draw what this would look like if you could see it from the outside. Use as much color as you want. If you want to, just kind of trace the outline on a separate sheet, and draw it big. Create a visual representation of the actual, felt sense of what this feeling feels like to you, on the inside.

Summary

So that wraps up Step Two: Move It. You've brought a feeling state more into awareness using the mapping, feeling it more fully, creating a clear, tangible image, sort of a visual handle. And then, using that handle, you moved the feeling itself. You invited this part of you to reveal to you what it really wants to be feeling.

Can you see the connection between the first feeling and the second one? It's the same part of you. It's trying to do the exact same thing for you, but in the second case, it's doing it in the context of possibility, of what could this be if your life was truly as it wants to be.

Now, we're going to take that new feeling, in Step Three: Live It, and we're going to explore, what does it look like to bring this fully into your life? What changes want to happen naturally? So take a little time with your new feeling state, and then come along for Step Three.

Use the worksheet on the following pages to record your notes. Make copies, use separate sheets of paper or a journal, or download a template from FeelingPath.com to print as many as you need.

STEP 2: MOVE IT.   **Date:**

Original Feeling:

New Temperature:

New Substance:

New Color:

New Location:

New Movement:

New Sound:

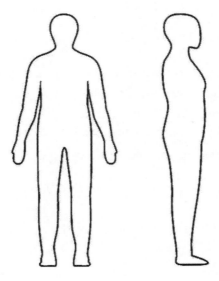

New Feeling Name:

New Beliefs

Other Notes:

Reflecting and confirming

So what did you notice? Pretty fascinating experience, isn't it?

(If you had any difficulty, please do go to Part 3 where I provide a bit more guidance, and consider getting together with a friend who can lead you verbally through the questions. It can be a lot easier to do the work when you are completely free to just focus on the inner sensations of feeling, and you have someone else to take the notes and track your progress.)

Let's take a look at a few examples from Olivia again, so you have a reference point for your own experience. The following three maps represent the ideal feeling states Olivia arrived at in doing the moving process with the three original states we mapped earlier.

Core Strength

(Formerly Crumbling)

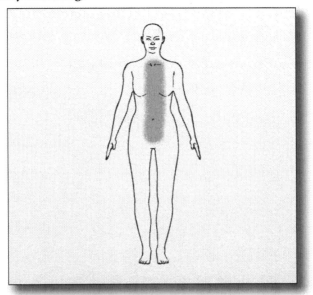

Feeling description: Hot bath temperature; slowing down, lighter weight, like a solid, all holding together, all the particles, hard, heavy, upright, like sandstone; a warm, yellow-gold, shimmery solid color; up through my core, a foot in dia., through whole torso; has weight but not heaviness, solidity but not rigid; there's energy movement in it; energy that takes the form of a solid; a pulse all the way through it, heartbeat-speed. A warm, humming sound like a beehive or something. Seems like the pulse would change and adjust depending on circumstances.

A few thoughts/beliefs that come with this feeling: Forward movement, a reaching out into full experience and true understanding and awareness. Fully awake, aware and receptive without fear of threat. "It's OK." It's a safe state of just being.

Inclusive

(Formerly Isolated Outside)

Body temp; lighter, pure energy; gold, shimmering, translucent; moving with a lot of energy, constant movement, little particles vibrating, humming; radiating out from my core in all directions; pulses in and out, very gently; there's a pulse but there's no real end; it's continuously radiating out of my core. Going out and coming back, like breathing, rate of comfortable breath. Sound is like a breath.

You carry all the protection you need inside of you. It creates a space that other people can move into; there's this gentle pulse, allowing things in, including other people in the pulse of the interaction

Infinite Self

(Formerly Longing)

Slightly above body temp; energetic light; luminous gold/yellow, warm, rich egg-yolk color; steady, expanded, coming into me from above, all the way through. my body; a real sense of awareness of the different chakra points illuminated; peaceful and quiet, with a feeling of all sound, an energetic hum of everything.

Feeling of connection. I feel this real height, like my whole being is really tall. This feeling of this constant supply of love. It's a feeling of being perfect in the moment, not perfect as a closed, achieved thing, but more an energetic balance in the moment, the feeling of being perfectly supported, prepared; perfectly comfortable in the moment and present for the moment. I have everything I need, and it's just there.

Before and after

OK, so I'm assuming you've had your own experience of mapping and moving a negative feeling state, revealing an ideal state you didn't know was there. (If you haven't, please go do it before reading further.)

What do you make of this? If you were on your own, and happened to conduct the experiment I did myself 17 years ago, turning a downward depression into an upward cheerfulness, what would you think? If you're like me, your first impulse might be to dismiss it.

Seriously. There is no way to make sense of this within currently circulating ideas and understandings of the mind. Cognitive psychology tends to argue that emotions result from cognitive assessments, and you need to change your assessments to change how you feel about something. Neuroscientists tend to treat emotion as primarily brain-based and instinctual, happening automatically outside of awareness, with conscious thought and feeling layered on top of it. Much of psychotherapy suggests that emotions have a history, and changing a strong emotion requires digging into and changing one's understanding of (or otherwise processing) that history. Various personal growth and spiritual practices argue for specific disciplines or beliefs being necessary to change one's emotions.

None of these makes any distinction between feeling and emotion, with the exception of the neuroscientist Antonio Damasio who has identified specific portions of the brain responsible for feeling as distinct from emotion, but still considers feeling to be primarily a higher-level assessment of body state. And none of these make allowances for directly interacting with a feeling state and deliberately changing it at will in just a few minutes. None of them.

So no matter what you might have studied or practiced or been led through, you will have no basis from which to make sense of this experience. For most of us, when we find something for which we have no existing conceptual structures, we will argue to ourselves that it is an anomaly, that we have experienced it incorrectly, or that somehow it actually proves what we already believe. That's just how we are.

I did the same thing. Frankly, I was a bit freaked out. I had invested a great deal of time and energy in other ways of approaching my emotional healing. Most of it was focused on my thoughts and my history, and I had plumbed the depths. So for me to admit to myself that I had done something that should not have been possible was to also admit that I might have wasted a good deal of my life chasing specters and ghosts of no value. It was hard to swallow.

So I ask you right now: how much do you have invested in other methods and ideologies for dealing with unwanted emotions? Can you put those aside for a moment, just for a moment, and consider there is truly something new at work here? Something you don't yet understand?

Discovering the feeling path

So let's look at this. We started with one strong, viscerally tangible feeling state. We elicited a multi-sensory image which brought that feeling state even more strongly into our awareness. Then we interacted with the image, inviting parameters of the image to shift. And what happened? The image shifted. Not only did the image shift, but the feeling state shifted with it in a seemingly meaningful way.

If you did this, you'll notice the feeling state you ended up with has a clear relationship with the first state. These are not two randomly occurring states with a haphazard connection. They feel like they are the same part of you. They feel like they're about the same thing, trying to do the same thing, fulfilling the same function at some level in your life.

The second, ideal state feels like it is doing so with higher fidelity, shall we say, higher purity, greater clarity, more authenticity. It feels more like the "real" you. The first, reactive state feels like you, yes, but a version of you that is off balance.

Notice too that in the second state, your thoughts and perceptions have changed. They have changed spontaneously, with no particular effort on your part. You did not have to analyze the thoughts of the reactive state. You did not have parse the beliefs to identify where they were non rational. Nor did you have to logically or rationally construct new beliefs, thoughts, or perceptions to replace them.

All that happened completely without your intervention. Bingo. You found yourself feeling the new state and simultaneously you found yourself thinking the new thoughts. And they weren't just any new thoughts. They were your new thoughts. They felt authentic, real, and as comfortable as your skin, (even though they might have seemed strangely new and unfamiliar if you were encountering them for the first time).

How did this happen? Or more to the point: what exactly did just happen? Let me share my best understanding with you.

When I first started doing this work, I assumed it would be possible to take any feeling state and turn it into any other feeling state. One application I discovered was to help create emotional states for performing artists. I started working with a professional dancer out of New York City who wanted to create her own performance, to help her craft her dance as a journey through her emotions.

The arc of the dance was to take her from the emotion she called Fear to a different emotion she called Stand Tall. Seemed like an easy enough journey. Map the first, map the second, and take her gradually from one to the other as she improvised her movements as expressions of the driving emotions.

But there was a problem. Fear wouldn't turn into Stand Tall. It just wouldn't go. Instead it turned into a different feeling she called Welcome, a type of connection with her audience. And no matter what we did, we could not get either Fear or Welcome to turn into Stand Tall.

So I reverse engineered Stand Tall. I had her shift it in a negative direction toward something that felt worse. It went to a dark feeling she called Withdrawn. OK then.

For the performance, her choreography was driven by the pair of feeling transformations: Fear became Welcome; Withdrawn became Stand Tall. As a technique for scoring a dance, it was a success. But this experience threw a wrench into my convenient understanding of what I had discovered.

Over the following months I explored the relationships among states. This is the investigation that led me eventually to the work of eliminating my bipolar disorder.

I tested the relationships of states that seemed to coexist. As it turns out, if we can feel two given states simultaneously, they cannot turn into one another. I also tested many states connected by their transformation. It turns out that at times, more than one reactive state can turn into the same ideal state. But any single reactive state cannot turn into more than one ideal state. And any two reactive states that share the same ideal state never coexist. They alternate between one another from one time to the next.

It became clear that a reactive state and its ideal were linked inextricably. They shared the same "thing-ness." I came to call these things to which specific states belonged "parts." It took many years to understand exactly what a part is, how a part works, and how parts interact.

More recently I have locked onto the terminology of "path" to describe this relationship of a continuum of states which share a single identity. A feeling path is the spectrum of available states defined by the ideal origin state at one end of the continuum, and one or more reactive states at the other. Each feeling path has one and only one ideal state, but it can branch into multiple reactive states to provide responses to different situations.

How do we distinguish one feeling path from another? How do we identify each? What defines their identity? Does there exist a finite set of feeling paths in any given person, or is there some other distribution? Does the set of feeling paths follow any fundamental, universal pattern, or is each person's set of paths unique? I will answer these questions to a great extent later in the section on Architecture.

For now, the important thing is to realize that a feeling path has certain qualities that will be helpful for you to know as you embark on Feeling Path Mapping. Let me summarize here.

1. Any two feeling states which can be experienced simultaneously fall on two distinct paths. They will resolve into two distinct ideal states.

2. Any two feeling states which, when moved, turn out to be the same ideal feeling state, are most likely branches of the same path. Test by verifying whether they can be experienced simultaneously: most often you will find that the explorer

experiences one state, then the other, rather than both at the same time.

3.   Any single feeling state which seems to turn into more than one ideal state is most likely a blend of two states, or the moving process is accidently including an additional state which has not been explicitly identified. Look for the extra state.

I've included the following graphic to illustrate these ideas.

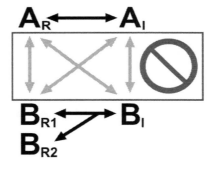

Feeling path A is different from feeling path B. Feeling state A-Reactive is experienced at the same time as feeling state B-Reactive-1, and so cannot be shifted into one into the other. The same goes for feeling state A-Ideal and feeling state B-Ideal. Feeling state B-Reactive-1 and feeling state B-Reactive-2 both shift into feeling state B-Ideal. These two reactive states are experienced at different times, and belong to the same path B.

Going back to the examples from Olivia, we can see how Crumbling turns into Core Strength but cannot turn into Longing or Infinite Self. However, Olivia also mapped a state she called Emptiness.

Emptiness

In my core, but it's a vacancy, an emptiness, cold. It's expanding, most intense in the center and then expands out between these two states (Longing and Support). Cold, white, empty color. Like a quiet pulling out both front and back. No sound.

Looking to the future but knowing that I'm stuck behind my own walls, knowing that I don't have strength or the courage to follow, to move forward. It's like giving up before I try. Wanting what's out there but not wanting to move towards it because I know I don't have the strength to reach it.

Emptiness also resolved into Infinite Self as its ideal state, the same as Longing. And it's easy to see how the Emptiness and Longing were connected. If Olivia was in a position where she felt a stronger longing toward something more specific, while at the same time feeling a stronger impossibility of having what she longed for, the emptiness would arise, as if the strands of longing pulled hard enough to open up this empty space. Emptiness and Longing are part of the same feeling path with Infinite Self as the ideal, origin state.

Why are we made this way?

Whenever we as explorers discover something new, the very next question that typically arises is, "Why is it this way and not some other?" I shall have more to say about this later in the section on Architecture, but at this point I think it is important to give you a preview.

Each feeling path fulfills a specific function in the whole of the self. Its job is to monitor a particular dimension of your experience, and to provide you ongoing feedback about your state of balance with respect to that dimension. For example, one path has the job of tracking what you have to give of yourself in this moment, in the specific context in which you find yourself.

When your highest good is being served and each dimension of your being is in balance, you experience optimal well-being. You are bathed in ideal feeling states. You feel good.

Good feeling states tend to be large, whole body states that blend into one another. There's not a whole lot of clear differentiation among feelings when you feel good. It's more like one big ocean of bliss.

But when things get out of balance, look out! Each feeling path crystallizes out of its ideal state into specific reactive states. A reactive state is uncomfortable, distressing. It is meant to call your attention to a specific way that you have fallen out of balance. And it's meant to call your attention to it right now.

A reactive state also has the characteristic of distorting your thinking and your perception. You will see, hear, and kinesthetically feel the world with heightened sensitivity to the source of your imbalance. If there's a threat and you feel fear, the source of the threat looks bigger than it otherwise would, certainly bigger than an objective measure of it would indicate. That's because this threat must be dealt with right away! All your attention must be mustered and focused on dealing with the threat.

The entire purpose of the distressing, reactive state is to help you identify the source of an imbalance and correct it. When everything is operating as it should, this is exactly what you do. You see the threat, (you can't miss it). You retreat and protect yourself or advance and confront. You take action to remove the threat and return yourself to comfort and well being.

But don't mistake this for emotion. It's not the same. The feeling mind operates on much more sophisticated terms. It is highly sensitive to complex social and environmental information that is beyond our simple emotional machinery to process.

Emotion is for survival, and it can't be beat for that. It kicks in instantly, and we don't need awareness for it to do its job. Our bodies are immediately mobilized and prepared to deal with threats, losses, opportunities or satisfactions for core survival needs.

Feeling, on the other hand, enables us to navigate the far more complex universe of social reality, of creativity, of spirituality and more. The feeling mind is able to process a great deal of information that lies far outside of our awareness. It is fully available to consciousness when we turn our attention to it, but most of the time that kind of awareness is unnecessary.

The feeling mind is elegant and wise beyond anything our conscious, rational mind is capable of. And it works beautifully if we don't interfere with its natural functioning. You'll understand more about what I'm telling you once you've mapped and moved a few dozen feeling states.

Step Three: Live It!

Once you've shifted a feeling from its reactive state to its ideal state, what's next? You might think the goal is to promote the ideal state, to seek to maintain that state at all times. This idea is based on outmoded concepts of how feeling works.

The ideal state you revealed through the Feeling Path Mapping process is not some kind of optimal state for continued existence. It is an ideal. It establishes the origin point for this particular feeling path, the ideal end of the full continuum of feeling states possible on this path.

This feeling path has a job to do. Its job is to provide you with accurate, highly responsive feedback about your state of balance in the world. It needs to be fluid, ever changing according to what is real inside and around you. If it were tacked at the positive end of the spectrum, it would be just as dysfunctional in serving your life as when it was stuck in the reactive state.

Some people live their lives seeking to achieve and maintain certain positive states. I call them state chasers. This is not what you want. State chasing is not full-on, wide-open living. It is not sensitive. It resolves not to be vulnerable.

Real life involves threat, loss and the potential for threat and loss in every moment. Real life is tentative and constantly changing. Nothing is secure. Nothing is guaranteed. Trying to force yourself to live perpetually in a state of bliss is an all-out assault on the nature of life.

What you have done though, in shifting your reactive state to its ideal, is you have opened up the full spectrum. This feeling path is now free to respond in all its beautiful magnificence, all the way from wide-open bliss to intense pain, according to what is real and true for you in your life at this present moment.

This is amazing. This is glorious. To live with the full capacity to feel, right here, right now, is beyond bliss.

I remember when I first cleared the paths which anchored my bipolar disorder. I was stunned by the richness of nuance and sensitivity I found myself feeling. Before that, I worshiped my highs. I lived to climb the pinnacles of inner sensation. Before my transformation, I would have declined any invitation to give those up.

But what I found was far more satisfying, far more fulfilling, far more soul-nourishing than anything I had previously experienced. Simply by walking down the street I could open myself to multitudes of various feeling states. Awe just by looking up at the sky. Shyness by noticing an attractive woman. Sadness seeing a panhandling drug addict. I was feeling it all. And not in these destructive waves which used to carry me high and leave me battered on the rocks. But in gentle surges, one after the other, several at a time.

I found myself thinking, so this is what "normal" people experience. I found myself grieving the fifteen years I had lost, where this fullness was pushed out by the falsely exaggerated highs and lows of my roller coaster ride. In my life with bipolar disorder, I lived within these grand symphonic moments: every instrument in the orchestra stuck in the same phrase, or even on the same note, for days at a time; then a dramatic crash into another phrase or note, again to be held for days as it pushed my nervous system to the limit and left me exhausted, depleted, empty. Now I saw the possibility for appreciating the little things, and I was grateful.

So this is what you get to have, doing this work. You get to become more fully alive. You might ask yourself, "Is this really what I want? Don't I simply want to feel less pain and more joy?" From where you are now, it might seem that is a move forward. But please trust me, as you do this work, as you open yourself to greater and greater sensitivity and responsiveness to the sheer grandeur of life, you will be grateful to be feeling more of both joy and pain. The pain you feel will be real, responsive to in-the-moment losses or threats or violations. You will feel it and you will respond to it, and the pain will have done its job and will subside. The pain you feel will do its job quickly, and you will no longer get stuck in suffering, disconnected from reality and perpetuating a reaction from the past. You will be grateful for your pain, your sadness, your fear, because you will recognize it for what it is: aliveness and truth, and the authentic engagement with the awesome mystery of being.

Alongside your pain you will also experience far greater joys. The moments of bliss you experience will break your heart open with their beauty. Any moment will have the potential of cracking open the doorway to eternity, and you will feel that potential within you at all times.

This is what it means to do this work. And for you to have this requires no more than to simply pay attention to your experience as you map and move first one state, then another, going ever deeper through the layers of separation from your birthright as a fully conscious, alive, beautiful being. You will awaken, simply by mapping and moving reactive states as they arise.

Nevertheless, most people feel more secure along the way if there is something they can do to reinforce their experiences. Let me offer a few suggestions for integrating the full-spectrum feeling path into your life.

Four-step integration

Now we have the opportunity to integrate the full feeling path, and the ideal state in particular, into your everyday life. Let's work through four key questions. You'll find a worksheet to copy at the end of these questions.

Noticing other feelings

Part of the integration process involves being open to including other feeling states that may be related to the one you've already mapped. Let's look at the first question,

"What else do you feel?"

What we've done so far is, you mapped one feeling state and you shifted it. You created a new image and a new feeling state that is more of the true or original or ideal state for this feeling path.

So let's turn back to the first feeling state you mapped. As you shifted that state, you might have noticed a little tug or pull in a different direction from some other feeling.

You can think about your multiple, reactive feeling states as points of a star. Each feeling state represents the specific location or coordinates of each point. If you want to change the configuration of that star, and you've taken one point and moved it, well, now you have a distorted star. The other points are going to try to pull that first point back into alignment with the others.

So right now, having moved one state, you have to work hard to nurture and to hold that new feeling as the center of the new direction in your life. But once you've moved all the states, the whole star reconfigures. In that case, you experience a release of the old pattern. The old issue that you had is simply not there anymore.

You find yourself making new choices, behaving in different ways, responding in completely different ways to situations that used to trigger you into the old pattern. It's an exciting experience, and it's one that you don't have to work at. When you get all the parts and you shift the whole system, you create a new configuration, a new direction to launch in your life.

So right now, you've shifted one feeling state. That's a great start. But I want you to pay attention to the other feelings that might be coming up, or that might be obviously connected to this one, and take them through the process, too. The more you do, the more the center of gravity for this pattern will shift towards your ideal.

New choices

But with that said, let's go through a process that will help any single part integrate, and will work even better the more parts you take through this process for any given issue that you might be exploring.

After you've shifted the feeling from its reactive state to its ideal, you're going to find that your impulses are different, your motivations are different, your beliefs and perceptions are different. But the shape and circumstances of your life, (as well as the stimulus/response habits in your brain), can often reinforce your old patterns. So it can help to be very explicit and concrete about what kinds of new patterns are wanting to arise, and make some specific choices about those.

So, the second question:

"What new life choices does this new feeling guide you to make?"

You might look at your life. Think about the shape of your life, the patterns of relationships and commitments and responsibilities, the furniture in your house, the clothes that you wear, the job that you have. At any moment of relative equilibrium, the external trappings of your life are a more or less accurate reflection of the inner state of your being. Now that the inner state has changed, what wants to change in the outer environment to match and support that change?

Many times you will find that after you have shifted a reactive state to its ideal, something in your life no longer fits. The thing that no longer fits can be relatively trivial: you may find you no longer like a certain color which dominates your wardrobe, or a painting you worked hard to acquire. Or it can be more significant: you may realize that the career into which you've invested 20 years of your life is no longer what you want to be doing, or that you really don't like the weather or the landscape where you live.

So being aware that there is that dynamic, and being conscious about making new choices in your life so that the shape of your life starts to take on the natural expression of the new shape of your being, that's going to lead you in a powerful new direction.

These choices don't have to be big ones. Little choices, like how you start your morning, or how you choose to interact when your boss is unreasonable, or how you choose to engage with your spouse, your partner, around having some fun.

Small choices about how you engage in your life will create new opportunities. Small choices will open new doors, and they'll start things rolling in a new direction. And, at first, the divergence might be small, nearly imperceptible. But as you start down a new path, that divergence gets wider, and your life takes a new tack, a new path, and picks up momentum.

That's part of why I wanted to call this work The Feeling Path. You are using feeling as a guide for choosing your path in life. It is the path of feeling, as well, to find your authentic direction and expression and contribution in this life. So asking yourself, "What different choices do I want to make?" can be very helpful.

I encourage you not to make fast, knee-jerk changes in your life, especially for the more significant things. Go ahead and toss that gaudy shirt, but keep the job until you have time to solidify a vision of your new direction and have a clear next step to take. In the meantime, find ways to incorporate your new insights and feeling states into the "how," the way you choose to engage or inhabit the significant aspects of your life which you're wanting to change. For example, you might discover that simply showing up differently in your job opens up opportunities you never could have predicted. Make incremental adjustments before taking drastic action.

New practices

The third question:

> **"What daily practices can nurture your new feeling?"**

One of the best ways we can change the patterns we weave in the tapestry of our life energy is by taking on new, daily practices. Many truly transformative practices seem innocuous. They don't take long to do, yet they can set grand new patterns in motion, especially when they have the power of fully free feeling paths behind them.

What new practices do you want to consider taking on? What current practices do you want to alter in some way to make them more meaningful or supportive of your highest good?

I recommend changing your patterns in small, easy ways, rather than jumping into grand new lifestyles. The most useful and successful approach to changing your daily habits is to make sure you are receiving positive reinforcement at every step of the way.

For example, if you want to get more physical exercise, start small by going for a 10 minute walk each day. Your goal is to experience feeling good as a result of the new practice you choose. You want to enjoy the activity itself, as well as the result of the activity in other areas of your life. You want the positive feeling states that come from the changes you make to motivate you to incrementally increase your new activity up to but not beyond the point where it is contributing real value to your life. And you want the opportunity to find out early on, before you've made major commitments, whether a new practice really doesn't serve you, so you can more easily redirect your efforts into something more suitable.

To offer a contrasting example in the area of exercise, joining a gym and making a commitment to a 3-hour workout every day is a pretty sure strategy for quick burnout. You won't like it. You'll be in pain. You'll have to sacrifice too many other things to accomplish it. And all around, the net reinforcement will be negative.

To choose your new practices, spend a little time with your new, ideal states. Ask those parts of you if there are things you used to do which you would like to revive in your life. Ask if there are things you've always wanted to do but never gave yourself permission to enjoy. Ask if you are inspired by something you've seen others do, or have read about or watched a program on.

In your new states, notice where your attention is drawn. Where do your idle fantasies wander? What little scenarios do you find yourself indulging? These are all clues.

If you decide to enter some new territory, for example learning to play an instrument for the first time, avail yourself of guidance from those who can help you make your experience a positive one. Seek out teachers or books you can learn from. Find other people with similar interests who can offer you support and tips. Be open to resources showing up from surprising directions.

How do you want to express your new, fully alive feeling paths in actual daily practices in your everyday life? Make sure your primary sources of guidance for the new practices you choose are your new, ideal feeling states. Don't override the wisdom of your feeling with other ideas, judgments, or expectations. Trust the natural, spontaneous impulses and satisfaction that arise from the authentic new feelings and thoughts.

Think of your practices as a container that can hold the unique expressions and needs of each day. You may, for example, start your day with morning pages from "The Artist's Way." And it might be that you find yourself zeroing in on one particular feeling path as a way of expressing the day: "What does this feeling wisdom have to offer me today?"

You might find yourself in a physical practice – a yoga practice, for example – putting your attention on the image of that feeling and noticing, "Where is it in my body as I do this asana?" You might choose to focus on it in a meditation practice, or in a simple walk in your neighborhood or at the beach. Putting your attention on the new feeling state, deliberately, will bring it into new places in your life. Using various practices that are comfortable and easy for you is a great way to make this a daily habit.

New actions

And so finally we come to the last question in the brief version of the worksheet for Step 3.

> **"What new actions arise naturally from this feeling?"**

This question is really a way of inviting both new practices and new choices.

Start with the new feeling, and imagine yourself in a particular situation or context where the old feeling used to be. Ask yourself, "What will I do here instead? Having this new feeling as a way of being, what action naturally wants to come from this place? How will I be, how will I behave, how will I interact, how will I express myself differently, coming from this new place, this new feeling state?"

There's so much rich opportunity for re-patterning your life when you start at the core, at the center, at the heart of feeling and allow the natural expressions – your words, your thoughts, your behaviors – to emerge naturally from that place.

Feeling is the foundation. Every conscious experience has an anchor in feeling. And we're working with that foundation right now. By going to feeling and bringing it into awareness, and by inviting it to return to its original, ideal state, you are creating the conditions where everything in your life can realign to your authentic presence, your authentic being.

The gift of feeling

In conclusion, I'm going to wrap back around to that first question, "What else do you feel?" Be vigilant. Pay attention to what your feelings are telling you. And when you find yourself feeling something again that you've felt at different times in your life that has maybe steered you off track, that's an opportunity to take that feeling through this process.

And when you find yourself feeling something that's getting in the way of fully experiencing this ideal state that you've just mapped, that's an indication that there's a part that's asking to be involved in this process, to be taken through the three steps, so that it can be your ally, your resource, so it can offer you its gift.

That last word is important: its gift, its resource. I want you to understand here what you just did. You mapped a feeling that was a problem, a challenge. It felt as though it was not contributing to your highest good. You shifted it. You invited that feeling to reveal itself. In essence you asked, "Hey, who are you, really?" And in showing itself to you, it revealed something that was purely positive, purely good, purely of benefit to you.

Every single part of you has that truth at its core. There is no part of you that is bad. There is no part of you that wants anything less than the absolute best for you.

By welcoming every feeling and inviting it to reveal itself, you bring back into your awareness and your ongoing, everyday being all these different parts that have been split off and buried.

The gift of wholeness

The idea of wholeness is pervasive and revered among those in certain circles. But what exactly does the term refer to? I'll have more to say about this in the section on Architecture, but for now we can learn something important that can help us understand what wholeness might mean when applied to our experience of being human.

For one thing, even the act of mapping and moving a single feeling state opens up our experience to be more fully present in the moment and responsive to everything inside and around us. We move from being stuck in a single feeling state, seeing the world and experiencing ourselves through its distorted lens, to being more fully alive. I think we can think of that aliveness as wholeness.

In addition, when we are driven by a configuration of feeling states locked in the past, very often we find that certain of the reactive states are strongly defended. They remain outside of awareness while other states occupy the more comfortable foreground.

As we go through the experience of mapping and moving our reactive states, we clear the way for these deeper states to come to the surface. As they do, and as we map and move those as well, feeling paths which were previously unavailable to serve us come back into active participation in our well-being. This too, this reclaiming of parts of us long-ago lost, can be thought of as an increase in wholeness. When we have more of our feeling paths active and in service, we get to experience more of ourselves in this present moment. That, I believe, is a pretty good way to understand this idea of wholeness.

STEP 3: LIVE IT.   **Date:**

New Feeling Name:

Original Feeling Name:

What else do you feel?

Your new choices:

Your new practices:

Your new actions:

Deeper Integration

Let's take a look at some ways to take your work even further.

Practicing the path

Our old way of managing our internal environment was to highlight some states and diminish others. It can be tempting to engage in this state chasing after you've mapped and moved a really uncomfortable feeling. However, that is neither necessary nor desirable if what you want is to enhance the quality of your inner life. Instead, it's important to reinforce the idea that negative feeling states are actually your allies in the ongoing quest for balance. We need to reinforce this because of the unfortunate pervasiveness of messages to the contrary.

I highly recommend that you create index cards with the maps of the reactive and ideal states for each feeling path you map. Here is an example of the template I use with my clients. (I'll post a blank template for you to download at FeelingPath.com.)

Take a few minutes with this card soon after you map the path. Reactivate the ideal state in your awareness. Then deliberately reverse the ideal state back into the reactive state.

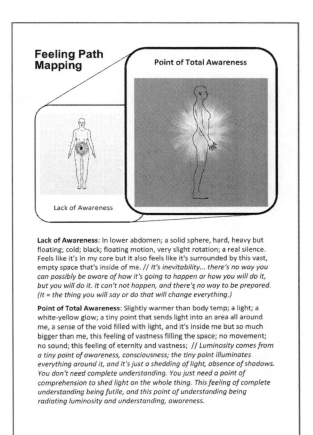

Feeling Path Mapping

Point of Total Awareness

Lack of Awareness

Lack of Awareness: In lower abdomen; a solid sphere, hard, heavy but floating; cold; black; floating motion, very slight rotation; a real silence. Feels like it's in my core but it also feels like it's surrounded by this vast, empty space that's inside of me. // *It's inevitability... there's no way you can possibly be aware of how it's going to happen or how you will do it, but you will do it. It can't not happen, and there's no way to be prepared. (It = the thing you will say or do that will change everything.)*

Point of Total Awareness: Slightly warmer than body temp; a light; a white-yellow glow; a tiny point that sends light into an area all around me, a sense of the void filled with light, and it's inside me but so much bigger than me, this feeling of vastness filling the space; no movement; no sound; this feeling of eternity and vastness; // *Luminosity comes from a tiny point of awareness, consciousness; the tiny point illuminates everything around it, and it's just a shedding of light, absence of shadows. You don't need complete understanding. You just need a point of comprehension to shed light on the whole thing. This feeling of complete understanding being futile, and this point of understanding being radiating luminosity and understanding, awareness.*

Allow yourself to feel the reactive state, knowing you no longer have to fear that state. Let yourself notice the positive intention it always had for you. What was it trying to do for you, back then when it first took this form?

Now reverse and shift the feeling state back into the ideal. Recognize that the ideal is just that: a beacon, a direction, an invitation to shape your life in ways that create harmony. It is not an arrival place. You are never "finished" your journey, residing in bliss, but rather you are forever engaging in the ever-changing richness of life.

When we are fully alive, we fear no feeling within us. We welcome all feeling states as essential awareness, helping us orient and engage. And when we are fully open to our feeling experience, we find it is very rare than a situation will ever arise in which the original reactive state will authentically express with the same disabling intensity. We become far more sensitive to changing conditions around us, and far more responsive. We take action at the slightest indication that things are moving out of balance, that one of our needs is not being adequately met. And when we take action, we restore our balance. There is no need for the extreme states we were consigned to suffer with and attempt to control in the past, when our feeling mind was locked into configurations of past pain.

It's a good idea to review your cards from time to time. Allow yourself to practice the full range of each path. You might even allow yourself some creative expression. Cultivate the reactive state and write a poem about a particular topic. Now shift to the ideal state and write a new poem about the same topic. What can you learn from the two poems, side by side?

Or explore your states through movement. Bring up the reactive state. Intensify it, and allow it to inform and motivate your dance. Gradually shift the feeling state toward the ideal, allowing your movements to evolve and express the full spectrum of feeling. Return to the reactive, back to the ideal. Let the two states talk to one another through your movement.

And what about visual explorations? What kinds of photographs will you take from the place of the reactive state, versus those you are drawn to in ideal state? How might you capture in a painting the full spectrum of a feeling path, from the most extreme reactive state all the way through the most ideal state.

Have fun with this. The more comfortable you are with the full continuum of states in every path within you, the more comfortable you are with the full continuum of experiences in life. You become free to engage without holding back, without controlling, without hesitation. You become free to show up, fully alive and present for all the wondrous experiences available to you.

Rewriting the past

The past does not exist. All we have of the past are our memories. And memory is notoriously unreliable as an objective record of what actually happened.

But even if memory were infallible, and we could faithfully recall and fully relive exactly what we experienced the first time around, our experience in that moment was limited by our narrow perspective on the whole situation. Our experience was a small, filtered fraction of the complex richness that is real life. Even if our memory were a perfect record of our actual experience, it would still be a pathetically incomplete record of the full reality of our past.

Take any childhood incident involving one of your parents, for example. What could you possibly have known of the real, fully alive, complex, flesh-and-blood person who was your parent? What could you possibly have understood about their motivations, their fears, their inner conflicts, their history? How could any memory of that incident be complete?

Even the most dreadful histories have within them the seeds of strength. Human lives are profound journeys through mystery, and every life is wide and rich beyond our small knowing. You begin to gain access to this deeper wisdom when you access your ideal states.

When you shift into an ideal state, take some time with your past. You don't have to do it right away, but at some point within a few days of shifting a state, look back on those times in which the old, reactive state used to be triggered. Look all the way back, if you can, to the original situations in which that reactive state was first set in place.

Now, hold your ideal state, and look through its lens at those past experiences. What do you notice? What stands out to you? What can you learn about yourself, and about the others around you, as you maintain access to your ideal and review your history?

This is a powerful practice for developing compassion. As you review your history with the new wisdom of your ideal states, you learn to recognize the many ways you have shut yourself off from the beauty of life, the ways you have judged and limited and diminished yourself and others. And you learn that you always have the choice not to do that. As you practice this through reviewing your past, you begin to find that you become larger in inhabiting your present. You are much less likely to get caught in those moments of judgment or withdrawal. You are much more likely to see the full humanity of whoever is in front of you, no matter what struggles they may be undergoing, no matter how they might be acting to deny or restrict their own humanity or yours. You will learn to inhabit a place of understanding and compassion, both for those difficult times in your past, and for those moments in the present where others' challenges interface with your own.

Rehearsing the future

In the same way that we can go back and rewrite our interpretations of the past, we can imagine ourselves into the future to re-craft our expectations. By doing so, we can make it easier and more likely that we will respond in new ways to situations that used to trigger our reactive states.

The way to do this is simple. Think back to recent situations that used to trigger your old, dysfunctional patterns. Particularly focus on situations in which you strongly felt a specific reactive feeling state. Choose situations which are likely to occur again in the future. Common examples of these are challenging interactions at work or difficult encounters with family members.

First go backwards. Imagine what would be different in that situation in the past, if you had access to this new, ideal feeling state. How would you perceive things differently, if you were able to go back? What would you do or say differently, if you could do it all over again?

Now project into the future. Having easy access to your new, ideal state as a way of being, what seems true, or real, or important about that situation? What can you imagine doing or saying differently, the next time you find yourself in that situation? How might you expect other people might respond differently to you as a result? What opportunities are available, now that you have access to the full spectrum of your feeling path, that were not available to you in the past?

Spend a little time and energy making your rehearsal as clear, and vivid, and life-like as you can. See what you anticipate seeing, hear people's voices and other sounds, notice the physical sensations of your posture and surroundings.

Take a few notes. Write the new scenario in present tense, as if it is happening right now. Be as specific as possible, noting various details that come to mind.

Follow through into the time after the situation has ended. Imagine how you will feel, having responded differently. What will you appreciate about your new way of being?

Also be alert for what might remain difficult. What did you notice in your rehearsal that might get in the way of your being fully present? Did you notice any other feeling states that came up in your mental scenario which you might also want to map and move? Do so, and when you finish, conduct your future rehearsal once again. Continue until you feel as comfortable as you want, that you can handle the situation in a way that feels authentic, preserves your integrity, and respects all the people involved.

Single state vs. full set

An integral part of The Feeling Path practice is actively seeking related feeling states. As you will read in the section on Architecture, every experience of self is constructed from a set of nine feeling paths. When a pattern of dysfunction is driving a challenging issue, those nine paths are most likely locked into nine (or potentially more) specific, reactive feeling states. Finding all nine states, mapping them and moving them is the most effective way to fully release and transform a limiting pattern.

However, identifying the full set of nine can be difficult in some cases. The skill and experience required to clear the entire set may be more than you are likely to acquire simply through reading this book. So there will almost certainly be times when you choose to do the integration step with a partial set of ideal states, or even a single state on its own. Please don't hesitate to do this. Working with even one state can provide relief and movement in a positive direction.

Think of the full set of nine paths as a system. In its open configuration, with all nine paths free to respond throughout the full spectrum of possible states, the system is fluid and responsive. It seeks to maintain equilibrium with the totality of itself plus your inner and outer environments. When there is imbalance in the whole, the set of nine paths adjusts to highlight that imbalance and motivate action to regain balance.

However, when the set has become compromised and is locked into a configuration of reactive states, it seeks equilibrium only with itself. It becomes separated from a relationship with its changing environment, and its full purpose seems to be to maintain its own pattern. In this situation, mapping and moving a single state is unlikely to change the pattern without a great deal of work.

That work may be worth doing. Choosing to engage in integration activities with a single ideal state, to support the continued freedom of the full feeling path, can begin to shake up the rest of the system. Movement can begin to happen over time. The more energy you put into the free path, the greater its influence over the whole set and more traction it gets in changing the system in a positive direction.

As within, so without

We tend to think of ourselves as individuals, with our interior clearly separated from our exterior. However, fully one third of our feeling paths are specifically oriented toward what is outside of us, and an additional third are oriented toward the whole which includes us. Only three out of nine paths governing our experience of being a self in the world are concerned with what is inside of us.

It is more accurate to think of ourselves as a dynamic balance between inside, outside, and context. And so as we release inner patterns, as we change the inner configuration of feeling paths, we find our relationship with the outside world changing. Our relationships change, our preferences for food and furniture and landscapes change, our satisfaction with various activities changes.

In doing the work of The Feeling Path, it is natural for us to gradually evolve our outer lives to more fully match our inner lives. Sometimes that natural evolution can be obstructed. If we live in a situation in which we have very little power to make those changes, if we are confined to a rigid structure of relationship, of job, of home, of community, then we may find our inner work stifled. We may do the necessary work to free the inner feeling paths, but because we are unable to make the necessary changes to our lives to mirror our greater inner freedom, we may continue to feel many of the challenging states that defined our pattern in the first place. The difference is, those reactive states may now be freely and accurately providing feedback about the state of balance in our world. But because we are not free to take the action to restore that balance, we may find ourselves slipping back into a rigid inner configuration.

In these cases, it can be very important to draw the focus of change inward. Even though it might be difficult or impossible to change external circumstances, one thing that no person or circumstance can take from you is the freedom you have within your own heart and spirit. If you bring the focus of your change inward as much as possible, there is the hope to move forward with your inner freedom despite your circumstances. It is not an easy path, but it is one with its own special rewards.

In cases where you do have freedom to change the circumstances of your life, I encourage you to be thoughtful about the changes you do make. Take your time. Include others in your deliberations. Create a clear vision for yourself but focus on your next steps, allowing the vision to evolve as your current circumstances evolve.

There is no way for you to fully know from where you stand today what future is fully yours to inhabit. Getting there is a unfolding process, one step at a time.

Spontaneous re-patterning

It might seem that changing a life is a lot of work. It might seem after you have mapped and moved half a dozen feeling states, or a full set of nine, that you should take a step back and make a five year plan. I can tell you that is unnecessary.

All that is required to change a life is to show up, moment by moment, with your newly liberated feeling paths. You will find yourself making dozens and hundreds of small choices differently than the choices you previously would have made. They may be infinitesimally small, these differences in choices, but together they begin to accumulate. By a thousand small choices a life takes off in an altogether new direction.

When you allow yourself the freedom not to know what the ultimate outcome is, when you support yourself in being fully present to the moment, you set in motion the grand forces of creation. Creation is rooted firmly in the present. It is not attached to the future. It is not trapped in the past.

When you stand fully in the present, you are open to notice your next step, and the next one, and the next. When you are open fully to the sophisticated and wise feedback of your feelings, you make your choices incorporating not just conscious preferences but you also include deeper threads and pulses outside of your awareness. Some of those pulses arise from within you, while others you are sensitive to arise from outside you. Your feeling mind has the power to synthesize the full spectrum of influences bearing down on this moment, in your life, in you. And it has the power to know, to simply know, what is next.

In the old days this might have been called intuition, or "gut feel" if you were a guy. What it is, though, is presence as a fully conscious human being. This is what it means to be alive, aware, free. This is what we are born to experience in every moment, to be caught up in the flow of life, fully at choice yet paradoxically fully surrendered to the current.

Inhabiting this place of presence, you will find the world responds differently to you. You experience yourself as yourself, with nothing in the way of the real you. Others around you can sense that. They respond to it. They want some of it for themselves. You find yourself with more opportunities for friendship, for work, for fun, than you imagined possible. And it is all just simply because you are showing up. Now. And now. And now.

And through this showing up, through the gradual accretion of dozens and hundreds and thousands of moments, your life transforms. It transforms not because you have transformed it through an act of will. It transforms because you have opened yourself to forces greater than yourself, forces from within as well as those from without, and together those forces reconstitute the experience of your life in shapes and shades you find more authentic, more satisfying, more fulfilling.

Revisiting developmental stages

The deeper the work you do, especially when you work with full, nine-path sets, the more likely it is for you to find yourself in a place where you feel like a raw novice in some area of your life. This can be true no matter how old you are or how much experience you may have in that area.

The natural flow of a life passes through certain developmental thresholds. For example, when we start dating, we need to construct an all new persona with all the required perspectives and behaviors by which to navigate relationships. Often that persona is founded on defenses and compensations, designed to protect some underlying, intolerable feeling state or express some long-ago injury or resentment.

In these cases, when we clear that persona through the Feeling Path work, and reset it to its ideal configuration, the old M.O. no longer works. We find ourselves without our longstanding frames of reference, habitual ways of communicating or behaving, standard judgments and interpretations. We no longer feel the same attractions or motivations, are no longer limited by the same repulsions or defined by the same preferences.

It would be nice if clearing an old persona like this left us with a new set of healthy beliefs, perceptions, and habits all ready to go, just push the button and you're off to the races. But it doesn't work that way. Instead we find ourselves rewound to the beginning, needing to figure out all over again how to navigate this territory.

We need to take the time it takes to place ourselves in the relevant environments, pay attention to our authentic likes and dislikes, learn how to know what's what in our environment, make mistakes, and gradually come to know our true selves in this context all over again.

I've had to do that with relationships once or twice, finding myself feeling more like an adolescent than I ever actually did during adolescence. Unsure of myself, I engaged tentatively, but authentically. I learned for the first time what was important to me, how to be discerning, what my preferences were. It was strange for a period of months at least, and I have to say that while my life experience helped, (for example, my communication skills were far more advanced than they ever could have been as a adolescent), I did have to go through a protracted re-learning period. It was awkward at times, uncomfortable at times, and at the same time wonderfully fun.

Depending on the focus of the work you do, the pattern(s) you clear, you may find yourself starting all over again with your work, in relationships, in your social life, or any of a number of various contexts. Give yourself permission to be a beginner. Seek mentors and close friends who can support you. Allow yourself to make mistakes and trust yourself to learn from them.

It's a wonderful opportunity to be able to truly start over, free of the baggage you used to carry around. Enjoy it.

An issue versus a life

When working with a focused issue – an ongoing challenge in your life, a longstanding habit you want to change, a recurring experience of difficult emotion, an experience of limitation in pursuing a goal, etc. – the work will most often remain somewhat limited in scope. For most issues, you can fully clear the pattern by mapping and moving the nine paths of the relevant persona, or what I call the Surface Self. In doing so, you often find the problem simply vanishes. It is relatively easy to make new choices and set in motion a new pattern, a new direction in that area of your life.

But it is rare that anyone has an issue which is truly isolated, a challenge that has no echoes into other areas of their life. In most cases, clearing this issue will lead to your finding yourself in new situations, situations which may have a tendency to trigger another pattern which had previously been hidden.

For example, let's say you were terribly shy. So you had very few close friendships. You clear the shyness, and all of a sudden you find yourself having a close friend or two. In those friendships you notice the issue of jealousy coming up. The potential for jealousy was there all along, but because the surface issue of shyness kept you safe from close friendships, you never had to deal with it.

You may find it helpful to migrate from one issue to the next, clearing them as they appear. But eventually you will start wondering if there is any end to the hang-ups you have stored inside you. And frankly, it is possible you could find no end.

In my own growth work, I cleared many sets of nine-part Surface Selves. Eventually I grew tired of it. I decided I didn't want to map and move another feeling state, ever.

That's when I started looking for the deeper pattern. All the surface patterns seemed to share a certain DNA, a kinship, a theme. I went in search of the theme, and I found the Deep Self. I'll have more to share about this in Part 2 on Architecture.

Now whether you are doing this work on your own, or you are choosing to work with me, or someone I've trained, or a self-taught therapist, eventually many of you will want to take on the work of the Deep Self. This work is not so quick to put behind you. This work is not so easy to move through. It takes a level of commitment and support which is serious and substantial, and I just want to let you know that up front.

Think of the example I shared of myself starting all over again as if I were an adolescent, dating for the first time. That was a result of clearing a Surface Self. Now imagine that same level of disorientation, newness, and naivety applied to your deepest sense of identity, your sense of who you are as a person, your sense of connection to the people around you, to your work, to your deepest decisions and preferences in your life.

That is the level of transformation you will most likely experience as you map and move the Deep Self. This is not simply clearing an issue, a pattern. This is like hitting the reset button on your entire being in this life.

It's wonderful. It's exciting. It is also terribly frightening at times, extremely uncomfortable and disorienting at others. There is no experience you are likely to be able to compare it to. It really is like starting over.

Fortunately, although you wipe the slate clean on the core issues that define your persona, and the template that shaped the formation of all your personas throughout your life, you do find something solid in its place. You find an exquisite, robust, embodied sense of being yourself. The language eludes me right now. The experience is so simple as to almost not be worth putting words to, yet so profound that only poetry might approach its essence.

The longer you inhabit this new self, the more experiences you accumulate, the more choices you make, the more memories you lay down, the easier it becomes to be at peace with this new self, and the more confident and secure you become. You learn by doing, just what are your preferences, just what do you care most about, just what will you go for when given the chance. And so gradually, imperceptibly, you come to redefine your life and the way you choose to inhabit it.

My first big transformation

To give you a little perspective of what it's like to do this work in depth, let me share the story of the day I dismantled my bipolar disorder. I awoke on April 4, 1995 at about 4:30 am after a disturbing dream. I knew the dream had to do with some deeper issues I was wrestling with, and I used the material of the dream as the starting place for my work.

I didn't know about these things at that time, the nine-part architecture, the Surface and Deep Selves. But somehow I believe I got lucky. By working with a dream, I think I was tapping into a very pervasive set of paths underlying much of my life. And although I only found seven parts at that time and did not do a complete transformation, the change was profound.

The previous few days, I had been flirting on the edge of a manic episode. I believe all people with bipolar disorder have the capacity to "increase the voltage" of a state at will, and I know I used to use that capacity to amplify both my highs and my lows. I had been amping up my high, (most likely in response to feelings of insecurity and aloneness brought on by my girlfriend leaving town).

The dream was fraught with intense fears and a deep sense of sadness and longing. At that time in the development of the work, I had worked at most with three or four parts at a time. I didn't draw the states, didn't even give them names, either before or after moving them. I was flying by the seat of my pants.

Also at that early time I hadn't become very practiced at facilitating my own work with myself. I had to provide some kind of an external structure to lead myself through the questioning sequence. That day I used the structure of typing out the conversation on my laptop between the guide asking the questions and the explorer answering them. I still have the dialog I captured.

Overall I mapped and moved seven feeling states. So I didn't get an entire set. But one of those states was what today I would call a pivot. It a feeling state which was so uncomfortable, all the other states were arrayed around it in such a way as to keep that state out of awareness. "The feeling which must not be felt." The entire array pivots around this central state.

I called it "the fear thing." In my notes I described it as "ovoid in shape, about half the size of a human… four feet behind me… It seems gray and smooth, but more like a gas than a solid, and more like a dull, soft smooth than shiny… It's scary as hell."

It was pulling on me, as if to pull me backwards into itself. When I asked what would happen if I gave into it, the answer was that I would die – whether literally or figuratively I didn't know; it felt chillingly real either way.

In the course of moving this state, I discovered that the fear's function was actually to protect me, to keep me from being pulled apart by people wanting things from me. The presupposition was that I was not strong enough to withstand such forces.

When it moved, it came into my body, relocating to my lower abdomen, and became a powerful source of light and energy inside me. The power was formidable, and it had the sound of a rocket engine. I described it this way, "white-hot, small. I have a sense of being able to expand it if I want to tap into a greater source of energy. This is raw energy, raw source, raw power, the source of creation."

I worked hard that day, digging into very intense and difficult feelings, mapping and moving them, taking breaks at times to get my bearings. But at the end of the day, I was not the same person woke up that morning from a bad dream. Over the next two weeks or so I felt like a stranger in a strange land. I felt things I had never felt before, with a subtlety and nuance which was stunning in its richness. I felt as though I finally had some window into the experience of other (normal) people.

From that day forward I never had another manic episode. Not only that, but I did not miss those highs. (I had always thought I would never choose to give them up.) The highs were nothing compared to the richness of full-on feeling. I wouldn't trade back again for anything.

My life also took a strong turn in a new direction. I had dropped out of school in my early 20s after a few years of trying to finish up my bachelors degree at the University of Pennsylvania. I assumed I would never finish because I could not bear the thought of suffering with the structure a class or degree program would impose.

Within a few months of shifting "the fear thing" into the "source of creation," I had signed up to audit a class, to test the water for a program to complete my degree. Two years later I finished it, and I went on to complete my masters as well.

The changes unfolded organically out of the mapping and moving I had done. My thoughts changed. My spontaneous feelings and moods changed. My reactions to specific things and people changed. My life orientation, ambitions, and attitude changed.

All of these things changed without any direct effort on my part to change them. The changes were the natural outgrowth of the deep shifts I had made within my feeling mind. I simply could no longer live in the ways to which I had become accustomed. And so little by little I carved out new paths, made new choices, reached out in new directions.

This is what you can expect in doing this work. The deeper the work, the more profound and effortless the changes. Often times those changes create some disruption or discomfort in your life as you break off from one path and take up on another. But these are the ordinary discomforts of a life on the edge of aliveness. I believe you will welcome them as I have, and appreciate the gifts that come to you as you bring more of your authentic self to every day.

The importance of support

Whether you are working with the Surface Self or are at the point where you are doing the serious work of the Deep Self, I strongly advise you not to do this work in isolation. By setting out on The Feeling Path, you are choosing the road not taken in comparison to almost everyone else on the planet. This road is new, and few people know about it at this point. You will have experiences others will not be able to relate to. As you tap into your deeper wisdom, you will gain insights others may not share. And you may find yourself struggling to connect with people who are still operating by the old paradigms.

If you can, bring someone along with you. Or link up with someone who is already on the path. I will be creating opportunities for people to connect and create community at FeelingPath.com. I invite you to join me there.

Using with other practices

The Feeling Path Mapping process supports and accelerates your growth along other paths.

No matter whether you're going to therapy, involved in a self-help group, practicing meditation, working with an executive coach, or involved in any other growth or spiritual practices, you'll appreciate how quickly you'll get unstuck and move your progress forward once again.

Compatible with somatic therapies

Feeling is rooted in the body, and the experience of feeling intermingles with the experience of embodiment. Many times, somatic issues are interwoven with feeling states. For example, simple pain is far more tolerable when it is not complicated by the suffering of a dreadful feeling state which overlaps the physical area of the pain. Pain management goes more smoothly when accompanied by effective feeling hygiene. And all somatic practices and therapies are improved when we are free to clear any feeling state obstacles that may be in the way.

Complementary to cognitive therapies

All conscious activity is grounded in feeling as its foundation. Even so-called "mental" activities like calculation and judgment, or states of numbness or confusion, can be traced to somatosensory-based feeling states. And when you identify the underlying feeling states of dysfunctional patterns of thought or behavior and clear the reactive states, the thoughts, beliefs, perceptions, and behaviors naturally and spontaneously re-calibrate to a healthy and whole state of being. So any effort to change beliefs, thought patterns, or behavior gains effectiveness when combined with a strong program of clearing the underlying feelings.

Augments personal growth and spiritual practices

Any prolonged pursuit of personal or spiritual development eventually runs into roadblocks. These roadblocks can easily be traced to underlying configurations of reactive feeling states. Identifying and clearing these states is easy now, so anyone can maintain forward motion in their chosen practice.

Creates leverage for personal coaching

Coaching usually focuses on goals and actions. But even the best intentions often go off the rails when we encounter deeper issues. And most coaches are inadequately prepared to help their clients move through those issues. The Feeling Path gives an opportunity to create movement by releasing small, internal obstacles. For most emotionally competent clients, judicious use of Feeling Path Mapping results in faster and more consistent progress toward chosen goals.

Accelerates the pursuit of professional goals

When the next rung on the promotional ladder involves managing subordinates, giving presentations, or making high-stakes decisions, people who are otherwise highly qualified often find their careers stalled. When that next advancement involves actions that take the professional outside his or her comfort zone, The Feeling Path can help by clearing fear, hesitation, anxiety, or self-doubt and establishing new feeling states that promote success.

Explore the many ways you can apply The Feeling Path to the pursuit of your own personal goals by joining in with the community at FeelingPath.com.

Part 2:
The Architecture
of Wisdom

Nine Paths

Within every conscious moment lie nine distinct feeling states, all active, all playing a role in creating your experience of a self-in-the-world. When the feeling mind is fully present, fully alive and free, each of these states is a momentary expression of an ever-changing feeling path. These nine paths comprise an elegant, interdependent system.

Each feeling path is sensitive to a particular dimension of existence. Each path has a unique function to play within the greater context of the nine.

Three domains

Think for a moment of a living cell as a model for consciousness. For the cell to exist as an entity in this infinitely complex world, it must define itself, set itself apart from the whole. Yet it must remain integrated with the whole. This differentiation and integration take place within the wider context of the environment and its limitations and resources. For example, the environment on earth three billion years ago could only support sulfur-metabolizing bacteria because there was little oxygen. Today, those sulfur bacteria still exist in places where the environment requires it, in deep sea vents for example.

So a cell has a boundary, a cell wall. Inside that boundary is one domain. The area immediately outside that boundary is another. And the wider context, the properties and broader environmental characteristics which provide limitations and resources for how the inside and outside can interact is the third domain.

In the same way, we find these three domains operational in the feeling mind. Three feeling paths generate your experience of what is inside of you, what you have to contribute to your world in this moment. Three paths generate your experience of what is outside of you, what is available to support your being in this moment. And three paths generate your experience of the context within which the relationship between your inner world and your outer world is supported.

These three domains exist in dynamic balance. Changes in one domain require adjustments in the other two to maintain that balance.

Inside

The inside triad governs the experience of what we have within us, that is uniquely ours to give and express. In different contexts, this triad may encompass our capacity for vitality, creation, will, caring, voice, understanding, or meaning.

In its ideal, the inside triad holds what is possible for us to give, and the optimal ways of being which bring that to fruition. In its responsive states, the inside triad gives us ongoing feedback about the state of our freedom to be, to give, to express our true nature. When the inside triad falls into reactivity, it can often compensate with states and behaviors that undermine one's capacity for giving.

Outside

The outside triad governs the experience of what is available to us from the outside. In different contexts, this triad may encompass available (or unavailable) sources of health, sexual connection, the physical world, a loved one, the community, knowledge, or spiritual presence.

In its ideal, the outside triad holds what is possible for us to receive, and the optimal ways of being which bring that to fruition. In its responsive states, the outside triad gives us ongoing feedback about the state of our being supported by others and the world. When it falls into reactivity, the outside triad can often compensate with states and behaviors that undermine one's capacity for receiving.

Context

The context triad governs the experience of what holds the space within which the inside and outside aspects of our selves are free to interact. In different situations, this context can encompass the larges frames within which we conduct our giving and receiving with respect to our body, our sexuality and creativity, our will and agency, our capacity for love and intimacy, our engagement in community, our exploration of knowledge and meaning, and our experience of ultimate purpose.

In its ideal, the context triad holds the largest frame for what is possible, and supports optimal ways for us to bring what is possible into being. In its responsive states, the context triad gives us ongoing feedback about our broadest environments and what they enable or limit in our ability to sustain full aliveness in our giving and receiving. When this triad falls into reactivity, it can often shut down the other triads because it compromises the frame within which the others operate.

Three roles

The three parts comprising each triad – inside, outside, and context – hold three specific roles. Each role is present within each triad. Each one of these roles has a particular structure and function within the whole. You will see examples of these very clearly when you do your own work, shifting reactive states to ideal states. The three ideal states from Olivia in Part 1 were clear examples of the three different roles.

We can think of these roles as necessary structures for the smooth operation of each triad. Take the inside triad for example. In order to generate the experience of what is available to give from within oneself, and to be able to act in such a way as to optimize that function of giving, we require three specific roles. No more are necessary, no less will do the job.

Each role finds clear expression in the actual structure of a feeling path in its ideal state. The role of a path is also evident in the type of beliefs and perceptions it tends to hold in the ideal, and the scope of influence it exerts in all states including the ideal.

Source

The structure of the source role is clear and unequivocal. As the feeling path moves toward its ideal state, it takes on a quality of limitlessness. There are three types of this limitlessness, one for each of the domains.

- The inside source is experienced as a limitless supply of some feeling substance flowing, radiating, or otherwise emanating from a single point on the midline inside the body. Very often these inside sources take on qualities and find optimal locations that suggest chakras from certain long-standing traditions.

- The outside source is experienced as a limitless supply of some feeling substance flowing, radiating, or otherwise emanating from some place outside the body. The direction of movement is toward and into the body, continuing all the way through the body into the space beyond it. Olivia's Infinite Self was an example of an outside source.

- The context source is experienced as a limitless supply of some feeling substance occupying every point in space, inside and outside the body, extending infinitely in all directions.

The source role takes on the job of representing the field of possibilities. It answers the question, "What is possible or available?" It defines the broadest boundaries of the playground in which we get to make our choices moment to moment.

The source paths are the most powerful in a triad. The other two paths adapt to the state of the source. If the source is open, close to its ideal state, the presence and guidance paths are free to choose their state for optimum well being.

If the source is shut down and the supply of essential feeling-substance is limited or halted, it communicates a fundamental lack or absence of choice. In this case the presence and guidance paths are forced to compensate in various ways, sometimes quite painfully.

In some cases, the source will occupy an even more extreme state in which the experience is one of feeling-substance actually leaving the space of one's being. These are inverted sources, an example of which might be described as a "black hole" or "draining" state, where life energy feels as if it is being sucked away. These inverted sources are among the most painful and debilitating states we know. We call them names like despair, hopelessness, and abandonment.

Fortunately, these inverted sources also tend to be among the most easily and dramatically shifted states. When you map a state and discover its image is that of a feeling substance disappearing or escaping, there is almost always a directionality to that migration. The first quality to shift is that direction. Simply ask the question, "What would happen if that feeling substance were to move in the opposite direction?" Often the shift is instantaneous and powerful. My original experiment with moving the depression from a downward pull to upward was an example of this.

Presence

The structure of the presence role is more contained than that of the source. Ideal presence state images tend to be comprised of a finite amount of feeling substance located in the general area of the body. Often it is a full body state, many times it will extend outside the body as well. Sometimes it may be circulating within its own space, while at others it is simply present.

In contrast to the source paths, I have found no clear distinguishing features to help identify which domain a particular ideal presence state is serving. The only way to establish that is to explore pairings of each presence state with each source, to find out which ones seem to go more strongly and naturally together.

The presence role takes on the job of tracking the current state within the field of possibilities. It answers the question, "What is real?" The presence role is all about being. I gave it the name presence because most often that is how people describe it, simply as a presence of being. Olivia's Core Strength was an example of an ideal presence state.

Guidance

The structure of the guidance role is somewhere in between the source and the presence. Its ideal state images tend to involve a more or less finite amount of feeling substance which actively interacts between the space of the body and the space outside the body. There is a circulation inward and outward, a breathing, an ebb and flow, a bidirectional radiation, or some similar interchange.

Similar to the presence paths, there seems to be no clear way to easily identify from the structure of the ideal guidance state whether it serves the inside, outside, or context domain. Again, the best way to ascertain its affiliation is to match it up with the source paths to find out which one fits best. At the same time, you will often find there is a dominance of inward or outward directionality to the interaction between inside and outside with a given ideal guidance state, and that often matches its domain affiliation. A guidance path which belongs to the inside triad will be experienced as primarily an outgoing feeling substance, with the incoming circulation experienced more as a replenishment or simply completing the circuit.

The guidance role takes on the job of orienting. It answers the question, "What is my intention?" It serves as the intelligent interface between current reality and the field of possibilities. It makes selections, decides what is most important, guides action in the world and within oneself. The guidance role is all about becoming. Olivia's Inclusive was an example of an ideal guidance state.

The three by three matrix

These three domains and three roles intersect to create the nine-part matrix of feeling paths which comprise the conscious experience of being. It is only at the ideal end of the feeling path that the path's role is revealed, in its structure:

- Is it experienced as a limitless supply of some feeling substance issuing from a point inside or outside, or distributed everywhere? If so, it is most likely filling the source role.

- Is it experienced as a finite amount of some feeling substance, generally occupying the space of the body and its vicinity? If so, it is most likely filling the presence role.

- Is it experienced as a finite amount of some feeling substance exchanging or circulating between the body and the space outside the body? If so, it is most likely filling the guidance role.

It is also only at the ideal end of the feeling path that the path's domain is revealed, in its preferred relationships with other paths. Which ideal presence state seems to fit naturally and synergistically with the ideal inside source? Which ideal guidance state seems to fit most naturally and synergistically with that dyad? When you establish a felt heightening of the tangibility and significance of each of the paths when brought into association with the others, you have identified the inside triad. You can do the same with the outside and context triads.

You will see. At this point, with the information I've given you so far, you should have no trouble identifying source states when you encounter them. You may have some luck identifying presence and guidance states as well. It may require further instruction, however, before you are equipped to successfully elicit the full, nine-part set and shift it completely into its ideal configuration of three optimized triads. Stay tuned. In the meantime, here is an example of a 3x3 matrix of ideal states I mapped for myself recently. This shows visually the relationship among the different paths, and the qualities typically associated with each.

3x3 Matrix example

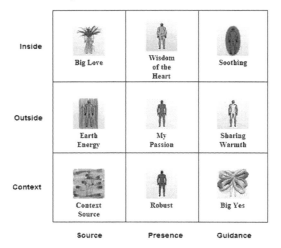

	Source	Presence	Guidance
Inside	Big Love	Wisdom of the Heart	Soothing
Outside	Earth Energy	My Passion	Sharing Warmth
Context	Context Source	Robust	Big Yes

The deep and surface selves

A number of years ago, a curiosity prompted a question while I was working with a client.

> So we've been working for a while here. You've been going into one feeling, then another, again and again. Yet you have maintained a connection with me throughout, and a kind of witness awareness of these different feeling states. What would you call that part of yourself that has been engaged in this process, that witness or self part of you?

The answer might have been "Me," or something like that. Then I asked the standard location question, asking about the actual, felt experience of "Me." We mapped this client's experience of this witness self very easily, the same as if we were mapping any other feeling state.

OK, I thought. Interesting. So this witness is the self the explorer inhabits as she is mapping the various feeling states. And it, too, is grounded in feeling. So it seems we have to, in a way, step outside the feeling state in order to map it. But what outside position did she inhabit in order to map the witness? I asked again:

> **So when you mapped the experience of "Me" just now, you had to step outside it to another witness position one step removed. What would you call that place, that observer of the witness?**

She named it "The Observer," and we mapped it. Interesting! How far could you take this? I asked the same question again, referencing this observer state.

This time she paused for a very long time. Her eyes defocused, and it was as if she was looking a very far way away. When she came back, she shared something like this: "There are no words for it. It's like god, or something like that. Something infinite, and intelligent." Whoa. This I wasn't expecting.

Many more times, with other clients, I did the same sequence of questions. Each time, when I got to the third level, the explorer tapped into some other dimension or experience they found very difficult to put into words. And there wasn't any way to go beyond that. This wasn't an infinite, nested Russian doll sort of thing. The third level was the limit.

Over the years since then I have done extensive investigation of this witness self. For a good portion of that time I became accustomed to work with the following three-part witness.

- The first level is the experience of the primary self. This is the "me" which experiences the mapping process and can provide the one-step-removed perspective necessary to generate the image. I sometimes call it the driver of the bus, or the First Witness. In its ideal state it clearly occupies the presence role.

- The second level is the experience of a kind of higher self. It makes the choices, holds the values, generates the attitude. I call it the navigator, or the Second Witness. In its ideal state it clearly occupies the guidance role.

- The third level is the experience of the ultimate context for one's life, the world one inhabits. It holds the broadest definition of what is possible. I call it the universal mind, or the Third Witness. In its ideal state it clearly occupies the source role in the context domain.

I realized that the witness was also often locked into a reactive configuration that supported the pattern the person was trying to change. Mapping and moving the reactive witness significantly increased the effectiveness and power of the transformations people experienced as a result of the work.

To elicit the three reactive witness states I used straightforward language. I would generally elicit them in this order: first, third, second. It was pretty reliable.

The First Witness

> Who are you, this person who experiences this combination of feeling states we've mapped? How would you describe your experience of self in your life, in these contexts where this issue is most alive for you?

The Third Witness

> How would you describe the world this self inhabits? What is this world, which gives rise to this experience of your Self in the context of this issue? What adjectives would you use to describe this world, and what name do you want to give it?

The Second Witness

> How do you navigate this world, as this self? What is your primary attitude? How do you decide what to do, and when? What do you want to call this part of you?

After naming them, it was easy to map and move them like any other states.

These witness paths were particularly powerful in creating more complete transformation in someone's life. Doing the witness work made the changes more pervasive. The transformation felt deeper, more completely authentic, and positive shifts would show up in other parts of the client's life outside of the initial issue we started with.

Over the years, as I worked with myself more extensively, mapping and moving many sets of nine parts, I became familiar with my particular ideal witness states. Each set I worked seemed to contribute to a further slight evolution of my witness. The first witness gradually became more robust. The third evolved to be more magical (the only word that captures it). The second more playful and willing to take risks. But every time, whatever reactive state these three paths started in, they always wound up in the same place when I shifted them.

At the same time, I was starting to see themes in the various Surface Self sets I worked. It was as if there was an underlying personality or type which governed the shape of the reactive configurations. This was true for myself and a few others with whom I did more extensive work. For me, there was always a sense of isolation in one form or another, for example. This stood in contrast to the typical themes I'd see in other people.

Recently I began to search for that underlying theme. I discovered another feeling state which I had long buried, but which seemed so much a part of the fabric of my personality as to be unquestioned.

This state felt on par with the other witness states. Yet when I moved it, it shifted to an ideal that fell outside my standard three. It became an inside source, yet it was clearly connected to my other three ideal witness states.

At first I hypothesized I had found a third level, occupied by only one part. But when I started to apply this model to work with others, the assumption didn't hold up. I quickly found the witness self, which I had originally defined as three paths, actually was a complete nine-path set. This was a surprise, and very exciting.

Immediately I went back to my own work. Now that I knew what I was looking for, it was pretty easy to find the missing feeling states in myself. I mapped and moved them as quickly as possible. At the same time, I was able to take two more people through the mapping and moving of this deeper witness self.

The experience was profound for all three of us. All three went through a period of destabilization, of having our old "programs" removed but not having new ones immediately available to replace them with. We also experienced various levels of health issues showing up lasting from one to three weeks or even longer. It was as if our whole system, our primary mode of operating and making sense of the world, was disrupted – in a good way.

Each of us began seeing things differently, experiencing life more fully, making different choices. I began to finally tackle this book, for one thing, and made a commitment to move toward success with this work.

Today I call this witness set the Deep Self. It is more than a witness. The context triad of this Deep Self is the former three-part witness I used to work with. Working with the context triad is a good way to get some significant change, but it's not enough. Especially if someone has significant obstructions or inversions in one of the other two sources.

That was the case for me. My inside source was inverted, which made it impossible for me to consider that I truly had something of value to offer. My primary assumption was that I inhabited an unalterable reality in which what I saw as possible was forever separated from the reality of what could be actual. So I held back, tried to perfect and perfect and perfect, as if that could overcome this unbridgeable gap. That underlying configuration is why I've been toiling away on this discovery for 17 years and I'm still working in obscurity.

Working with the Deep Self is the most profound work you will ever do, whether with yourself or in facilitating someone else. My knowledge of this work is still nascent. There is much I don't know. Pioneers take chances, that's how things get discovered and advanced. But I suspect that until we understand more about the structure and dynamics of the Deep Self, we are best to do this profound work only with people who are relatively high functioning. We need to understand above all how to re-knit the fabric, how to put the nine parts back together again after the lifetime-long pattern is disrupted.

Working with the Surface Self is not so disruptive. Typically, you map and move the nine paths, re-integrate the nine ideal states, and the issue or pattern is gone. That's it, simply gone. The person no longer falls into the same holes, and they are free to make new choices and take on new behaviors that feel more supportive of their overall well-being.

The question that remains, though, is this. How many Surface Selves does a person typically have? Is there one fundamental self with many permutations? Or are there several fundamentals?

One bit of data that contributes to the uncertainty is the fact that when people work multiple Surface Self sets, almost always the ideal states for those sets align themselves uniquely. In particular, the inside source for each set will locate itself somewhere different along the core axis of the body.

The different locations of the inside source suggest the possibility that there may be multiple fundamental Surface Selves. Each Surface Self may govern, or be governed by, a particular dimension of a person's life. For example, the Surface Self in which the ideal inside source aligns itself at the root position of a person's physical core seems always to concern itself with very physical or survival issues, while the Surface Self in which the ideal inside source aligns itself at the throat is very different, seeming to concern itself with the person's expression in the world, or their participation or belonging in a community.

Beyond that, I have seen even further differentiation. For example, I have experienced multiple different ideal configurations each with an inside source locating itself at the same location. In these cases, the various ideal configurations seem to concern themselves with different roles or focuses.

For example, three variations of a set with the ideal inside source located at the throat may include one set focused on the experience of membership within a group, one focused on finding ways to contribute to a group, and a third focused on leading the group. One set seems more oriented toward the outside domain, (focused on belonging), the other more oriented toward the inside domain, (focused on contribution), with the third oriented toward the existence of the group as a whole in the context of the broader society, (focused on leadership).

Obviously, this is an area which needs research. At the moment, I don't have the answers. At the minimum, we have a single Surface Self which is highly flexible. This flexible Self can get trapped in specific reactive configurations triggered by specific contextual cues. In its ideal, it has the capacity to generate configurations which optimize adaptation to a variety of situations.

At the maximum end of the spectrum of possibility, we may have three or more Surface Selves possible for each of seven or more different "levels" of existence. I lean more in this direction, with the expectation that we don't come ready-made for the full set, but rather develop Surface Self configurations as needed, as we enter various stages of life and take on various roles in our families and communities.

For example, a person would probably not have a Leadership Self ready-made when they find themselves in a new position of leadership for the first time. They would go through a developmental phase where the new self would get constructed. Its raw material would be the person's ongoing experiences in the new role, models offered by other people, the other relevant Surface Selves being applied and adapted to the new situation. Its ultimate shape would most likely be guided by the underlying template of the Deep Self.

If I may be so bold, I believe we may find the exploration of how Surface Selves come into being may lead us to a new, potentially more accurate model of human development.

The available unconscious

You might think to yourself reading this section on architecture, "That's a lot of moving parts. My mind isn't that complicated." And you'd be right, sort of.

I'd say most of us operate with only one to three feeling states in awareness at any given time. It's a challenge to accommodate in conscious awareness all nine states in a given set at the same time, let alone simultaneously the full active Surface Self at the same time as the Deep Self.

Yet at the very least, these two full sets seem to be in operation at every waking moment. It's a bit like an iceberg; with 18 states active at any moment, and one to three states in awareness, we're aware of about 10 percent of our feelings at any given time.

However, even though 90 percent of our feelings are beneath the horizon of conscious awareness, it is generally a pretty simple matter to turn attention to those states under that horizon and identify them.

One way to do that is to notice the procession of states through time. A given reactive configuration of a Surface Self will tend to raise one or two states at a time above the horizon, cycling through the entire set in the course of living out a particular pattern of being. It's pretty easy to pay attention to the progression, note the different states, and go looking for them. And it's generally pretty easy to find them.

The natural state and its obstruction

In its natural state, this system operates fluidly. Each part is sensitive and responsive to actual conditions in your life. Feelings rise and fall, ebb and flow, in symbiotic relationship with your inner world, your outer world, and the context within which you find yourself. And each feeling responds exquisitely to the other feeling states in the system.

All together, there is a beautiful weaving of experience, a loom of feeling colors, a chamber orchestra of feeling tones. No feeling stands out from the others, and you experience life as seamless, "in the flow." This is a further refinement of the definition of wholeness I introduced in Part 1. When we experience wholeness, we are open to the emergent expression of the full set of influences bearing upon our existence from within and without. None are blocked or excluded. All contribute freely to the experience of the whole.

But when something in your world, whether inside or outside of you, disrupts the balance, one or more feeling states will respond strongly. They will indicate the imbalance with feeling states that are uncomfortable. By way of the discomfort, they will call your attention to them.

When a feeling is responding to something out of balance, there is distress. In that distress, there is a heightened perception which exaggerates the source of the imbalance. Fear will make the intruder appear larger and more formidable. Anger will make the violation appear more egregious and hurtful. Sadness will make the loss appear more dramatic and wrenching.

Our feelings color our perceptions and our thoughts, and through that coloring they shape our responses. Feelings of discomfort and distress are meant to motivate us to correct the imbalance.

When the flow gets interrupted

Two things can interfere with the natural rebalancing process.

1. We are prevented from feeling the distress signal.

2. We are prevented from acting on the distress signal.

When this happens, the imbalance remains out of balance, the signal remains in the ON position, and the nine-path system begins to adapt. Over time, the adaptation gets frozen in place and the person develops a pattern of thought, mood, and behavior that is rooted in the past and dysfunctional in the present. We all know the experience of this.

Reactive configurations

The feeling mind operates differently when its natural flow has become obstructed. It is rare that a single feeling path gets locked into a reactive state while the rest of the set continues to function normally. More common is that early experiences of being prevented from feeling or acting on feeling have a paralyzing effect on the entire set. The entire set of nine paths of the Surface Self takes on a rigid configuration. Each feeling path is locked into a reactive state, and each reactive state reinforces the others. No longer is the set of paths free to provide ongoing feedback about the person's actual state of balance.

Learn more at FeelingPath.com

The entire system is set up instead to preserve its dysfunction. Each path, locked into its reactive state, is stuck in the past. The state is lodged, as if the original, triggering situation still exists today. It distorts perception, magnifying threats for example. Most likely, source paths are compromised, stuck in closed or inverted states, and the other paths align around these to protect and compensate for a reality which is perceived to be limited or even dangerous.

Typically, these reactive configurations paradoxically drive the person to select exactly similar circumstances as those which originally triggered the reaction. When the source paths are compromised, the presence and guidance paths become highly active in compensating. It becomes important to play out the dramas of compensation in order to deal with the "fact" held strongly within that the sources of life energy are blocked or inverted. The person becomes invested in inviting others into the compensatory drama, and they become locked into a perpetual reliving of the original situation.

We know someone is trapped in this kind of reactivity when their feeling states are strong, when the same states are recurring and familiar, and when the standard behavior tends to lead to further triggering of the same states. Often, one or more of the underlying reactive states are so strong as to be intolerable, and the entire configuration makes adjustments to suppress this state, investing even more into the surface compensations. But over time, feeling states that have been suppressed actually get stronger and require ever-greater measures to keep them under wraps. The dysfunctional pattern escalates until it precipitates a crisis.

Alternatively, reactive configurations can look like progressive deadening. When someone is particularly successful at suppressing the intolerable state(s) and walling off entire portions of themselves, their life takes on ever more rigid qualities. Over time, allowing themselves to experience any kind of feeling at all becomes dangerous, potentially leading to an eruption of the suppressed states. Some people are relatively successful at managing their lives into smaller and smaller boxes to prevent this eruption.

The structure of belief

I don't want to go too far into this – someday it may become an entirely separate book. But there is a clear relationship between belief and feeling. Let me try to give you the short version.

Each feeling path generates its own mental imagery. You can find visual, auditory and kinesthetic imagery, and occasionally olfactory or gustatory imagery as well. In any given instance of a Surface Self, we have nine different feeling paths generating nine different sets of imagery at any given time.

Some of this imagery is brought forth from memory. Some of it is created fresh, imagined. And the same imagery fields play a role in shaping and filtering our perceptual experience as well.

This imagery is our interface with the world. It is how we order and make sense of it. It is how we navigate.

Language connects images. Link image A to image B and we have a semantic expression. Those images might be generated from the same feeling path, the same "module" of consciousness. Or image A and image B might reside in two different feeling paths.

Belief is a recurring semantic link between classes of images, particularly across feeling paths. We have links of three primary types:

1. A has an equivalence relationship with B. (A equals or does not equal B, or is the same or different from B in particular ways.)

2. A has a time relationship with B. (A happens before or after B, or at the same time.)

3. A has a causation relationship with B. (A causes B or is caused by B.)

As you might expect, beliefs generated by feeling path configurations which are locked in reactive states tend to be much more rigid and unyielding. Beliefs generated by fluid, responsive, alive configurations tend to be much more open to new experience and responsive to alternate perspectives. As we shift configurations from reactive to responsive, people's belief systems tend to become more open, more fluid, less rigid.

There is so much more to say about this, and a great deal to learn about it as well. But opening this door any further is beyond the scope of this first book.

How I discovered this architecture

I have every expectation that people will question this model. Where did it come from? How can you be so sure I'm not just really clever at making stuff up? Answering that question requires that I disclose my guiding principles. There is method to my madness. Let me share it with you.

My background is in science. I was pre-med at the University of Pennsylvania, in the engineering school, (so there's a practical bent as well). My original career aspiration before I went off the path with bipolar disorder was to become a neuroscientist, researching consciousness. I continue to read science books for fun.

I'm also an inquisitor. I challenge reality. I want to understand, on my terms. And I am practical. Grew up on a farm, shoveled lots of manure, tossed many bales, fixed machines. If an idea or method doesn't work, I'm not interested, no matter what kind of credentials or pedigree it might have.

Finally, I have the kind of uncommon intelligence that eats ordinary academic learning and testing for breakfast, and goes hungrily looking for real challenges. Conventional "wisdom" often tests my patience. I see through intellectual posturing and ideological obfuscation. I prefer to go back to sources and make sense of things myself. I'm a pattern seeker, a meaning maker, a dots connector. Can't help it. Somehow I was born with this.

Bottom line, my modus operandi could best be described as a hybrid of science and design. In developing this work, I went back to the source. My area of inquiry is feeling, mood, emotion. So my source is the actual data of raw, lived experience, both within myself and as reported by people when asked direct, incisive questions. When I started I had no interest in theories already made; it was clear to me they were inadequate.

The design part of this is in the model making. You can't make a model without something to base it on. You need experience, observation. As you've seen, I've discovered the most precise method of observing the world of feeling. So I've had the most amazing source of information to base my models on.

Here is a brief summary of the way observation and design interact in the conduct of scientific investigation as I practice it:

1. Try something, and carefully observe what happens.

2. Make sense of what you observe by designing a model that explains what you've observed and predicts what will happen in a situation you haven't tested yet.

3. Go back to step 1. Test your model by trying something new with the intention of disproving your prediction. Carefully observe, seeking data that your model cannot explain. Continue the cycle.

You can't make a good model without being willing to tear it apart. Often. Over the first fifteen years of my investigations, I tore my model down to the ground on average every few months. Again and again I put my designer hat on. Again and again I subjected my new model to the test of rigorous observation, inquiring into my own experience and that of hundreds of willing subjects. The observation part of this process involves rigorously and intentionally seeking evidence to <u>disprove</u> the model you worked so hard to design. Again and again I found the raw data of experience contradicted my model.

Eventually the cycle of revision became shorter. Eventually the scope of revision became smaller. Today I present to you a model which is the best of scores or even hundreds I've tested. And today I say with confidence this model is good. It is reliable. It is adaptable. It is broad in its application.

I might argue that every good scientist is both an investigator and a designer. We are not discovering reality as scientists. Rather, we are designing models which enable us to navigate reality with greater reliability. The models are not the reality. They are mere maps. We fall into dangerous territory when we confuse the two.

I am very clear that what I am presenting to you here is a design. It is not "reality." The reality lives within you, and within each person. This is a model, though, which offers superior results in navigating the reality of feeling, mood, emotion, thought, behavior, consciousness. If you want results in this domain, no matter what your intention, you are best served by using the most advanced map. I present you here with the most advanced map.

Of course, if you are a scientist you are used to seeing incremental developments of a model over time, with peer-reviewed testing all along the way. What I'm giving you here, though, is a giant leap without the interim steps. I understand that we will have to start all over again for the academic community, to re-discover and test the elements of the model within a peer-review environment.

We can do that. And there will be much to be gained by doing so. My suggestion is to start by investigating the hypothesis that the inner experience of feeling is constructed of a somatosensory capacity that transcends the physical boundaries of the body. It shouldn't be too difficult to test that in various ways, and doing so will break new ground for many avenues of research. Start there, and the rest will unfold. Please include me in the planning of your research – I can help you design it for maximum effectiveness.

An optimal configuration

Before I close this section, I want to make an important observation about this nine-part architecture. If I were designing the structure of consciousness from scratch, I can imagine no more elegant solution. As suggested by the comparison to a living cell, there is something essential about the division of inside, outside, and environmental context. And I can imagine no more elegant solution to managing each of those domains than the three-part triad governing the field of possibilities, the state of current reality, and the vector of creation.

I fully expect we will find such a nine-part structure as we more fully investigate the brain. Not only that, but I expect we will find that we share this structure of consciousness with other sentient beings including at the very least the other vertebrates on this planet. I imagine that the key difference between human consciousness and that of other animals is that we have evolved the second layer of the Deep Self which gives us an advanced self awareness that is not otherwise possible.

We will learn much more about this architecture in coming years, especially as other people dive in to replicate and build upon the work I've done. I believe I've barely scratched the surface. The more we learn about the feeling mind, I have a hunch the more we will learn, not only about human nature, but about the nature of consciousness and life itself.

I'd like to make a suggestion to the AI community. Consider using this nine-part, modular structure to design new processing for artificial intelligence. It has evolved over a great deal of time, and it obviously has advantages. I can't imagine a more fruitful place to start designing the next generation of intelligent machines.

An Example Set

I share this set of feeling states as I mapped and moved them two years ago. It should help you see the bigger picture of what is possible with this work.

The ideal states are labeled according to the universal taxonomy I shared with you in the previous section.

Reactive: "No Place in This World"

When mapping the reactive states of a feeling configuration, it's difficult to predict what type of ideal state the feeling will become. Over years of doing this work I've become somewhat proficient at identifying cues which suggest the outcome, but I get it wrong as often as right. (The mind is astonishingly creative in its compensations!) So I'm sharing the following list of feeling states without any identifiers. In mapping the feelings associated with a specific issue, that's how you would encounter the states in the raw. No labels. No assurance of what they will become. As I said, you never know for sure what any given feeling will become until you move it.

I called the issue I was working "No place in this world." It arose after Father's Day 2009, as I was reflecting on what I never received from my father, what felt missing: a sense of belonging in the world, a conferring of value, a validation from the "elders." An idle reverie led to discovering a crucial step in my liberation, as you will see.

I began exploration of the set in a tentative list of states I wrote in late June:

- Bereft – abandoned / orphaned by my ancestors / father.

- Something Missing – like a cog in a machine essential for its operation. The machine sits idle without it.

- Sadness – a heavy grieving in my chest.

- Unworthy – a shrinking back from opportunity ($, dating)

- Dregs / Scavenger – seeking castaway stuff to sustain myself

- Outsider – seeing others have resources and opportunity, and knowing I am excluded from those. No question about it.

- Acceptance – this is the way things are >>> Hopeless.

- Failure – I tried. I failed. At least I tried.

- Body Corruption – the whole body breaking down.

- Tension / Worry – tensing myself against the complete breakdown.

- Anxiety (anticipated) – about success. If I "get the girl" or "win the prize," it will be taken away by someone with appropriate validation. I don't deserve any good stuff, so if I have any, I'm in danger.

Later, in early July I wrote the following meditations:

This started as an exploration of the absence of dad's conferring of validity upon me in the context of a larger community. But it seems to be deeper than that. I had opportunities to be "fathered" into legitimacy. There was Dr. B, the dean. There was the guy who helped me get the Edinburgh scholarship. There were the men at the St. Andrew's Society. My boss at the lab. The MD/PhD student who was mentoring me. Plenty of opportunity.

But I kept a distance, did not open to their influence. Why?

Last night in meditating on this I found an underlying anxiety, a tightly-held tension deep in my upper body. Last night in sleep it showed up even more. It seems to reach back to very early childhood, and when I go into it, I notice a fear of all adults and especially men.

These people were so dangerous, so not alive, not nurturing, not safe. They were strange and repulsive to me. I was isolated in their world. And it wasn't much better with other children. They didn't seem to see what I saw, couldn't talk about it. I didn't know how to talk about it either, because there was never anyone to talk with. No practice saying the words, "this is crazy."

Later in the month I began mapping. It is only in mapping that the list of feeling states becomes clarified. Some distinct names turn out to be for the same feeling state. Others morph upon examination, revealing their nature more fully by the light of the mapping questions.

I often spend a few weeks "sitting with" a set of feelings, getting to know it, noticing its influence in my everyday life. This one was no different.

After about three weeks, toward the end of July, I spent about four days mapping each feeling and moving it. Here are the reactive states I mapped.

Grief

Generally very weak, a soft cloud in and around my whole body, emphasis on upper body, gray, moist, like Seattle overcast, still, a little heavy; can become much darker, with movement and precipitation of tears throughout, heavier; **Holding** keeps it from intensifying. (This surrounds, helps soften **Pain** and **Holding**.)

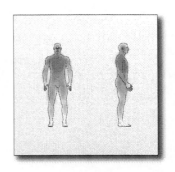

About the pain and separation of this life. I may never get to experience the full joy that is possible in this life, because everyone is so damaged, and I am alone.

Becomes "Spirit."

Pain in My Heart

Ground meat in a tough, protective container sac (**Holding It Together**), like a pericardium. Feels connected to the "other world" of deep anxiety (**Higher World**). Hurts more, the more separated I feel from that world. Red, bloody, slightly less than body temp, very mushy and formless without the container. Very passive, unmoving, as if 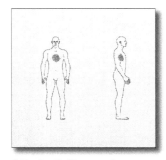 dead, (although the red color indicates it is not fully dead). No sound.

*It hurts too much to be alive in this world where everyone is crazy and hurtful. I don't want to be here and be fully aware, I don't want to leave the other world (**Higher World**) behind. I don't want to commit to this. It hurts too much.*

Becomes "Joyful."

Holding It Together

Very thin, tough, pericardium-type sac around the **Pain**. Tendon/connective tissue color; body temp; squeezes a little to hold a shape for heart, blob-like. No sound. This seems to be echoed in my upper body with tension and holding.

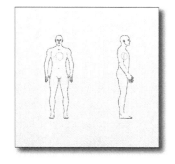

Just for now, and for now, and for now. Holding back. Not jumping into this, or this, 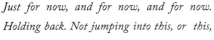 *or this. Waiting. Perhaps things will change enough, perhaps the right things will come together, that I can let go, commit.*

Becomes "Powerful Purpose."

Higher World

Deep in my belly. Like a portal down and back, through the solar plexus as a starting point and out behind me, arcing down, out and back like a tail, but with the cone opening outward. Filled with particles and clusters of shimmering, iridescent/pearly light. Extra-dimensional, entire worlds inside. Movement is galactic. Inside are

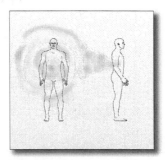

immensely wise beings. Neutral temp. A kind of white-noise choir.

I am between two worlds. My connection to the larger world keeps me on track, holds me true, makes sure I do not lose truth and fall completely into illusion.

Becomes "Ancestor Support."

Massive Strike

Size and power of a massive trash compactor piston, but can move extremely fast; intense energy, usually pent up, not striking; plane of my body, several feet thick; the substance of cut-up rubber tires like boat/ship or loading dock bumpers, super indestructible (but made of energy, not rubber); pressurized. (Held back by **Restraint**.)

I want to destroy stupidity, (not the people, just their stupidity). Connects with **Higher World**. *To release this strike would pull me irrevocably into this world. The* **Restraint** *is connected behind, to this* **Higher World**, *to keep* **Strike** *from activating.*

Becomes "Beckoning Instigator."

Restraint

A pervasive holding back on expressing what I want or striking out at stupidity. It's like **Massive Strike** is poised but holding itself, cued by a kind of sleeve around it, a thin, white canvas restraining jacket over the massive strike piston, camouflaging it and cueing it to hold back. Tentative. Pulling back from points behind me. Neutral temp.

Steady. Like a dog that's well trained, a gentle touch holds it back but its power may be considerable. Sound of "ah ah," gentle.

*I can't let this out because I am unprepared, too **Vulnerable / Empty**. I hurt too much (**Pain**), I am too unsure / uncommitted (**Holding**) to sustain effort.*

Becomes "Receptive Presence."

Extreme Vulnerability

A very, very thin, fragile glass shell around my body, extremely delicate, a vacuum inside; everything of this is located in the shell; clear with pink/red tint; body temp; no movement, and it doesn't want me to move. Doesn't want to be put at risk.

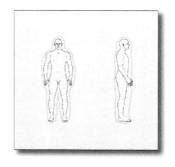

People seem crazy and dangerous. The world is a scary place, and I am fragile, at extreme risk.

I am in danger; I am weak, **Empty Inside**; anything that strikes me could shatter my protection and I could implode.

Becomes "One Dance."

Hurtful Heathen

Like one of those iron man torture devices, where huge, sharp shards of metallic glass come toward me from every direction, sometimes all at once, penetrating me all the way to my heart (or threatening to do so). Cold, shiny, silvery w/iridescent color. Always there, just outside me; I have to be careful not to set them off and trigger their  plunge into my heart. Strongly connected to **Vulnerability** and **Empty**.

The pain I experience surrounded by intensely fucked up people, who are unconscious, conflicted, and hurtful. People suck. They are dangerous to me. So ignorant of their own truth.

Becomes "Dance Body."

Empty Inside

The vacuum inside of **Vulnerability**. Actually a very thin gas; slight drifting; clear/yellow tint. Large silence.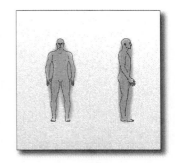

I don't know what I'm doing. I'm empty. I'm not being fed. Nobody is feeding me. I'm alone.

Becomes "On Fire."

Ideal: "The Divine Dance"

This work opens up dimensions in us that are highly transpersonal. I'm not a woo-woo kind of person in any way, but my experiences reached into a very different space than I inhabit in my everyday life, and brought me deeper meaning and connection on many levels. The examples earlier in the book are more typical, but I figured I'd include these to show you the full scope of what you may encounter in your own explorations.

I also want to say I don't subscribe to any spiritual beliefs, yet the experiences I had in moving these states could easily be adapted to certain belief systems. Personally, I maintain an agnostic approach, and prefer not to impose strong interpretations on experiences such as these, but rather to remain open to possibilities.

Inside Source

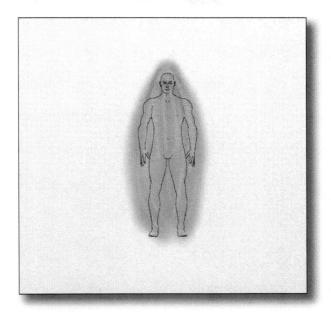

Spirit

Previously "Grief."

Light, a quiet glow, slightly cool; color a warm yellow, transparent; full-body and out three feet... Emanating from a source at my crown, strong and gentle; warm; just above my head but still "inside" me. Sound of a very faint white noise.

I am one with all divine beings. All spirits know me and I can know all spirits. I can be present with someone within a frame that transcends this life. I can know myself and others as more than this body, this life. I am filled with spirit and I embrace all beings.

Inside Guidance

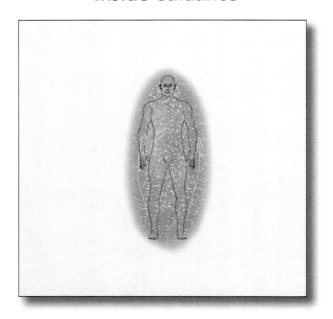

Joyful

Previously "Pain in My Heart."

Lighter, softer, an effervescent energy, with "bubbles" rising; silvery/clear with a blue tint; bubbles can wiggle as they rise; a laughing from within (my laugh); full body and one foot all around. Sound of fizzy bubbles.

*There is nothing in my life so serious I cannot laugh through it; everything is an expression of the **Divine Play**, and I thoroughly enjoy the patterns and connections I see all around me.*

Inside Presence

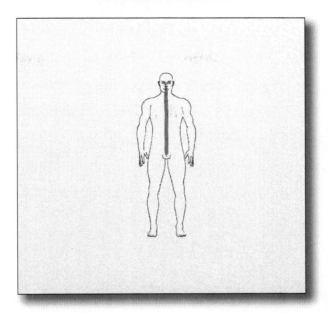

Powerful Purpose

Previously "Holding It Together."

Flexible, strong spine; dancing/pulsing energy; holds my head erect, easy, with strength and poise; deep, magenta red; one inch diameter; the strength and flexibility of big-cat muscle; dense, feels like muscle but it's pure energy; sound of a jungle beat; impulse to move with undulating dance movements.

I am strongly connected, open; my head is connected to my tail; I am integrated, whole; I am strong and flexible in my life; I have a powerful core/spine; I easily commit to and live into my purpose. I easily move forward to manifest my purpose.

Outside Source

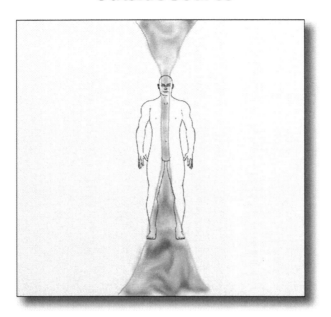

Ancestor Support

Previously "Higher World."

Comes in both at top and bottom; connects to **Spirit**. Similar qualities as **Higher World**, but it is always with me, no matter how I move, as I engage in the **One Dance**. A little brighter, more vivid, warmer, connects through my core ~ 3 inches diameter. Its influence filters outward into my body. Opens out above and below, connected infinitely. Brings the **Higher World** into direct interface with this world, this life.

I am supported by the ancestors. I have access to anyone. The ancestors get to dance through me now, with others.

Outside Guidance

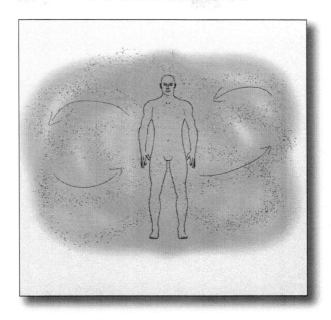

Beckoning Instigator

Previously "Massive Strike."

This becomes an eager, welcoming excitement, inviting others into the dance with me; actually, inviting others to notice the **One Dance** they are already in. Soft, high-frequency, sparkling energy, multi-color; like a mist in & around me, extending ~ 6 feet, more if desired; sparkles are traveling simultaneously toward and away from me. People feel drawn into the dance through me and they feel me drawn into the dance through them. Sound of the ocean, with waves.

Come with me into this beautiful dance! (I am reminded of those moments at ecstatic dance when I instigate broad, multi-person interactions.) I invite you as you are; you are already dancing!

Outside Presence

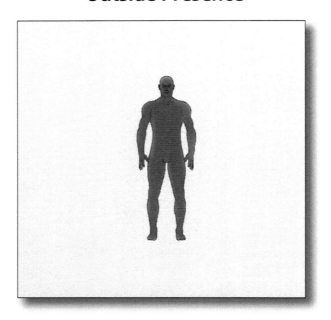

Receptive Presence

Previously "Restraint."

Becomes a solid presence from which to receive engagement in the dance. Whole body. Quiet, still, soft, dense. Feels solid but is more of an energy; porous. Accommodates others without losing itself, can conform to other shapes but its mass is steadily present. Dark, forest green.

I am here and you can feel the play of the dance through me. We don't need to move. We don't need to do anything.

Context Source

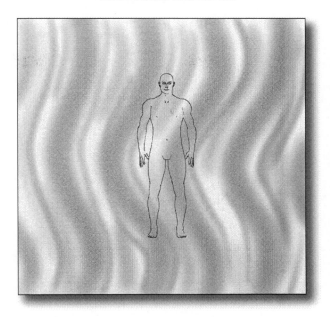

One Dance

Previously "Extreme Vulnerability."

Permeable, open, a field of connecting energy; there is no separation; infinite; shifts to & fro like the movement of downhill skiing. Like a magnetic field in its effect on me, gently pushing one way then the other. Silvery yellow, glistening/ shimmering. Sounds of waltzes and hearty laughter.

We are all one. I embrace the play of the universe through you, as you "play out" the many parts of yourself with my presence and cooperation. I am strong in the ways I show up; I have a role to play in the dance we dance together. I speak my truth, I share what I see, engage with authenticity.

Context Guidance

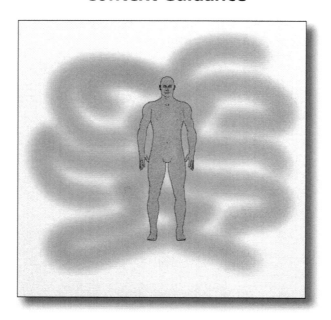

Dance Body

Previously "Hurtful Heathen."

Comes into me, extending outward, extending both my presence and my sensitive perception; this is my dance body, and interaction with others in the context of the **One Dance**. Sound of laughing with gusto. Golden yellow light, but it is light with substance, opaque and luminous, warm, soft both in appearance and to the touch.

Taking things lightly yet sensitively and respectfully. This is my respect for others as they are, and my willingness to engage in service to my purpose and theirs.

Context Presence

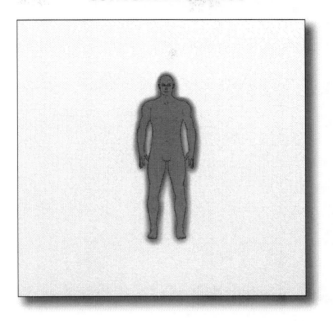

On Fire

Previously "Empty Inside."

Solid, powerful muscle, full & present; sound of a pure, intense vocalization of my presence; warm to hot, as if during a workout; full body and a little more; red, deep, intense, opaque. On fire, intense, red, short, steady flame over my whole body.

I am fed simply by being, by this immense, living universe. I am here. I do what I want, trusting that is the right move in the dance, knowing that with my awareness and presence, all movements get woven into the dance, and there is no right or wrong movement.

The set all together

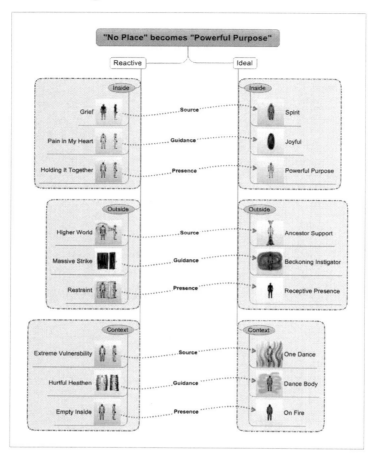

The impact in my life

As a result of doing this set, I became more comfortable with my masculinity. I felt supported in a more transpersonal way that let me release my resentment at not having that kind of support in my early life. This led me to taking myself more seriously, and feeling anchored in this world as someone who belonged, particularly as a man who belonged.

On the day I completed this work, I went to dance as I usually did on Wednesdays. And on that day I finally asked someone out I had been attracted to and dancing with for a period of several months.

We became partners and moved together to start a life in Port Townsend a few months later. My relationship with her was of greater depth and authenticity than any I had experienced before. I feel the work I did with this set cleared the way for me to show up in relationship with the possibility of being a full partner, supported by my community in a way that I could feel inside me even though it was not yet evident on the outside.

We are still close, and I consider her one of my best friends although we are no longer living as partners. Over this past two years I have learned that it is not enough to do the inner work. We must also create the changes in our lives to reflect the inner changes. I did not understand that so well, and did not do such a good job of it. Today I am returning to this work of becoming a man in the world, making my contribution, claiming my place in my community. This book is a very important step on that journey for me. So I suppose it is fitting that I share this set here.

Why All This Might Matter to You

Emotional pain is one thing. Suffering is another entirely. The threshold between the two is crossed when we lose power and meaning.

When we understand what causes our pain, and when we feel it is natural or that we know what to do to respond to its origin, emotional pain remains simply a state of discomfort. It holds no sway over our internal equilibrium. It poses no threat to our future. It presents no disruption to the meaning and purpose in our lives.

But when our emotional pain comes from unknown causes, when it compels us to act in ways that harm ourselves and those around us, and when we are at a loss to make it weaken or stop, then something comes unglued at our center and we enter the land of suffering.

Most of us will do anything in our power to avoid experiencing this. I believe the greatest human fear is to be overcome by something out of control arising from within our own selves, and to be bound forever in suffering beyond our capacity to bear. Whether our individual, most-frightful demon is sadness, hurt, rage, emptiness, or fear itself, we build elaborate schemes and personas to protect ourselves from ever having to face the beast.

Recently I have been recognizing the power of these deeply hidden states. I have seen how entire lives full of compensatory activities can be assembled around a pivot of intolerable suffering, the awareness of which must be avoided at all costs. And I have been driving like a laser in search of these pivots in all my work with my clients, and with myself.

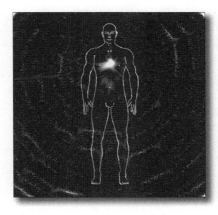

In January this year I found myself tearing my own life tapestry apart in abject deference to one of these deep states. But I sensed its power and followed the trail to its lair. It revealed itself as a state I called Infinite Agony, a feeling of the entire universe collapsing inward on my heart.

I experienced this as what I called "the gap" between what I felt was possible in my life and what I was consigned to endure. On the one hand, I was highly sensitive, often excruciatingly so. On the other, my home life was dominated by my father, a cop at work and at home, for whom feeling and empathy seemed a distant memory.

I hated my life at home. To me, the way things were conducted seemed brutal and ignorant. Yet I had no choice but to suffer with it. I compensated by building up my smart-kid ego at school and escaping into books, both of which supported my vision of the possibilities that lay forever out of my reach and exacerbated my experience of the gap.

I believe this state was the origin of my bipolar disorder. It drove my flights into manic explorations of possibility, yet kept my line tethered to the ugly limitations of the reality surrounding me. As I left home, the entire human world took on the qualities that home had represented. It felt brutal and ignorant to me, and the ways of men, especially those with the greatest authority, seemed appalling and heinous.

In many ways the entire path of my life, even including the development of this work, I have undertaken in an effort to avoid this intolerable state. It remained entirely unconscious. And so as an adult, I have lived with the unexamined, deeply limiting expectation that the world I inhabit is similarly foreign and hostile to me. This has been my unquestioned "reality." Even in developing this work, I have focused many of my efforts on studying my anticipated enemies and refining my models and arguments to withstand any attack. I have wasted interminable periods on this distraction, rather than putting my ideas and discoveries out into the world expecting them to be received with appreciation.

In fact, this book has been written a half dozen times over the years, each time finding an early death before I actually released it. I always had "good reasons" to kill it, but the truth of it is, outside of my awareness I was unwilling to risk experiencing the intense suffering of this Infinite Agony.

But now I have finally brought this state to my awareness. When I shifted it, it opened into the most amazing experience of love, a love bigger than for any one person, bigger than my entire existence as a single being, a love that feels transpersonal and vital. I call it Big Love.

Discovering this Big Love within myself started a journey this year of transformation and discovery. For one thing, I've moved forward with this book. If you are reading this, it is because I have finally overcome this imprint and liberated myself from the unconscious suffering of my Infinite Agony and the invisible prison within which it held me.

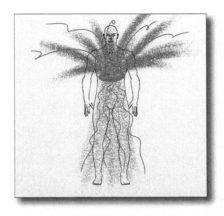

For another, this Infinite Agony to Big Love feeling path did not fit my model. That's one reason it stayed out of my awareness for so long; I wasn't looking for it, didn't consider the possibility of its existence. Finding it led me to inquire deeper and uncover the Deep Self, the nine-part template that shapes our lives.

I share my personal story with you to illustrate what is possible now with this work. In the past, these deep, hidden states of pain without power ruled our lives. (It's an irony, isn't it, that the states we experience ourselves as having no power to control exert ultimate power over our own lives?)

Today we are free to liberate ourselves at will. Do the Feeling Path Mapping practice with a few dozen feeling states, and it will eventually sink in for you, that you never again need fear any feeling, mood, emotion, thought, impulse, or behavior that arises from within you.

Never again! No matter how intense, or dark, or seemingly insidious in its power, you now have ultimate freedom. You can turn to face the shadow, to walk directly into the heart of it, to turn it upside down, inside out. You can reveal once and for all the inspiring glory that is within every dark corner of your soul.

This is not trivial. It is a wholesale reshaping of our relationship to our own emotional realities. When we can be blindsided by forces arising within ourselves, we must work hard to guard against them getting the upper hand and wreaking havoc in our lives. Now we can let down our guard, and begin to carry forward, open to the shadow, curious about what delightful resources we might liberate from within ourselves.

Every inner discomfort, every distressing feeling, every impulse to withdraw or lash out or sabotage – every one! – represents an untapped force for positive well being. Every negative feeling state, especially those we experiencing as recurring and disruptive, has within it some unknown light which most likely has not shone forth for quite some time. I say it's time to pull up the shades, throw open the windows, and let fresh air blow through our long-shuttered psyches.

What I am telling you here is a Big Deal (with capital B capital D). One of the foundational assumptions our civilization holds about human nature is that it either starts bad and must be controlled and contained, or that it can go bad for various reasons and must be punished and contained. Ideas about evil, animal drives, etc. shape discussions about justice, accountability, and privilege. We assume almost without question that people who take actions motivated by greed, hate, and other dystopian states are bad people.

What I have discovered in my work mapping and moving thousands of states, is that even the most ugly, hateful, so-called evil, black, hurtful, vicious, and frightening states have their ideal. What I have discovered is that even the blackest of inner states is driving without question toward light. Contrary to some of our most defended moral beliefs, every evil is goodness trying desperately to survive.

Before I bring this little rally to a close, I want to open up our perspective to see the big picture. I believe humankind has been ruled since the dawn of consciousness by the overriding fear of untrammeled forces within. To almost everyone, even more frightening than the most dangerous animal or catastrophic natural event are our own irrational impulses. Terror that overcomes us in the night, rage that renders us helpless to stop the destruction we wreak, grief that incapacitates us and makes even the sun seem pure darkness, these are the things that we fear the most. Even our fear of another's irrationality has mostly to do with how craziness can elicit our own very powerful reactions against which we are helpless. Civilizations throughout history have developed ingenious ideologies and practices to keep the inner demons reined in. Ours is no exception.

Consider this an invitation to a much larger conversation. The new assumptions:

1. We no longer need fear <u>any</u> feeling state that arises within us.

2. We know without any doubt that <u>every</u> feeling state, (in every person), has an ultimately positive intention.

3. Consequently, we know that every person is inherently and essentially good. Our overriding purpose should be how to nurture and bring out the best of the unique goodness in ourselves and in everyone.

If these principles are true, what kind of life do you want to choose for yourself? What kind of society do we want to create together? What kind of community do you want to live in? How do we want to parent?

Or love? How do we want to shape our professions? Our businesses? Our schools? Our governments? What new choices do you want to make?

Three Simple Practices for The Feeling Path

Feeling Path Mapping and the discovery of the underlying architecture of the feeling mind provide new insights about how feeling actually works. These insights suggest that our standard, rational, command-and-control approach to many human challenges can be improved upon. The feeling mind operates by different principles, and as it underlies all of our human experience, these new principles present themselves as potentially useful in broader contexts. Let's explore the guidelines that emerge from this new work, then turn to how we might apply them.

The Feeling Path is a creative approach to life. It commands greater depth and power than planning or problem solving approaches. The creative approach can be thought of as managing a dynamic tension between current reality and desired reality. Planning focuses more intently on desired reality and often falls short because it gets too invested in the planned outcome and fails to maintain ongoing contact with an ever-changing current reality. Problem solving focuses more intently on current reality and often falls short because it gets too invested in outmoded expectations of what "should" be and fails to adequately envision future possibilities. The creative approach holds both current and desired realities equally and dynamically, recalibrating frequently to track evolving realities on both ends of the line of creative tension. The Feeling Path demonstrates the creative approach in the optimal engagement with the feeling mind, and opens up the possibility to apply this approach to a broader spectrum of challenges.

Origins

The Three Simple Practices originated directly from Feeling Path Mapping:

- **Practice 1: Embracing what is.** This practice derives from the first step in Feeling Path Mapping, where we open to our actual feeling states. It also is reflected in the Presence role in the architecture. Presence paths serve us by giving clear feedback about current reality.

- **Practice 2: Inviting what wants to be.** This practice derives from the second step in Feeling Path Mapping, where we ask the reactive feeling state to reveal its ideal. It is also held in the Source role in the architecture. Source paths serve us by giving clear feedback about what's possible.

- **Practice 3: Embodying the difference.** This practice derives from the third step in Feeling Path Mapping, where we integrate the ideal state into our lives. It is also expressed in the Guidance role in the architecture. Guidance paths serve us by giving clear feedback about our active engagement with life.

Let's take a look at each one of these in greater depth.

1. Embracing what is.

The first step in The Feeling Path is to identify existing feeling states and map them. Mapping brings each feeling state fully into awareness. It welcomes each feeling as valid, important, and useful in and of itself.

Mapping also seeks to identify the full constellation of feeling states that create and express a given way of being. Every feeling state is welcome. Every feeling state is actively encouraged to participate. Every feeling state is considered just as important as the next in mapping out the totality of the reactive experience.

It is only when we succeed in enrolling every feeling state comprising the experience of a specific life issue that we are able to fully shift the entire pattern and become free of it. Any single feeling state that is left unconscious and excluded from the process has the power to blockade the shift and pull the other states back into the dysfunctional pattern.

In the same way, whenever we are working in life with a challenging situation that involves multiple perspectives, voices, stakeholders, or intentions, it is paramount that we bring all the players to the table. Leaving any single voice out of the conversation opens the likelihood that the dysfunctional pattern will persist and perhaps even intensify.

Even more important, embracing What Is means we need to intentionally open to the full extent of reality. When we pay attention to what is real without barring it, suppressing the truth, or distorting it to fit some agenda, we are able to begin real work.

Embracing What Is, is our root connection with current reality. When we stand firmly in currently reality, we can hold the close anchor of creative tension firm, so that the force of the tension can work its magic.

This one practice has great power. It can also be extremely challenging because of our long-entrenched habits, both individually and collectively, of avoiding current reality at all costs.

Embracing What Is invites a different relationship with current reality than that employed in either the planning or the problem solving approaches to challenge. In planning, we "assess" reality at the outset, then execute the plan. As soon as we take our first action, however, reality has changed. But planning almost always fails to build in continuous monitoring. Instead it commits to executing the plan as designed, expecting to achieve the outcome as defined. Along the way, the plan and reality diverge, and the outcome is almost never what is expected.

In problem solving, we seem at first to focus on current reality. However, problem solving frames reality as having something wrong with it. And that wrongness is judged from the perspective of some previous or alternate right which is most often from the past.

Problem solving seeks to identify what is wrong and correct the failure. Along the way, it completely fails to notice many things which may be "right" about current reality, including the so-called problems. It filters its examination of reality to fit its problem/solution view of the world. Unfortunately, it therefore misses deeper patterns of dysfunction, interconnections with a broader context, positive benefits of and motivators for the current state of affairs, and other factors. Without a full and accurate assessment of reality, problem solving is unable to leverage available assets and forces which could lead more naturally to better outcomes.

Access to reality

I should probably step out of the flow here to clarify what I mean by "reality." Once you've had a few experiences of your beliefs and perspectives shifting when you move a feeling state from reactive to ideal, you'll recognize that most of what we cling to as "true," especially in the human world of relationships, community, and the like, is no such thing. Any given belief, perception, or judgment is a partial approximation of an infinitely rich and complex reality. No belief, perception, or judgment is complete as a representation or proxy for that reality.

Even the model I am presenting to you here falls into this framework. All I have done is design a map which does a pretty good job of helping us navigate the tangible reality of feeling. But it is partial at best, and most likely wrong in some aspects, wrong in the way that it will inadvertently lead some people down blind alleys or over cliffs in their own personal feeling mind. The Feeling Path model is a work in progress, and your experience of the reality of your own feeling mind trumps the model every time.

Not only that, but your experience provides a unique and non-replicable viewpoint on the reality of feeling. The full reality of feeling is beyond the sum total of every possible viewpoint, every possible perspective, every possible map and model of the territory. The full reality can never be accurately captured by a representation of it, an idea about it, a belief or perspective.

Nevertheless the reality of feeling exists beyond our ability to capture it in language or models. For our purposes, we choose to assume that. This choice is actually part of the map: we get better results when we take on this framework, assuming an objective reality that is beyond our ability to describe and fully know. So too with the reality of the needs of your family, or the dynamics of your community, or the engagement of your organization with its stakeholders – these exist but are impossible to fully understand conceptually or linguistically.

But just as we can never fully know the reality of feeling except through the direct experience of it, guided perhaps by our models but largely un-muddled by our ideas, we must allow that reality in any context is bigger than our thoughts about it. In order to embrace any given reality, we need to open to multiple perspectives, multiple viewpoints, multiple models, and we need to use these freely and creatively to engage the actual things and forces and energies and souls of our situation.

The prime requirement for the true creative approach is to ask "What else is true?" We all have our ideas and perceptions of reality, but those ideas and perceptions invariably leave out important portions of what must be included in the mix, if we are to discover What Wants To Be. Of ourselves, we must ask, "What else do I feel? What else do I believe? What else do I want?" And we must be open to all answers, especially those which conflict.

In community, we must ask, "What else do you want? What else do you experience? Who else has not yet been included in our conversation? What else are we affecting by our actions?" We must be open to all voices, all desires, all answers, especially those which conflict.

In The Feeling Path, embracing What Is instructs us to actively employ different methods, different frames, different ways of engaging with reality, in order to surface all of what is present. The deeper assumption is that until we have included all the players and factors in a situation, we will fall short in our attempts to shift toward higher states of being and wholeness.

2. Inviting what wants to be.

The second step of The Feeling Path is to invite the mapped image of the feeling state to follow its own natural impulses toward its ideal. The ideal is implicit in the reactive state, and the reactive state contains within itself the knowledge of its ideal. Not only that, but the spontaneous impulse, the underlying drive, for every reactive state is to return to its ideal. All that is required is to open the invitation.

Similarly, in the way of The Feeling Path, we can take that attitude into all dimensions of life. We can trust that whatever state of being we find within or among ourselves holds within it a natural drive toward wholeness, integration, and harmony. All that is required to release that drive is to open the invitation, to ask, "What wants to be?"

When we work with feeling states, it is important to trust the state itself to find its way to its ideal. We interfere with the natural forces leading to wholeness if we impose some idea of what we believe should be the ideal. When we trust each feeling state to find its own way, we are often surprised, and what emerges as that state's ideal is always more alive and wondrous than what we might have imagined it should be.

In the same way, when we are working with the complexity of real human relationships, real communities, real organizations, there is no way we can imagine the ideal for that set of forces. It is beyond our capacity. But when we create the conditions for What Is to seek its own ideal, to reveal What Wants To Be, we open to the power of mystery and genius that is far greater than that of any single, rational mind.

Planning relies on rational goal setting. It commandeers the process of becoming by choosing the outcome. The outcome can only be chosen from a privileged place, the place of the manager or designer, the parent or the politico. The choice of outcome is dependent upon a particular framing of reality, a specific perspective that holds this not that as valuable and defines the object of that value. It violates the first practice by selecting a particular version of reality rather than embracing and trusting the whole. By abandoning What Is, planning finds itself trying to force the goal into existence and failing egregiously.

Companies usually try to deal with this failure by setting goals in the form of narrow metrics. "Fourth quarter sales will be 1.2 million dollars." What happens then? The people in the organization do whatever it takes to reach the goal. (There are bonuses to be gained, of course.)

There is no accounting for the real cost of the actions taken to achieve the goal. The real consequences of these actions may ultimately undermine the health of the company, and they may seriously damage the well being of the employees, the communities within which the company operates, and the planet which sustains the whole. But as long as the metric is achieved this can be conveniently ignored. This is blinkered insanity.

Problem solving on the other hand fixes the outcome in the past. It compares What Is with "what should be" according to ideas, practices, rules and assessments previously made. Because problem solving is trapped in recreating the past, it requires itself to ignore great swaths of What Is, filtering perception according to the standard of "what should be."

There is no invitation in problem solving, only control. There is no opening to the natural creative forces of life, only shutting down and killing the spontaneous emergence of possibility. There is no joy or discovery in problem solving, only drudgery. When our focus is repairing a broken machine, the problem solving approach is adequate and effective. But when we apply this approach to human systems the result is ultimately destructive.

Planning and problem solving hold our culture in a death grip. They are strangling life out of individuals, organizations, nations and the global community. But what would it take to bring the true creative approach of The Feeling Path into broader human affairs? Is it possible? How?

I believe the first step is to recognize the humility involved in a true creative approach. It's not hard to see one place where the planning approach gets its hold over us. The origin story of our western culture involves an all-powerful god deciding on an outcome and creating it. We are enraptured by the possibility that we might fashion ourselves into gods, and we attempt to envision the outcome we want, and create it. This is grandiose fantasy, and wreaks ever greater havoc, the more power and wealth are brought to bear on these fantasies.

A true creative approach begins with "I don't know." We cannot know What Wants To Be until we invite it to reveal itself. What Wants To Be is emergent, and can only arise when we create the conditions inviting its emergence. How do we do this?

Facilitating wholeness

Within an individual, optimal aliveness emerges when we free up the feeling paths for unhindered responsiveness. We can apply this principle to groups as well. Every group has multiple "sticking points" and areas of unconsciousness. In the same way as an individual gets locked into dysfunctional configurations of feeling paths, collections of individuals can get locked into dysfunctional patterns of interacting that stifle the capacity to respond creatively to challenges. Freeing these stuck places can help the group return to optimal functioning.

My good friend Jim Rough has been working for the past 30 years on a process that is well suited to serve this function. He calls his process

Dynamic Facilitation, and I invite you to learn more about it at tobe. net.

I've been working on adapting Dynamic Facilitation to more fully leverage the opportunities of the creative approach. I plan to go into this a little further toward the end of the book.

3. Embodying the difference.

In Feeling Path Mapping, the third step of the work essentially comes down to getting out of the way. When we have mapped and moved only one feeling path, embodying The Difference takes a bit more work. But when we have successfully mapped and moved an entire nine-path set, the feeling mind is activated to recreate the reality inside and around you, and great changes unfold almost without effort. In the same way, if we are working the first two practices well, the third will take care of itself.

The most important aspect of the third practice is to hold the outcome lightly. With planning or problem solving approaches, we get attached to a specific outcome. That takes us out of relationship with current reality. When we hold equally the actuality of What Is and the possibility of What Wants to Be, and when we hold the possibility as an ideal with no attachment to specifics, we create a maximum-force creative drive.

Creativity is total engagement in the moment with total awareness of the ideal. In painting, it is an immersion in the media and the tools while holding the essence of the painting which is taking shape. Deciding ahead of time what you will paint, for example trying to recreate a photograph on the canvas, is a low level of creativity. That is planning painting. Surrendering to your paint and brush and canvas, holding an open sensitivity to what they are wanting in this moment as they engage with you, while at the same time holding an energy or idea or vision of something which has never existed – that is the creative approach.

In dance, creativity looks like total engagement in the moment, each dancer with their own body, with the bodies of the other dancers, with the space, with the sounds, with the audience in sublime, rapt communion in service to an ideal, the "score." Creativity in dance is wholeness with presence. It is an embodiment of the difference between What Is and What Wants to Be through the medium of the physical body.

In theater, this is what my friend David Robinson calls the direction of intention. Good acting happens when the actor's intention is clear. David carries this practice into classrooms and boardrooms through experiential workshops that assist participants in showing up with who they are, free of their story, in relationship with one another, present to the magic of emergent creation. Intention is another word for the vector of creation, the embodiment of the difference between What Is and What Wants to Be. It is not something your mind imposes on your self and your world, but something which emerges from full presence in the world. In theater as in life, there are choices to be made, but in the creative approach, those choices are made with the full influence and participation of the whole.

This is the same in any area of your life – in managing your office, holding a family meeting, planting your garden, participating in your community, enjoying a quiet moment with your lover. In the creative approach, we surrender to the dance between What Is and What Wants to Be, and trust the vector of creation to guide us simultaneously from within and without.

As we act from this place, every act changes the reality we inhabit but we remain open and alive to those changes. The evolving reality feeds back into our process of becoming. What Is informs What Wants to Be in a constant interplay of one influencing the other. There is only the present, but it is in thrall to the driving force of possibility.

Don't be fooled – this is not easy. Most of us have lived our entire lives clinging to planning and problem solving, and it takes earnest effort to learn how to show up in the present, surrender to the flow, and let go of attachment to the outcome.

Perhaps the best way to learn how to do this is through extensive Feeling Path Mapping. Clearing the old, reactive configurations makes us naturally better able to sustain this new way of being. But other practices can support our learning. Arts practices are among the best, especially those considered improvisational.

This seems such a simple thing, but it stands in such stark contrast to standard practices of planning and problem solving. Both these conventional approaches succeed by their own standards only by distorting perception. Currently reality is obscured by focusing only on what is relevant to either the goal (planning) or the fix (problem solving), ignoring most of what is real. What Wants to Be can not be taken into consideration at all without a full reckoning of current reality. Consequently these conventional approaches do violence in the world when applied to human systems. They run roughshod over real people in real communities surviving on the real planet.

This third practice holds the key to our moving forward. We are novices in living from this place. Let us learn together. Let us relinquish our attachments to the goal and the fix. Let us become masters of presence who channel the vector of creation into all we do.

176   PART 2: ARCHITECTURE

The Bigger Picture

Remember in the introductory pages where I spoke about the negative impact of controlling thoughts, behavior and the brain in our pursuit of well-being? I mentioned the negative impact on parenting and relationships in particular, making the point that when we operate from the intellect instead of from a wise, feeling presence, we undermine the foundation for healthy relationships.

But the situation is even more dire. An even more insidious consequence is that we create a strong feedback loop. The more we undermine feeling as the source of our wisdom, the more strongly we defend its replacement. Here's how it works.

When we sabotage the wisdom of the feeling mind by discounting distress and suppressing its impulses to correct imbalances, we set up the conditions for reactive, paralyzed configurations of feeling. When we overrule feeling with intellect, judgment, and rules, and when we operate by planning or problem solving instead of a creative approach, we intensify that paralysis.

Every person who adheres to narrow, rigid beliefs and a command and control way of operating in the world came into this world as a bright, open, alive child. But something happened along the way. Along the way, situations arose where that child felt very strongly about something that was out of balance in his or her young life. But the feeling was not permitted or acknowledged, or its expression was punished. And the power to correct the imbalance did not belong to the child. To survive and maintain belonging with family and peers, the child was forced to suppress the signal, and with it he or she was forced to suppress a living part of themselves.

I'm guessing you know exactly what I'm talking about. In my own life I can remember countless moments, one comes to mind just now that is too painful to recount, where something felt very wrong but there was nothing I could do about it, and the people who had the power to do something were actually creating or permitting the wrongness. I had to bury those feelings of helplessness and violation, and they became the sources of perennial melancholy and resigned obedience for my young life and the seeds of both resistance to authority and difficulty with intimacy as I became an adult.

After accumulating many layers of these suppressions, we can find ourselves locked into reactions, into patterns of thought and behavior, and into beliefs none of which feel true, none of which feel authentic, none of which give us the satisfying experience of wholeness with presence. We have lost something very important. Very important.

But along the way we have burned bridges and made bargains, and cannot see the way back. The prevailing messages in the family and in society are that operating on the basis of rules, of judgment, of intellect, is preferred. Our society greatly rewards those who appear to achieve this elusive, rational perfection. Our economic system is built upon rational principles, where all human value is abstracted into a measurable dollar amount. Those who can operate without feeling, who can adhere to a set of principles and practices regardless of the human or environmental consequences, those who can become more purely rational, are given the highest rewards of wealth and power.

In order to accomplish this worshiped standard of detached rationality and commitment to principles, one must sacrifice feeling with all its nuance, its messiness, its gray zones. One must sacrifice one's authentic presence and wisdom. One must take on instead a more rigid internal life, affixed to rigid beliefs and scripted behaviors. One must avoid true intimacy with its unpredictable emotions. One must control relationships of all kinds to manage unpredictable others. One must create distance as a result between oneself and everyone else, creating an island within which one can maintain the control which must be kept to preserve the original bargain.

Imagine doing this. Imagine you have invested many years and even decades of your life following a path given by the authorities around you. Imagine you have sacrificed your soul, yet you have in fact been given the rewards you were promised. You have wealth. You have power. You have freedom to control resources and make decisions that affect many people.

(This works in reverse as well. In my case, my inner sacrifices were made to position myself in opposition to authority and everything it stood for. I declared myself sovereign and was ferociously invested in maintaining my sovereignty. I had sacrificed my own nuances for leaps of manic intensity and plunges into "real" despair. I had bargained for freedom from, for superior to, for more creative than, and I defended the rewards I had gained in the sacrifice. Some of us are mirror images, same but different, from those who have aligned themselves with authority.)

What can you do but continue forward on the path you have chosen? How can you turn your back on this, especially if you have burned the bridge to your true self long ago beyond your capacity to remember?

But what is the consequence of hewing so tightly to your chosen path in these troubled times?

Now imagine being someone who has successfully traded your authentic wisdom, your wholeness with presence, for what our society has told you, (and you have believed), is more valuable. And imagine being faced with real situations which threaten the worldview that says you have done the good and right thing. Maybe the threat is the collapse of our economic system and the more severe oppression and disenfranchisement of real people. Maybe the threat is a rising tide of people similarly committed to principles at odds with your own. Maybe the threat is an encounter with death, or with your own suppressed self screaming out through behaviors that run counter to your own professed beliefs.

What do you do when you encounter these threats? You must, you must, you must double down. If your house is shaken you must reset the foundation. You must strengthen your commitment, defend your principles, intensify your passion for what you believe in. You must do this at all costs. The alternative is to question your position, doubt the bargain you have made, and open the door to those long-buried agonies.

But the more you double down, the farther you drift from your own humanity. The more you recommit, the more insane you become in the eyes of children and those who have not lost the wisdom of feeling. And the farther you drift, the more destruction your powerful actions and decisions propagate.

This is not to say that every wealthy and powerful person has sacrificed authenticity in service to the goal. Many have come by their privileges while maintaining access to the wisdom of feeling. What I am saying is this: The abstracting of human value into money, combined with a political economy which promotes its accumulation in the hands of a few while conferring greater power upon those same people, is a recipe for the widespread corruption of the human spirit.

All of us are susceptible to this corruption, whether or not we succeed in gaining the rewards of wealth and status. Every time we walk past a homeless person because we can't help everyone in need, every time we say nothing about an injustice at work because our chances for promotion might be compromised, every time we quell the voice inside that begs for a little more time with our loved ones because we must earn the paycheck that covers the bill for the wide-screen TV, every time we suppress our deepest human impulses in favor of gaining or preserving this abstraction called money and all it can buy, we lose a little piece of our soul.

There is so much more to say about these things. I've been observing the trends over the past 10 years and I am deeply concerned. The heightening of conflict between tribes of people clutching to positions so narrow as to be completely untenable in any real human universe troubles me. The use of religion of whatever kind justifies those narrow positions – whether Christian or atheist or utter nonsense – troubles me. The growing reliance upon grandstanding and browbeating and sheer gamesmanship to win points troubles me.

I have sat with hundreds of people for thousands of hours as they have inquired within themselves. I have seen their bodies open, relax as they have embraced some part of themselves which had long been banished. I have heard their words, wise words "beyond wrongdoing and rightdoing" they have spoken as their feeling has responded to an invitation to return to its true nature. I have sat at the feet of mystics and seers, ordinary people with ordinary lives who, when they lay down their command and control to embrace what is and invite what wants to be, become wise beyond measure.

Every time we sacrifice a true human impulse on the altars of principle and materialism, we lose part of our spirit. That feeling path becomes locked in a reactive state; it goes underground and we lose access to the wisdom it is meant to offer us. As we accumulate such sacrifices, we are pushed into smaller and smaller corners of aliveness. Over time we become crippled caricatures of the magnificent and beautiful humans we once were. When I watch or listen to what is called public debate today, whether via the media or directly piped from the halls of congress, I see humans who have lost their humanity, who are operating as caricatures of what they once were, of what they might one day become again. They speak as my students speak when they are caught in the dream, in the nightmare of reactivity where enemies reign supreme and agony is expected. They look nothing like those same students when they open to the wisdom within.

Wisdom is not knowing all the answers. Wisdom is the humility to know you don't know, the temerity to ask questions, and the courage to hold the answers you receive with open hands and an open heart. I want to live in a world in which the people making the decisions that affect millions are making those decisions with full access to the wisdom I see and hear within every one of the people I work with. We all have access to it. Let us find a way to bring this wisdom into the places where it is most important.

I hope you are able to see what I see: the importance and significance of restoring the freedom and wisdom of the feeling mind to our individual and collective lives. Our future depends on it. Together we can do this.

Part 3:
Facilitator's Guide to Mapping & Moving

The Practice

Feeling Path Mapping is best conducted as a facilitated practice. You can do the practice alone as well, (see Part 1 for help with that), but it's a little easier when you have someone to guide you through it.

The Feeling Path Mapping questions engage the centers of your brain devoted to multi-sensory imagery and feeling, simultaneously. They aim the perceptual field of your attention toward a specific feeling state, and use the sensory mind as an interpreter of your experience. The questions invite you to be creative, to "make up" a sensory image that "matches" your feeling state.

Feeling Path Mapping questions explore the following kinds of imagery, inviting you to find the qualities that best match your feeling state:

- Location, size and shape
- Substance qualities including solid, liquid, gas, light, energy, etc.
- Temperature
- Color and other appearance qualities
- Movement, force or pressure

- Sound or voice

- Occasionally, smell or taste are important

This isn't the kind of imagery you are familiar with. You're not using images as metaphors, saying for example that your loneliness is like a windswept tundra or your anger is like a volcano about to erupt. Instead, this imagery is more directly in alignment with the way your mind actually processes feeling. There is something "tangible" about these images, something "real" in a way most people haven't experienced before. There's no interpretation going on here, it's more like a discerning perception.

You find that certain imagery strongly matches the feeling, while other imagery clearly does not. For example, you may find yourself quibbling about the exact shade of turquoise, "no, it's a little more green than that…" or temperature, "it's a little warmer, about 78 degrees I think, the way sun feels on your skin on a cool day." (Here you're using a metaphor to describe temperature more specifically; there is no sun, only a specific temperature that can be described by comparing it to something familiar.) Through the questions, you create a complete sensory image that closely corresponds to your experience of the feeling state. We refer to this process as mapping.

The Feeling Path Mapping experience can seem odd at first. Most of us have never had anyone ask us explicit questions about what a feeling actually feels like, so giving a feeling state this much attention is unusual in itself. More often, we're familiar with talking at length about what we think, remember, believe, perceive, or do when we feel a certain way, but almost never does anyone ask what it actually feels like. Because of this, sharing the mapping experience with someone can be quite special. The mapping questions allow you to share more of the reality of your inner experience than is common, and it can be nice just to have someone be a witness to that awareness. Being a witness is a special privilege, like being welcomed into a private sanctuary.

The questions can seem odd as well because we're using our brain in a way that is at first unfamiliar. Like any new skill, it can take a little time to get the hang of it. For some people, it will feel like there's no "right" answer and they're just making it up.

So it's important to know that yes, you *are* making it up. That's exactly what you're doing. And you're making it up with full freedom to change and adjust until the image matches the feeling. You're the only one who knows when you've achieved that best fit, so no, there are no right answers. For most people, by the time they map their third or fourth feeling state, they've become comfortable with the process and have learned to trust the images that arise in response to the questions.

When you have completed the mapping questions, you will have created a tangible image of the feeling state you mapped. The process of creating this image does two things. First, in order to answer the questions, you must "step outside of" the feeling to examine it as if it were an object. As you will discover if you continue in your study of The Feeling Path, we all have within ourselves a "witness" or higher self. This witness self is the place we stand in order to have greater choice and freedom to respond to our feeling states in ways that serve our highest good. Many times, a feeling state that is occluded in our awareness and recurrent through time can be confused with the witness state. The two parts of our selves can act as if they are collapsed into one another, and we identify with the distressed feeling state as if it were our total self. We've all experienced this at some point or other, when we are so immersed in suffering that nothing seems to exist outside it. The mapping process gently teases the witness self back to its differentiated state, where it can better serve our whole self. We regain access to the reactive feeling state as something we *have*, rather than something we *are*.

The second thing that happens in the process of mapping is that we establish a strong link between the sensory image and the feeling state. I don't know enough about neuroscience to cite research supporting this, but I suspect that this property of entrainment is a natural function of the most basic structures of our nervous system which allows us to track moving objects, manage the continuous movement of our bodies, and follow the complex storyline of a movie.

The result is that we can deliberately alter the sensory image and the linked feeling state follows appropriately. For example, if we have mapped a feeling state to the sensory image of a hot, black stone in our solar plexus, altering the sensory image to be cooler, brighter, and softer will directly change the discomfort of the feeling state, probably toward something that feels better.

The Feeling Path Mapping practice of mapping and moving feeling states can be both fun and challenging. It can be fun because there is an element of lightness and creativity to the process, and because you are interacting with yourself in a new way. It can be challenging because it is a new skill that requires focused attention in ways that can take you to some pretty deep territory within yourself.

Mapping and moving several feeling states in a single session can feel exhausting. Give yourself the time and space after a session to reorient yourself and integrate your learning. And consider starting out by mapping and moving one single feeling state at a time, to get the hang of it.

The Role of Facilitator

The facilitator is a guide, a holder of the safe space, and an anchor for the process of self-exploration. As the facilitator, you put aside the functions of advice, empathy, passive listening, commentary, analysis, and other activities often found in the roles of counselor or friend. Through asking the Feeling Path Mapping question sequence, you simply support the explorer's own self awareness and discovery.

The facilitator's job is to control the entrance and exit to this practice space, being clear about beginning, maintaining and completing the work. Outside of Feeling Path Mapping, you are free to pick up other activities again, moving back into the space of friend, partner, or counselor. If you are in a close relationship with your Feeling Path Mapping partner, don't assume you can enter the role of facilitator at any time. At all times, the practice is ultimately managed by the explorer.

Another important function of the facilitator is that of focused attention. The facilitator puts self aside during Feeling Path Mapping and focuses all attention on the explorer. Strive to honor and mirror the explorer's experience, and to assist the explorer in gaining clarity and awareness about that experience.

Although these requirements of clarity and focus seem to imply that a facilitator must have advanced training to be effective, that is not the case. The qualities of clarity and focus are well present in the structure of the Feeling Path Mapping questioning sequence. Even a beginning guide can assist an explorer in coming to a much deeper self awareness simply by reading the questions aloud.

As a facilitator, be mindful that you occupy a privileged role. The experience of self discovery through Feeling Path Mapping is uplifting and affirming of the deepest goodness of a person's being. The explorer is choosing to share that with you. It is one of the most special gifts you can receive from anyone.

Not therapy

For many people, the idea of supporting a friend or loved one in any inner exploration is frowned upon. Psychotherapy has taken over the territory of personal support for inner healing, growth and transformation. The role of therapist is complex and requires a great deal of training to do well. And therapeutic interactions can trigger old projections and patterns of relating that make clear communication difficult for someone who hasn't been trained in how to manage and leverage these "transferences" and "counter-transferences." So personal intimates are discouraged from doing anything resembling "therapy" with one another.

Be assured that Feeling Path Mapping is not therapy. Your job as an Feeling Path Mapping facilitator is simply to support your explorer's self-discovery. You won't be interpreting their experience. You won't be directing their explorations. You won't be taking on any role beyond that of a simple witness and facilitator of their attention on their own experience.

I've done this work with people in all the varieties of relationships I have. It's easy to take the facilitator hat off and return to whatever relationship you already have.

In fact, because this work highlights gifts and capacities we all have, people generally find their connections grow closer as a result of sharing this work. Feeling Path Mapping goes beyond the surface stories that keep us trapped and gets to the deeper truth of feeling that connects us all.

At the same time, Feeling Path Mapping in the hands of a gifted therapist can yield great treasure. In the hallowed safety of a healthy therapeutic relationship, Feeling Path Mapping can enable deeply profound self-discovery and transformation. It can dramatically shorten therapeutic plateaus, eliminate "resistance," and clear the way for steady progress in therapy, no matter what the issue. I welcome all therapists who desire to learn this new methodology to train with me and learn to integrate Feeling Path Mapping into your practice. I'll be making training opportunities available as part of the community at FeelingPath.com.

The surprise of discovery

As the facilitator, you are going to find yourself being surprised at times. Be prepared for that and check your expectations at the door. The interior world of another human being has ways of defying any preconceptions you might have. For example, if the explorer is mapping a feeling she calls sadness, you might feel as if you can relate, as if you know pretty much what to expect when she answers the questions.

Don't count on it. There are more varieties of "sadness" than there are people using that label to name a feeling state. One thing you'll discover if you facilitate this process for more than one or two people is the magnificent diversity of inner experience. It's quite a wonder to behold, so allow yourself to be fully open to whatever the explorer shares with you. Cultivate your sense of wonder and curiosity.

Also support the explorer in letting go of her expectations. She will be just as surprised as you are at some of the images she gets in response to your questions. And assure her there is no need for her feeling states to obey the laws of physics or adhere to what she has learned in psychology class. The world of her feelings obeys its own laws which only it can know.

Space and materials

I've done Feeling Path Mapping, both solo and with others, in locations as varied as an outdoor park, on the bus, in a coffee shop (my favorite place to work through the worst dreck of my own), or in the quiet comfort of my office. The most important factor is that once you get started, it's best to avoid interruption. As a rule of thumb, quiet is good, but some people may prefer the anonymity of a bustling public space or the strains of a favorite genre of music in the background. It's all up to the explorer's preferences.

Comfort is important, though. It's best if the explorer can settle into a comfortable posture and give up control of her body, easing into the experience of attending to feeling states. Whenever possible, provide that comfort for the explorer. She may want to close her eyes to get more in touch with a feeling, or lie down, or even move through the space to express what's there.

As for materials, you should have at a minimum these materials on hand.

- Blank paper or Feeling Path Mapping templates with the appropriate gender of body outline. (See male/female templates to trace or copy on the following pages, or download templates at FeelingPath.com.)

- A reasonably hard surface to write on, either a table, a clipboard, book or magazine.

- Multiple writing instruments. It's a bummer to run out of ink or mechanical pencil lead when you're in the middle of mapping an intense feeling state.

- A set of colored pencils or pens. Pencils are the most versatile tool, and it's best to have a box of 24 or more. Colors can be combined for maximum accuracy, and can be used to simulate many textures.

You can easily assemble a complete set of tools for under $10 or spend hundreds if you're wanting to do this professionally, and it can be fun to put a travel set together for mapping on the road. I have a matchbox-size set of colored pencils that I sometimes carry in a cigarette case with little sheets for notes and drawings.

If you like, you can also explore tech solutions to the documentation. Here is a list of options using computers and other devices:

- **Note taking and organizing:** Consider a mind mapping application like Mind Manager or FreeMind.

- **Drawing:** Use an application that supports layers and a stylus (or finger) for drawing. I like using a tablet PC with ArtRage software. Consider something like Brushes for the iPad or even the iPhone.

- **Take-Away:** I assemble map images and notes into PDF templates and print on index cards.

For all of these solutions, a high priority is that they be in formats the explorer can use. Index cards or a PDF deck make for easy reference.

Female Outline

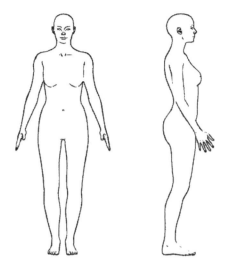

Notes:

Male Outline

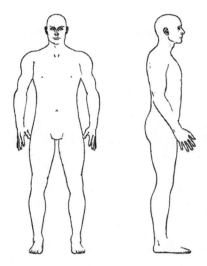

Notes:

Map It: Somatosensory Imagery

Mapping a feeling state is often like making a new friend. You take the time to get acquainted by inquiring into the subtle sensations of the feeling, and showing you're listening by reflecting back those sensations through the emergence of a creative, sensory image. My students will sometimes share that the part of them we are mapping is grateful to be acknowledged after toiling long years in obscurity.

All feeling paths are trying to serve our highest good. What has happened when we experience recurrent patterns of negative feeling states, is that these particular paths have become locked into a pattern based on a situation long in the past. Through mapping, we bring attention to each locked feeling state, breathing new life into each path, freeing it to begin to move again, to respond authentically and sensitively to our ongoing present moment.

Our feelings are meant to provide rich, sensitive feedback about our state of wholeness in the world. Every feeling state, no matter how distressed, was once trying to signal you about a significant disruption to your wholeness. If at that time you were powerless to do anything to correct the situation and restore your wholeness, or if you were prevented from turning your full awareness to the signal, that feeling state became frozen in time, the signal calling and calling and calling without getting any response. Very often, it went completely underground, becoming a force directing your life from a place beneath consciousness.

As you proceed through the mapping process, you will be recovering these parts of you, restoring them to awareness. For some people, some of the time, this restoration to awareness is all that is necessary. That part will return to its natural responsiveness and the feeling state will no longer create a recurrent pattern in your life.

Most of the time, though, awareness by itself is not enough to release the feeling. Whenever possible, undertake the mapping process with a feeling state when you expect to be able to take the time to move it to its ideal state within a day or two. Many times you will want to do that in the same session. It's a great way to dive in and experience relief right away. The entire process, identifying the feeling, mapping it, moving it, and befriending it in its ideal state should take an hour or less. The actual process of moving a feeling state that's been mapped, uncovering its ideal state, takes about 15 minutes.

If you don't have that kind of time though, it can still be helpful to map a reactive feeling state. Taking ten minutes to run through a few of the basic questions can provide a helpful distance from the feeling and return you closer to an identification with your witness self. And even if you don't have time to run through the entire moving process, knowing the sensory image map of the feeling allows you to interact with that image to tone the feeling down and reduce its intensity if it's causing problems for you. It's a fabulous emotional triage system.

The mapping process in a nutshell

The Feeling Path Mapping process has four parts:

1. Identify and name the feeling state.

2. Ask mapping questions to elicit sensory imagery.

3. Ask belief questions to elicit the underlying "contract."

4. Draw the feeling state.

We'll walk through each step.

Getting started: Identifying a feeling state to map

A good candidate feeling state for mapping is any one that's "up" for you right now, or any one that was dominant in your recent experience.

As a facilitator, ask the explorer to share a bit about the feeling, and if she wishes, its context. Your job as the facilitator does not depend on knowing the context, but it can help the explorer make an important connection to relevance. And talking about it can help start a kind of reframing process. Already at the beginning of the mapping process, there is an expectation that this feeling state is going to get special attention, and knowing that can help relieve any distress that might be present.

As the explorer, find a name for the feeling state that fits for you. This name does not have to be part of the standard lexicon for emotions. Allow yourself to be descriptive and creative. Names people find useful range widely, from descriptions of sensations, to the effects of the feeling, to the intentions of this part, to the behavior it motivates. Here are a few examples taken at random from my files:

- Intimidated
- Playing It Safe
- Threat
- Withdrawn
- Hatred
- Fog / Shut Down
- I Want
- I Can't Have It
- Contempt
- Rigid Control
- Essence
- Shut Down

- Doubting Myself
- Disbelief
- Get On With It
- Twisted Stomach
- Cutting Ties
- Mental Fireworks
- Catapult
- Heebie Jeebies
- Bafflement
- Simple Me
- Quicksand
- Disconnecting

Please put aside any training you may have had about what constitutes a "real" feeling name. Most existing systems of identifying and working with feelings are semantic in nature. Semantic systems rely on careful definitions in an attempt to categorize what is inherently an infinitely complex field of experience.

We want the explorer to feel free and supported in defining her experience in whatever way is relevant and meaningful to her. In addition, semantic systems of working with feelings assume that feelings are a special class of experience, different from cognitions, for example. What we discover in The Feeling Path – and this is very important – is that *every conscious experience has its foundation in the felt sense.* Even if the explorer wants to map the experience of "thinking," or "distracted," these experiences have at their core a feeling state which can be mapped just as any other feeling state. Even something called "numbness" – which is often interpreted as the absence of feeling – is itself a feeling state fully amenable to the mapping process.

Taking notes

The explorer will benefit from a thorough capturing of the mapping process. Note their answers to the standard questions and any other relevant thoughts that may arise in the process.

As you take notes, capture exact, relevant words and phrases whenever possible. As the facilitator, you may wish to allow the explorer time to try out various answers to the mapping questions, and wait until she settles on something specific before capturing that in your notes. But if you hear a vivid phrase along the way, write it down – there might be something fruitful in the imagery to explore further. It's OK to pause the process and ask for clarification to write down the details. The explorer will appreciate your attention, and may discover something new about the feeling state while you're writing.

Suggestions for drawing

As the explorer, be creative in your drawing. At the same time, be precise and capture the feeling state as you described it. This is your visual representation of the feeling state you are mapping, and it will serve as a literal map to enable you to return to this state, to understand it, and to learn your way through and out of it.

Sometimes you will want to draw a white feeling state, and that will be difficult to do on white paper. Try outlining it in another color, or gently shading the negative space around it.

You may at times find yourself wanting to draw a detail that is too small for the body outline on the template. Try drawing a "magnified" view in another part of the page with an arrow to show its location.

For these and other challenges, feel free to start with a fresh sheet of blank paper for your drawing. Just make sure to label it and keep it attached to the notes for that feeling state. And if you think it could be useful to use different paper or other media, go for it.

Asking the mapping and beliefs questions

Read the following questions on the following pages verbatim, and as much as possible, write down the important parts of the answers word for word. If an answer isn't clear at first, invite different possibilities until one feels like it fits. As the facilitator, speak slowly and from the heart. Repeat the explorer's answers back to clarify.

Substitute the appropriate language in the areas indicated by *[italics in brackets]*.

Mapping Questions

FIRST IMPRESSION: What is your first impression of this *[feeling state]*? How would you describe to a friend what this feels like, or what it makes you do, or how it makes you think?

PREAMBLE (for the first few times): Now I'm going to ask you some specific questions about what this *[feeling state]* actually feels like. At first, these questions may seem unfamiliar or awkward. It may even feel as if you are making up the answers. That's OK. Go ahead and "try on" different answers until you get one that seems like it matches the feeling pretty well.

LOCATION: If you were to say that the actual, felt experience of this *[feeling state]* were located in or around your body, where would you say that is? What size and shape would you say it has?

SUBSTANCE: If you were to say this *[feeling state]* had qualities of substance, would you say it seems more like a solid, a liquid, a gas, some kind of light or energy, or something else? What other qualities does this feeling substance have?

TEMPERATURE: What temperature would you say this *[feeling substance]* seems to be?

COLOR: If you could see this *[feeling substance]* and it had a color, what color would you say it is? And does it seem to be transparent, translucent, or opaque?

MOVEMENT: Does this *[feeling substance]* have any qualities of movement – does it seem to be flowing, or pulsing, or vibrating? And does there seem to be any force or pressure?

SOUND: If you listen internally, do you notice any inner sound or voice? If there is a voice, it is your voice or someone else's? What other sound qualities or tone of voice do you notice?

OTHER: Is there anything else you want to notice about how this *[feeling state]* actually feels before we move on? Would you like to make any adjustments to your description?

Identifying key beliefs

PREAMBLE: Now we're going to explore the thoughts that typically accompany or express this *[feeling state]* for you. You could think of these thoughts as beliefs or as a contract between the feeling and other parts of your world.

STATEMENT: From the perspective of feeling *[feeling state]*, how would you capture in words what seems true, or real, or important? What's true about yourself, about your world, or about a significant someone else? What thoughts naturally arise from this state?

Drawing the feeling state

Drawing the feeling state is an opportunity to get even more clear about the match between the image and the feeling state. For many explorers who are strongly visually oriented, drawing leads to further insights. Perhaps the size and shape are a little different than the explorer described. Perhaps the color is actually a little more blue than green. If the drawing elicits further significant information about the sensory image matching the feeling state, record or correct any important aspects in the notes.

It's pretty important that the description you've captured be a full representation of the sensory image that provides the most satisfying fit. You'll be using this description in the moving phase of the Feeling Path Mapping. And at times, the moving process may occur days or even weeks after the feeling state was originally mapped. Having a clearly explicit description helps the explorer access the original state so the moving process can proceed effectively.

The mapping process in more depth

Let's take a look at what kinds of answers you can expect from the mapping questions, and how best to facilitate the explorer coming up with the absolute best sensory image to match her feeling state. One useful strategy for all of the explicit mapping questions, (not including First Impression and Other), assists the explorer to create a more satisfying image match for her feeling state by making suggestions. You'll see this technique in action as we go into detail, but in general it works by providing a specific example or selection of examples for the explorer to accept or reject. I have found that when someone is new at this, it is far easier for them to reference a concrete example and agree or disagree that it offers a useful match, than to come up with their answer with no prompting at all. More experienced explorers sometimes still appreciate the choices, while at other times finding the imagery coming very easily with the bare minimum of questioning.

You can see a good example of offering choices in the standard question about substance: "…would you say it seems more like a solid, liquid, gas, light, energy, or something else?" This question is best delivered with a slight pause between each option in the list, so the explorer can "try on" each one in turn and either accept or reject it. To best support the explorer in finding just the right image, it's best to explicitly allow for rejection of all the choices by adding, "or something else," "or not," or some other escape clause.

Some people might question whether we are putting words in the explorer's mouth. The best answer to this is for you to try it, and see what you think. In my experience, explorers very readily reject any suggestion which does not fit, and in rejecting a suggestion they become more clear about what image does fit for them. It is far easier for most people to try on a suggestion, notice their reaction to it, and move quickly toward a more accurate representation, than to start with no boundaries and have to come up with something out of nothing.

If we think of the sensory imagery centers of the brain as our instrument, we are trying different imagery settings and monitoring the agreement signal. We are in fact "making it up" as we go, keeping track of what images feel like they "fit," and adjusting for optimization. It's a little like playing the childhood game "hot and cold" where a toy is hidden and the hider calls out temperature readings indicating how close the seeker is to the treasure. The seeker's best strategy is to move around a lot at the beginning to get a quick temperature map of the territory, then to zoom in on the "hot spot."

We can also use this technique to help the explorer confirm an image. When people are first getting used to this new skill, they sometimes question the images they get. "Where did that come from?" is a common exclamation. If the explorer expresses that she thinks maybe a feeling state has a certain imagery quality, but she's not sure, ask a specific question about opposite qualities. For example, if she says, "I'm not sure, but I think it's blue." Suggest, "Well, let's try on some other colors. Is it possible that it's red?" Most of the time, the explorer will express something like, "Oh no, it's definitely not red." It's a great way to let the explorer know she's on track and help her feel more secure about the image she's creating.

Another important technique built into the mapping questions is that of permissive language. We use phrases like "If you were to say," "If you could," "…would you," or "seems to be." These phrases give the explorer more explicit permission to experiment, to operate within a "what if" frame and avoid getting hung up on trying to get the "right" answer.

Now let's go treasure hunting and dive into the details, question by question.

First Impression

The First Impression question provides an opportunity for the explorer to begin turning her attention toward the feeling state. It's not so important what comes out of this question, only that the explorer make an attempt to answer it, and through that attempt to become more aware of the actual felt experience of the feeling state. It's also a great way to establish a deeper level of rapport between the facilitator and the explorer. The facilitator should mirror back key words, tone, and gestures, to let the explorer know she is being heard and seen.

Location, size and shape

> **If you were to say that the actual felt experience of this *[feeling state]* were located in or around your body, where would you say that is?**

If the explorer has difficulty identifying the location of the feeling, assist by narrowing down the field of possibilities. Do this by applying a technique of asking highly specific questions about its location, beginning with the legs and moving upward toward the torso and head. Even after the explorer affirms a particular location, continue until you've completed a scan of the whole body, noting all places where the feeling seems to be located. Only ask the final question about locations outside the body if you've gotten a clear no to all the body questions.

- Is the actual felt experience of any part of this *[feeling state]* located anywhere in your legs or feet?

- Is any part of this feeling located in your hips or lower abdomen?

- Is any part of this feeling located in your torso or chest?

- Is any part of this feeling located in your hands, arms, or shoulders?

- Is any part of this feeling located in your neck or head?

- Is any part of this feeling located outside your body, perhaps in front or behind, to one side or the other, above or below?

Whole body

Sometimes a feeling state is experienced as filling the entire body. If the explorer indicates that this may be the case, ask explicitly:

- Does this feeling fill your whole body?

- Is there any part of your body which does *not* have this feeling in it?

- Does this feeling extend outside your body?

Then move on to exploring the size and shape. The feeling state may occupy the full body and more, extending outside the body a few millimeters on all sides, or as far as many feet in specific locations and directions.

Outside the body

Occasionally the explorer will be working with a feeling state she cannot locate anywhere in the body. The phrase "in or around your body" in the standard location question is there specifically to support awareness of this special case. If the feeling state is in fact located outside the body, you may have to help the explorer locate it. Here is something you can say to help lay the groundwork.

> Sometimes a feeling state is actually located somewhere outside a person's body. It can be located in front or behind, above or below, to one side or the other. Because a feeling state is not a body-based physical sensation, it can be located anywhere. But because of the way our brain is organized, a feeling always has a location, and that location is sometimes outside the boundary of the physical body. I wonder if it's possible that your *[feeling state]* might seem to be located somewhere outside your physical body boundary.

In most cases of a feeling state being located outside the boundary of the body, it is actually making contact with the skin, often penetrating the skin into the body to a certain depth. Very occasionally, a feeling is entirely disassociated, and may be as far as several feet from the body.

If the explorer is having no trouble becoming aware of this feeling state, continue with the rest of the standard questions. However, if you are having difficulty proceeding, this work is best left for more advanced skills to be covered elsewhere. For now, go back to the beginning and choose another feeling state to map.

Once the explorer has identified the general location of the feeling state, you can begin to get more specific by asking about the size and shape.

Multiple locations

On occasion, an explorer will reply to the location question with multiple locations. Sometimes this is a single feeling that extends through several parts of the body. Other times the explorer is referencing two or more distinct feeling states which have come into awareness at once. (Some feeling-sensitive people will answer the location question with a string of questions, starting into descriptions of half a dozen different feelings. They love the opportunity to share their awareness – the opportunity is so rare!)

It's important to help the explorer clarify their experience. Ask questions like the following:

- Is [location A] and [location B] the same feeling?

- Are [location A] and [location B] distinct regions, or does one extend into the space of the other?

- Do the feeling states at [location A] and [location B] seem like they are two areas of the same feeling, or is it possible they are two different feeling states?

If you identify they are two or more different states, ask which location seems more important to work with. Find out if that is the location which corresponds to the feeling name you chose to map. If not, name the new feeling state before proceeding. Either way, make sure to note the other locations for future mapping.

Size and shape

What size and shape would you say this
***[feeling state]* seems to be?**

If the explorer has difficulty identifying the size of the feeling, assist by offering a selection of choices.

- Is this *[feeling state]* really small? Is it smaller than an egg?

- Is this *[feeling state]* as small as a tennis ball, or is more the size of a loaf of bread, or a watermelon, or larger than that?

In the case of a whole-body feeling, you will want to find out specifically where the feeling ends.

- Does this *[feeling state]* stop somewhere beneath your skin, does it go precisely to your skin, or does it extend beyond your skin, outside your physical body? How far?

If the explorer has difficulty identifying the shape of the feeling, assist either by asking about specific shapes or by providing choices between shapes, taking your cues from any hints the explorer provides. Gestures are wonderful indicators for location, size and shape.

- Is this "square" feeling flat, or more like a cube?

- Is this "round" feeling spherical like a ball, flat like a plate, or more extended like a cylinder?

Be prepared to elicit some unusual shapes. Anything is possible in the form and structure of the felt sense. Some possibilities to be aware of include the following.

- **Hollow objects** – These may include spheres, cubes, ovoids, cylinders and other shapes. Other forms may be inside these or they may be empty. Ask specifically if an apparently homogeneous object is the same all the way through the center. Of hollow objects, ask specifically what is inside them.

- **Doorways or gateways** – These can be of any size or orientation, and seem to open or connect to "other dimensions," other people, or some experience of energy. Don't try to understand what "another dimension" means (or for that matter anything else that doesn't make complete sense to your way of thinking). Simply accept that these words correspond to some aspect of the explorer's experience that is important, and use the same words to refer to the experience. Continue with the standard questioning sequence.

- **Multi-part shapes** – These are sometimes connected and sometimes not. If you continue the questioning process and discover that they have different properties, then you are probably working with two different feeling states and should probably do the complete mapping process with each. If they have highly similar or identical properties, they may be apparently separated forms of the same feeling state.

The felt sense is very sensitive in some people, allowing for a level of detail that can be surprising. Don't take too much time to get overly specific. Many times, shape will become more clear when the explorer draws the feeling state. When you have a pretty good description of location, size and shape, it's time to move on to substance.

Substance

> **If you were to say this *[feeling state]* had qualities of substance, would you say it seems more like a solid... a liquid... a gas... some kind of light or energy... or something else? ... What other qualities does this feeling substance have?**

Most people have never thought of a feeling as a substance, but when you ask this question, almost everyone has a very clear sense of what kind of substance a specific feeling resembles. Becoming aware of the feeling state as a substance makes the experience of the feeling much more vivid and clear.

A feeling state can have qualities like any substance that exists in the physical world, but can just as easily take the form of a substance that defies the laws of physics. After asking this question, if it seems the explorer is reaching for a description, I'll often say, "**The laws of physics do not apply here. You might turn out to have a feeling that's like a solid gas or a liquid energy. That's OK.**"

Once you have identified the general category of substance, ask a few questions about details of the substance qualities. Getting specific about a feeling substance's characteristics provides the explorer with even more vividness.

Try to strike a balance between expediency and thoroughness. Identifying every last detail can become tedious. Your goal is to assist the explorer in providing enough detail to become clearly aware of the feeling state and to create a workable sensory image of that state.

Following are specific details useful to inquire about for solids, liquids and gases. Use these as suggestions, choosing ones you perceive as most relevant for the particular feeling state the explorer is mapping.

Solids

- Heavy / light
- Soft / hard – (like putty or foam versus metal or stone)
- (If soft): Resilient / malleable – (like a rubber ball versus putty)
- (If hard): Rigid / brittle / bendable
- What is the texture of the surface?

Liquids

- Thick / thin – (like paint versus water)
- Heavy / light

Gases

- Thick / thin
- Heavy / light
- Moist / dry

Other kinds of substances you might encounter include the following. This list is not exhaustive, and you are likely to encounter other qualities of substance. Be open and supportive of whatever the explorer's experience indicates.

- **Plasma** – something between a liquid and a gas, or between a gas and energy.

- **Gel** – something between a solid and a liquid, like jello or toothpaste.

- **Electricity** – often with a buzzing quality.

- **Energy** – pure energy in whatever way the explorer understands that; it can be helpful to inquire into other substance qualities the energy may carry such as density, weight, and viscosity.

- **Light** – no substance per se, but with a presence all the same; similar to energy.

- **Infinite space** – a region within which the normal laws of substance do not apply, where space takes on a different dimension and infinity can fit within an area as small as a grapefruit.

- **Slurry** – a mixture of a particulate solid and a liquid.

- **Particles** – perhaps moving through space, perhaps clustered in clumps or solid shapes.

- **Pieces** – discrete, often contiguous, solid chunks, shards, balls, etc.

- **Sandy** – particulate solid with qualities of a liquid.

- **Aggregate** – two or more different particulate solids in a mixture; this may turn out to be a single state or two intermixed states.

Often, the best way to describe a solid is through analogy: it is "like" something else. If the explorer volunteers an analogy, that can be enough detail. Simply make a note of the item the substance resembles. Feel free to ask the explorer explicitly if the substance resembles anything in the physical world.

Once you are satisfied you have adequately captured the important qualities of substance for this feeling state, move on to ask about temperature.

Temperature

> **What temperature would you say this [** *feeling substance]* **seems to be?**

Temperature is often very obvious to the explorer, especially when it is extreme. At other times, though, you may need to provide a gentle prompt such as the following.

> **Does this substance seem warmer, or cooler, or more neutral like body or room temperature?**

Some explorers, for some feeling states, will have a very refined sense of temperature and will actually give you a specific degree reading. For others, the following distinctions are useful and sufficient designators for temperature.

- Very cold or extremely cold

- Cold

- Cool

- A little cooler than body temperature

- Body temperature

- A little warmer than body temperature

- Warm

- Hot

- Very hot or burning hot
- Nuclear hot

Neutral temperature

Occasionally, an explorer will relate that temperature does not seem relevant. They can't get a "reading." In these cases, check to see if the feeling substance is simply at body, room, or otherwise neutral temperature by asking about that specifically.

When you're finished with temperature, proceed to ask about color and appearance.

Color and appearance

> **If you were to say this *[feeling substance]*
> had a color, what color would you say that
> is? ... And does it seem to be transparent...
> translucent... or opaque?**

Color is a simple property that adds a lot to the sensory image's ability to connect strongly with the feeling state. When mapping, I generally keep the color question brief, not going into too much detail. The detail will emerge in the drawing.

Having an extensive set of coloring tools available can also help the explorer choose the appropriate color. Explorers often scan my hundreds of colors and pick exactly the one or two which match best. (And quite often, they can't quite find the right one. Colors in the feeling world can be far richer than we can easily represent using physical pigments on paper or pixels on a computer screen. This is especially true after the feeling has been moved to its ideal state.)

In addition to color, I ask about opacity or transparency. Here are the definitions of the terms.

- **Transparent**: can see detail through it, although the colors may be tinted; like some fruit drinks or tinted glasses.

- **Translucent**: light shines through but objects are not visible; like frosted glass, clouds, and lamp shades.

- **Opaque**: no light or visibility can be seen through the object; like a bowling ball, metal plate, or wooden bowl.

At times it can also be useful to inquire about luminosity – the property of a substance to emit light. Think of a glow stick, a flame, or a light bulb for examples. If it seems relevant, simply ask, "**Does this substance glow at all – in other words, does it radiate light – or does it simply have a flat color the way any ordinary substance would have a color?**"

One other property you might choose to explore is the surface quality. Does the substance appear shiny, dull, or textured in some way? Does it reflect light or absorb it?

Sometimes, a single feeling state can have two or more colors. If this happens, consider the possibility that you actually have two or more feeling states occupying very closely related spaces. Ask about whether or not the substance and/or temperature are different between the different colors. If the other qualities are the same even though the color is different, it is probably most useful to consider it to be the same feeling state and continue mapping. If the substance and/or temperature are qualitatively different, that may indicate the presence of multiple feeling states, and you may want to map those separately.

Once you are satisfied you have captured the essential qualities of appearance, move on to ask about movement.

Movement, force and pressure

> Does this [*feeling substance*] have any
> qualities of movement – does it seem to
> be flowing... or pulsing... or vibrating?
> ... And does there seem to be any force or
> pressure?

Properties of movement, force and pressure vary greatly. The possibilities are at least as wide as those in the physical world of solids, liquids and gases. As with the other properties, only go into as much detail as seems useful to help the explorer experience a strong connection between the image and the feeling state. Here are a few things to consider.

Types of movement/force

- Flowing

- Pulsing

- Vibrating

- Radiating

- Waves, ripples

- Whole-object movement

- Force or pressure

Qualities of movement/force

- Direction: Linear, circulating, inward or outward, expanding or contracting

- Intensity: Force, volume, or amplitude

- Speed: Rate of flow, frequency of pulse or vibration

- Variability: Steady, rhythmic, intermittent, or random

If the feeling substance seems to exhibit no movement, pulse or vibration, make certain that is the case by asking explicitly if it is "perfectly still" and unmoving. Often, the explorer will respond by saying it's "just there," and sometimes she will notice it is not actually completely still, but has a small amount of movement.

Sound or voice

> **If you listen internally, do you notice any inner sound or voice? If there is a voice, it is your voice or someone else's? What other sound qualities or tone of voice do you notice?**

For some explorers, sound is a natural element of their feeling state imagery. Others find sound a stretch. For many explorers, answering the questions about substance and color seemed like discovering properties that were already in place. Sound qualities may seem to fall more in the category of "making it up."

As a facilitator, try to strike a balance with an explorer who does not find sounds springing spontaneously to mind. Remind the explorer that making it up is entirely appropriate, that what you want is to find something that feels right, that fits.

I generally find that an overview of sound qualities is usually sufficient to be useful in the moving phase. I'll wait until after we find the ideal state to fully enhance and enrich the sound experience. Here are some qualities I've found most useful in mapping.

Vocal sounds

- **Voice**: the explorer's or someone else's; ask about gender, and note if there are multiple voices.

- **Attitude**: tone of voice and any meaning conveyed by tone; this can sometimes be a pointer to other feeling states.

- **Words spoken**: These can be quite significant – record verbatim. Often things like judgments, chastisement, laments.

- **Vocal qualities**: Rate, pitch, intonation, inflection, loudness (these are usually important to note only when the explorer volunteers the info, not so important to ask about).

Other sounds

- **General sound qualities**: pitch, amplitude, rhythm, tone

- **Single or multiple sounds**

- **Musical qualities:** instrumental, vocal, choral, natural

Silence

If the explorer states there is no sound, confirm by asking, **"Do you hear actual silence, or is there simply an absence of sound?"** There is a difference. Silence can be "deafening" or otherwise carry great meaning.

When you have completed a general description of the sound qualities of the feeling state imagery, it's time for one last check before moving on.

Other

> **Is there anything else you want to notice about how this *[feeling state]* actually feels before we move on? Are there any adjustments you would like to make to your description?**

All that's necessary here is a quick invitation to allow the explorer to share any background discoveries she may have made while answering the questions. Sometimes answering a question about color, for example, can lead to a clarification about substance. Make any changes or updates to the notes before moving on to the questions about thoughts and beliefs.

Belief questions in greater detail

The purpose of the belief questions is twofold. First, eliciting belief statements serves as a record of the explorer's starting point. Because the belief statements tie the feeling state to meaningful context, they can be helpful later in recalling just how distressing this state used to be. And that can add appreciation and continued motivation for the journey back to wholeness. Quite often I've heard an explorer exclaim upon reading her recorded beliefs a few weeks later, "Oh my god, I can't believe I used to think that way." I love those moments.

Another reason for the belief questions has to do with the more advanced skills for mapping and moving all nine feeling states involved in a given issue. We will look at a few basic skills for working with multiple feeling states at the end of this chapter, and more advanced practices will be covered in my trainings and future books. In brief, belief statements often connect thought images arising from one feeling state to thought images arising from another feeling state. Following the trail of belief statements is one way to seek out the full configuration of feeling states.

For now, in the basic practice, hold the purpose of the belief questions as a useful record of the meaning and context for the reactive feeling state you're mapping.

Basic belief statement

> **Now we're going to explore the thoughts that typically accompany or express this [feeling state] for you. How would you capture in words what seems most true, or real, or important, from the perspective of this [feeling state]?**

All we're going for here is a simple statement of what seems to be fact, regarding the explorer, her environment, the other people involved, or whatever other factor seems central to the perspective of this feeling state. Keep the statement simple, and make room to dig around the edges of it.

Sometimes the explorer will draw a blank with an open-ended prompt. If so, suggest some possible starting points for statements.

> **How would you complete the sentence:**
> - **I am, or I'm not…**
> - **I can, or can't…**
> - **I have, or don't have…**
> - **I need, or don't need…**

- **I want, or don't want…**
- **I should, or shouldn't…**
- **I have to, or don't have to…**

If appropriate, consider inviting the explorer to substitute "you," "they," or "it" for "I." If at any time the explorer continues to draw a blank with these more specific prompts, don't push it. Move on. Sometimes you are working with a feeling state that took shape before language and has been suppressed ever since, and it never developed a mature linguistic connection with other states in the form of articulated beliefs. When you have one to three clear statements capturing the general thoughts arising from the feeling state, you're done. It's time for drawing.

Belief statements and point of view

The explorer will have two choices of perspective available when eliciting belief statements. As one option, the explorer can speak as her whole self, having this feeling state. And it can be even more powerful to speak in the first person from the perspective of the feeling state itself. For example, a feeling named "withdrawn" might say something like, "I want to keep you safe, because I don't trust this person" where the "you" refers to the explorer and the "I" refers to this part of her which is protecting her by withdrawing.

Your first choice should be to go with the feeling state speaking from its own perspective. Especially as you map multiple feeling states, hearing distinctly from each part playing its role within the whole pattern can lead to terrific self insight. For some explorers, though, this perspective is more difficult to sustain. Or it can seem strange to have these parts speaking as if they were sub-personalities. Reassure the explorer that this is natural, that all of us have these parts of ourselves interacting with each other to create our experience. And allow the explorer to generate statements from either perspective. It's all good.

A pause for reflection

Before advancing to the moving phase of the work, let's pause and reflect on what you've just done. By asking questions inviting the explorer to engage with a feeling state using the filter of sensory imagery, the explorer created a rich sensory image which maps strongly to the feeling state. To the explorer, this image matches the feeling. It represents the feeling state better than any other image could do, and there is something tangibly "right" about it.

What does this mean? It means that *if the explorer interacts with the sensory image, deliberately altering properties of the image, the actual felt experience of the feeling also changes in real time, in direct proportion to the changes in imagery.* In this way, the explorer has created a "handle" on the feeling state and is able to intentionally and directly effect changes to the actual, real-time, felt experience of the state.

This is not a trivial accomplishment. *The explorer is able to effect these changes without recourse to any other aspect of her experience.* She does not need to review her memories. She does not need to examine her beliefs. She does not need to reframe her perceptions. She does not need to express her emotions. She does not need to alter her brain chemistry. These changes in her experience of the feeling state happen as a direct result of her intentional manipulation of a simple sensory image that is for all intents and purposes free of history and value and meaning. It's hard to bring judgment or interpretation to interfere in the raw experience of a cold blue stone or a swirling red gas.

If your profession has anything to do with helping people transform inner realities that have an emotional component, stop and think about this. This direct access to feeling states changes the landscape. The day I first tried this, and directly shifted a downward depression to an upward delight in the space of a few seconds, I was stunned. Flabbergasted. I had invested a great deal of energy, study, and time in working through my issues in many other ways that were infinitely more difficult and painful. Honestly, I couldn't believe it could be so easy to interact with and instantly shift some of my most difficult emotions.

If you are involved in any kind of research into the mind or the brain, stop and think about this. We now have a very simple tool with which to "scan" the inner states of feeling. We can convert these feeling states into precise images through which we are now able to compare one feeling state to another, within a single person and between people. This has never before been possible.

And not only that, but we can use those images to engage the feeling state, to directly manipulate it with intention and control as a way of discovering how feeling works. This tool opens up a tremendous new opportunities for people ready to break new ground in the mind sciences.

Using the image to reduce feeling intensity

One convenient benefit of having attached this dynamically-linked handle to the feeling state is the ability to reduce the intensity of a distressing state. Of course, if you intend to continue immediately after mapping to the moving phase, there's no need for this. But if for some reason there will be an interruption or there simply isn't time to continue the process, this can offer immediate relief.

To use the image in this way, start making adjustments to the sensory properties that seem most extreme. Make small adjustments at first – all you're going for is a bit of relief, not wholesale transformation. That will come later.

Usually, the direction of change to bring relief is the one that's intuitively obvious. For example, a feeling state that is extremely hot will probably benefit from cooling down a bit. One that is vibrating intensely will probably benefit from calming down a bit. A feeling state that is very heavy could probably use some lightening, and one that is very dark some brightening.

Once in a while, the obvious adjustment doesn't relieve the distress. In that case, first try the opposite direction to alter that property. And if that doesn't work, leave it as is and try another property. For most feeling states, just one or two properties will turn out to be "drivers." Making adjustments to these will effect the greatest change to the feeling. Try making small changes to discover one of these drivers, and go with that one.

As explorers, we may wish to practice altering that property back and forth between one value and another, almost as if it is a slider on an electronic device. Slide to one end to experience the strongest distress, and slide to the other end to experience the greatest relief. We have control of that slider at any time we need it.

The natural witness

Another way mapping contributes to reducing intensity of the explorer's feeling states is by helping to re-ground our point of view in what I have been calling the witness self. In order to answer the mapping questions, we must effectively stand outside the feeling and examine it as if it were an object of study. To do so, we must shift our origin of awareness to the witness perspective, observing our own inner states from a neutral position.

Our goal in this is not to make an object of our feelings. Nor is it to set up a permanent imagery interface for feeling states. We create an imagery map to provide the distance and precision we need to restore a distressed system of feeling states to its natural functioning. When we've accomplished that, (and it doesn't take very long), we don't need the maps any more. We create the maps because of where they're going to take us, not to become indelibly bonded to the maps themselves.

When more than one feeling state shows up

Feeling states never happen in isolation. There's never any question about whether other states accompany the one you're mapping. The real question is whether any other feeling states connected to the one you're mapping will interfere with your mapping and moving process. Sometimes feeling states have such strong interdependencies that moving one state, even in a direction that is clearly more pleasant, can trigger another state to flare up and take over.

Many times you can get a preview of this possibility while mapping. It may show up as a feeling of fear or fogging out that seems to take over while the explorer is mapping her anger, for example. The fear may prefer that the anger stays out of awareness because it remembers intolerable consequences that happened as a result of expressing the anger in the past. Or another feeling state may show up structurally, for example as a hot liquid core inside a solid metallic ball. The metallic ball may seem unwilling to shift its form or intensity because it's doing a job – keeping the molten liquid contained. In this case, you would need to map and move the core first, and then the container would be free to move as well.

I'll need to save the advanced strategies for working with multiple feeling states for another time. For now, just be aware of one important tradeoff.

As you are getting started with these skills, it is probably best to map and then move one feeling state at a time. Mapping more than one state brings multiple states into the explorer's awareness at once. Although we are creating some distance through the mapping process, mapping multiple states can lead to a sense of overwhelm. Whenever possible, leave the explorer feeling lighter and more resourceful at the end of a session by helping her to move most of the feelings she has mapped.

The important difference between "mental imagery" and a feeling state image

At times, you may find the explorer conjures some very specific images. She may describe a feeling as a "squirrel in my belly" or "like autumn leaves swirling all around me, each leaf shaped like a heart."

When you find this level of detail, question it. If you have difficulty understanding how someone would "feel" a few hundred leaves in the shape of a heart, it may be because the explorer has lapsed into using metaphoric imagery instead of tracking the actual, inner sensations of the feeling state.

This is a time to lead the explorer deeper into the "actual, felt" sensations of the feeling. Try this question:

> **Now as you allow yourself to fully experience this [*mental imagery*], notice the feeling that arises with that imagery. Paying attention to the sensations of this**

feeling, if you were to say the actual, felt experience of the feeling were located somewhere in or around your body, where would you say that is?

Usually, this is enough to shift the explorer's attention to the somatosensory information, and you'll be able to properly map the feeling state. If the explorer remains attached to the detailed, metaphoric image, go with it. Complete the mapping and continue with the moving process. The fact is, moving a mental image will often lead to similar breakthroughs as working directly with the somatosensory image of the feeling state.

More advanced methods can leverage this difference for various purposes. There's not room to go into those or other advanced methods in this book. If you are interested in learning more, please join me in the learning and collaboration community at FeelingPath.com.

Move It: Accessing the Ideal State

Now it's time for the fun part. If you are the explorer, the feeling state you've mapped most likely took its current form at some time in your past when you were prevented from feeling its message or powerless to change your situation. You have now created a convenient enhancement of your awareness of this feeling state, a vivid sensory image specifically linked to this feeling. This sensory image gives you a new power, the ability to directly interact with the feeling state and change how you experience it.

This feeling state is an expression of a feeling path that has always been within you. This feeling path has the capacity to express itself through an infinite range of feeling states. When it is free to function naturally, this feeling pathy spontaneously responds to the subtle changes of your life, both within you and outside of you, to provide ongoing feedback about your relationship with yourself and the world in the form of ever-changing feelings. This feeling path coordinates with eight other paths – two sets of nine – to give rise to your experience of being a self, a sovereign consciousness existing in a particular context. The natural experience of self is one of wholeness, a balance between what is inside of you and outside of you, and a harmonious interactive relationship between the two. Wholeness is dynamic, alive, aware, and present.

When something disrupts that wholeness, the natural response of these feeling paths is to signal that disruption through unpleasant feeling states. The purpose is to call your attention to the disruption so you can take appropriate action to restore wholeness in your experience of self. The distressed feeling stated both call attention to themselves and exaggerate the perception of what is disrupting wholeness, making threats appear more scary, losses appear more absent, and violations appear more egregious. Again, the whole purpose of this is to assist you in maintaining a harmonious equilibrium conducive to a pleasant and healthy life. Distressing feeling states are designed to motivate action to correct disruptions to wholeness.

In a healthy state of being, with feelings operating freely, we become aware of disruptions to our balance very early, while the perturbations are mild. And we act to correct them very early. The imbalances we experience remain minor and short-lived, and we exist in a general state of well-being.

But when those feeling states are prevented from doing their job in the moment, they persist. And if they are prevented from doing their job chronically over time, as happens in many childhoods or in other situations of oppression, those feeling states can become habituated. We become numb to the imbalances they are pointing to and come to assume that a disruption of wholeness is the standard condition of life. Our nine parts of self configure their functioning to compensate for the imbalance. The exaggerated perceptions get locked in place, the unpleasant feeling states get locked in place, and our entire being takes on a pattern that assumes wholeness is not possible. The only recourse is to make do with compensations that often distort and diminish our experience of life.

We'll get into this again in more advanced writing and coursework to come. For now, the important thing is to recognize that every part of you that took on a distressed feeling state, no matter how black, no matter how dark, no matter how oppressive, did so in response to something in your world. And its intention from the start was to support you in returning to a state of wholeness.

What we're going to do now is to support this part of you in restoring its access to that function by guiding it along the way to an experience of what this part of you wants to be feeling, what it would be feeling if you were in that state of wholeness. In order for this part of you to effectively support you in seeking wholeness in your life, it needs to be reminded of what wholeness feels like. Fortunately, its memory of that state of wholeness is built in and easily accessible.

What we are going to do is to use the linked sensory image you've created to directly make adjustments to the feeling state. As we do, you will monitor the feeling state, noticing what adjustments make the feeling more distressful and which adjustments make it more pleasant. We will continue making adjustments to the sensory image in directions that lead to a more pleasant feeling state, incrementally following the implicit knowing within this part of you, until we arrive at an ideal state for this part. You will know you have arrived because no further adjustments to the new sensory image yield positive changes. And you will know as well simply because it feels "right." It's like coming back to a true home after a very long journey.

The moving process in a nutshell

The Feeling Path Mapping moving phase has four steps:

1. Prepare the way by setting an inviting framework.

2. Ask the moving questions to elicit sensory imagery reflective of the ideal state.

3. Ask the belief questions to construct new beliefs congruent with the ideal state.

4. Draw the ideal feeling state.

We'll walk through each step, first with the basics, then with more extended guidance to help you get the best results.

On the following pages you'll find the standard set of moving questions. Proceed as you did with the mapping, taking notes and drawing the final feeling state. Note the date at the top of your worksheet as well as the name of the feeling state you're going to move. When you've finished, you'll name the final, ideal feeling state and write that at the bottom, under the drawing.

Asking the moving and beliefs questions

As the facilitator, read the questions on the following pages verbatim, and as much as possible, write down the important parts of the answers word for word. If an answer isn't clear at first, invite different possibilities until one feels like it fits. As you facilitate, speak slowly and from the heart. Repeat the explorer's answers back to clarify.

Substitute the appropriate language in the areas indicated by [italics in brackets].

Most of the questions follow this format:

1. Elicit a direction for movement along a property polarity. For example, exploring the polarity of hot to cold, "Would this part of you prefer to become warmer, or cooler…"

2. Follow up on that direction by inviting an optimal setting for that property. For example, "In becoming warmer, what temperature would this part of you most want to be?"

As soon as the feeling image shifts even the smallest amount, it no longer corresponds to the name it was originally given. For this reason, it is very important that you use the term "this part of you" instead of any specific feeling name.

Moving Questions

PREAMBLE: Before we start, I want to acknowledge this part of you. It took on this feeling state long ago in response to something in your life, and this feeling was an attempt to do something good for you, given your situation. As we move this feeling state, I want to reassure this part that you can always put it back if you should ever need to feel this again for any reason. We're adding choices, not taking them away, so moving a feeling state is safe.

Because it's safe to move, today we're going to help this part of you recover access to its ideal state. In this moment, just for now, we're going to explore what this part of you could be feeling in a perfect world, where all your needs are met, fully and completely, exactly the way you want them to be.

Finally, this feeling state is interconnected with others. I'd like to invite these other parts of you to participate in this process as passive witnesses, learning from the process about what is possible for every part of you.

Now, in this moment, in the spirit of exploration of what is possible...

TEMPERATURE: If this part of you were free to become warmer or cooler, which would feel better?... And in becoming *[warmer/ cooler]*, if this part of you could take on any temperature at all, what temperature would it most want to be?

SUBSTANCE: And in becoming *[new temperature]*, if this part of you could become harder or softer, heavier or lighter, more or less dense which would feel better? ... And in becoming *[new direction]*, if this part of you could take on qualities of any substance at all, would it prefer to be more like a solid, a liquid, a gas, some kind of pure light or energy, or something else? ... *Ask refining questions about qualities such as hard/soft, thick/thin, heavy/light.* Is there anything else you want to notice about the substance qualities of what this part of you wants to be?

COLOR: So in becoming *[new temperature and substance]*, if this part of you were free to take on any color at all, any color or colors of the rainbow, what would it most want to be? ... And would it want to be opaque, translucent, or transparent? ... And would it want to be luminous, iridescent, shimmering, or sparkling? Is there anything else you want to notice about the color or appearance of what this part of you wants to be?

LOCATION: And in taking on these new qualities of *[new temperature, substance, and color]*, if this part of you were free to occupy any location in or around your body, where would it want to be located? ... And if it could choose to occupy any size and shape, what size and shape would it most want to be?

MOVEMENT: If this part of you were free to take on any qualities of movement, would it want to be flowing, pulsing, vibrating, radiating, or moving in some other way? ... *Ask refining questions about qualities of direction, speed, intensity, or variability.* Is there anything else you want to notice about the movement qualities of what this part of you wants to be?

SOUND: And if this part of you were free to express itself in sound or voice, what kind of sound or voice would it most want to take on? ... *Ask refining questions about the qualities of sound or voice.*

OTHER: Is there anything else you want to notice about what this part of you wants to become? Are there any other adjustments you want to make?

Identifying key beliefs

PREAMBLE: Now we're going to explore the thoughts that naturally want to accompany or express this new feeling state.

STATEMENT: From the place of this new feeling, how would you express in words what seems true, or real, or important? What is true about yourself, your world, or someone else? What thoughts naturally arise from this state?

Most importantly, what does this part of you most want you to know?

NEW NAME: What name would you like to give this new feeling? What would it like to be called?

Name the new feeling and draw it.

When the explorer has named the new feeling state, write that name on your notes and allow the explorer to draw the image.

As with mapping, drawing the ideal feeling state is an opportunity for the explorer to get even more clear about what this feeling state wants to become. For many explorers who are strongly visually oriented, drawing leads to further insights. If the drawing elicits significant new information, record or correct any important aspects of the description in the notes. Having a clearly explicit description helps the explorer access this ideal state during integration exercises and at any time in the future.

The moving process in more depth

Moving a feeling state from its stuck, maladaptive condition to an ideal state is a treat, whether you're the explorer or the facilitator. As the facilitator, you get to watch transformation happen right in front of your eyes. The explorer's body posture gets more symmetrical, their face relaxes and sheds years of tension, and the lights in their eyes blaze forth, fresh and very, very present.

The words explorers speak after that experience always find me catching my breath and getting just a bit moist in the eyes. It's like you're sitting in the presence of a wise one. This ordinary person, who just minutes ago was seemingly entrapped in high distress, is now serene, optimistic, and joyful. And it's not fake. It's not put on. There's no effort to it, and the words people say from that place are poignantly ingenuous. It is a privilege to facilitate this process, and I am ever more deeply grateful for that gift.

And that's to say nothing of the explorer's experience! How does one go from despair to pleasurable enthusiasm in the space of twenty minutes? It can be hard to describe the experience in words. None of my clients can do it very well, and I myself have struggled for years to convey to the uninitiated what surprise and delight there is in such natural and effortless liberation.

What I'm saying here is that the rewards for excellence are phenomenal, so it's worth learning how to facilitate this process excellently. I only hope I can share enough of what I know for you to be able to learn well.

Preparation: Establishing the framework, setting the hook

Before we start, I want to acknowledge this part of you. It took on this feeling state long ago in response to something in your life, and this feeling was an attempt to do something good for you, given your situation. As we move this feeling state, I want to reassure this part that you can always put it back if you should ever need to feel this again for any reason.

We're adding choices, not taking them away, so moving a feeling state is safe. Because it's safe to move, today we're going to help this part of you recover access to its ideal state. In this moment, just for now, we're going to explore what this part of

> **you could be feeling in a perfect world,
> where all your needs are met, fully and
> completely, exactly the way you want them
> to be.**

Every feeling state you work with is but one of a set of nine distinct feeling states, typically interlocked in a long-held pattern. Moving one feeling state can seem to work at cross-purposes with the intentions of the other feeling states if they have not yet been moved.

As an example, I recall the feeling state of "heart wanting to break open" I mapped in myself at one time. I had difficulty moving it at first because of an underlying fear. This fear had the form of a shield and the intention of protecting that potentially vulnerable heart. The job it had taken on was to make very sure that heart stayed covered up. But when I tried to move the fear, it balked as well, not wanting to allow a third feeling, shame, to come to awareness.

This kind of interlocking can hold up the process. In earlier times in applying these methods, I used to follow the trail of interwoven states. In this case I moved the shame first, then the fear, and finally the heart. Since then, I've developed a more supportive framework that allows us to move almost any feeling state without necessarily getting "permission" from the other states connected to it.

The framework

We need to support the easy release of feeling states from their conjoined relationships with other feeling states, so they are free to seek their own ideal state independently. I have found the most effective framework to include the following elements:

- **Acknowledge the feeling state, and the underlying feeling path, for having a positive intention.** One of the ways other states keep a feeling state locked into place is through the interweaving of judgmental beliefs. Often, for example, an experience of fear is denigrated by a parent, and this judgment gets incorporated as a defensiveness both against the judge and against the feeling of fear. Both states were working hard to maintain the expectations set by the parent, thus maintaining the connection, belonging, and safety.

- **Affirm the freedom to return to the original feeling state at any time.** The fact is, in moving a feeling state, the part experiences a greater range of freedom of expression. It is able to choose to express as the ideal state it discovers, or the original compromised state, or anything in between. Asserting this reassures the feeling path that moving it is safe. There is no risk.

- **Narrow the time frame to "this moment," and set a spirit of exploration.** Within this moment, anything is possible. Narrowing the frame provides greater freedom to explore an "as if" world, without the limitations imposed by "reality." Using the word "explore" invites a sense of adventure and possibility. Who knows what we will find?

- **Set the frame for exploration to be "in a perfect world."** The definition of this world is one in which "all your needs are met, fully and completely, exactly the way you want them, and you know how to keep them that way." The purpose of every feeling path is to meet specific needs. If those needs are well met, the path signals this satiation with pleasurable feeling states. Taking on this frame encourages the path to reconnect with the feeling state associated with this fulfillment.

- **Give explicit instructions to the interconnected parts.** I have found the most effective way to avoid having another feeling come to the foreground and steal the stage is to give all the other states clear instructions. I suggest they participate as "passive witnesses," with the job of learning what is possible for themselves and "every part of you."

Creating this level of freedom and permission usually does the trick. The feeling path goes blithely through the process, winding up in a feeling state it most likely could never have predicted, and being quite pleased with its discovery as a result. Although we may emphasize over and over again that the path can always go back to its original state, once it discovers its ideal state, do you think it wants to? Not likely. Once a path regains access to its ideal state, it's going to work hard do what it can to maintain that access.

Of course, to fully support it in doing so requires moving all nine states in the full configuration of paths. If other paths actually did have an investment in its original state, they're going to work at getting this path to regress until they've had a chance to regain access to their ideal states as well.

Getting the "mind" out of the way

Another important aspect of the overall framing of the space for transformation is a deep trust in the wisdom of each feeling path of the explorer. Sometimes the explorer finds herself guessing about what the feeling state *should* be, according to some ideas about it. As the facilitator, whenever you hear language like, "it should be," or "I want it to be," that's usually an indication of another state butting into the process with its own opinion.

If this happens, remind the explorer to trust this part of her, to focus on what the feeling state actually feels like, and to go always in the direction of what feels best without making any effort to figure it out ahead of time. In this way, the path going through the transformation will almost always surprise the explorer. It has often become so out of touch with its ideal state that predicting what that ideal state should be is impossible.

In a general sense, this is why we can't actually ever know what we truly want unless we are first free to experience the ideal state of having everything we need. When viewed from the perspective of an un-centered, distressed feeling state, any idea of what we actually need or want is bound to be mistaken.

Setting the hook: entrainment

The process of mapping and moving a feeling state relies on a principle I call entrainment. Entrainment is the passive synchronization of complex, dynamic patterns – for example the harmonic vibration of a resting violin string when its neighbor is played. In mapping, we are establishing an entrainment between the brain patterns generating precise imagery and those generating the more nebulous feeling states. Once we have established that entrainment, we can deliberately manipulate the patterns of imagery to effect concordant change in the patterns of feeling.

The process works best when the feeling is strong. Although feeling state centers are located in different areas than the neural centers of emotion, and although the felt sense is an abstraction formed only in part from a map of the physiological state of the whole body, the two functions are strongly linked. When emotion is triggered in the body through instinctual responses, we typically experience changes in our feeling states. Similarly, when we experience the recurrence of a strong feeling state upon recalling an emotionally powerful memory, we tend to recreate the physiological state of the emotionally aroused body.

So when moving a feeling from its distressed to its ideal state, the experience will be more compelling when the feeling state is strong enough to engender some physiological response. When we have that mutuality of feeling and physiology, we tend to give it greater credence as something "real," and will mark it as a significant event in memory. This strength helps confirm for the explorer that the path itself is choosing its ideal state; it's not an abstract idea. It also helps lay in the neural pathways for easy transition between one state and the other in everyday life.

To establish this strong entrainment and feeling/emotion synergy, I have found the best technique to be a kind of "setting the hook," or "winding up." Before entering into the actual moving questions, I will first run a quick survey of sensory parameters with the explorer to identify which parameters have the biggest effect on the actual felt experience. I'll start with the obvious ones, whichever ones are most extreme in their qualities, and I'll ask the explorer to experiment with making small changes in both directions for that parameter. For example, if the feeling state image temperature is hot, I'll ask about the effect of making the image hotter or cooler. If the change results in a strong shift in the felt experience, providing great relief or higher intensity depending on the direction of movement, I'll note that, and move on to test another parameter.

In this way, I'll identify at least one, and possibly two or three parameters which are "drivers" for the image/feeling link. Then I'll share with the explorer the importance of feeling the state strongly for the process to work best, for her to get the clearest feedback about the direction to move. And I'll ask her to crank up the intensity, specifically asking her to make the changes in each of the parameters we've identified. I'm looking for a real experience of discomfort here. When I'm doing this, I generally also hold a sense of lightness and humor about it. I'm maintaining a rapport with her higher or witness self, working with her to facilitate changes that she wants. And we never tarry in the discomfort; just crank up the volume and get on with it. Usually, the explorer will only have to experience the extra discomfort for a few seconds.

This is a great technique for a couple more reasons. First, it demonstrates to the explorer that she is actually in control of the intensity of her discomfort. If she can deliberately intensify the feeling, she knows implicitly that it's also within her control to decrease the intensity. Second, it augments the explorer's motivation to follow all the way through with the move. We're all naturally wired to move away from discomfort, and when you intensify the discomfort, you elevate the force driving the part from its distressed state to its ideal state.

Generally, I'll only do this if it seems useful. Often the explorer is already experiencing the feeling state with a sufficient intensity, and I'll just go with it. But with someone who is in general reporting a low intensity of feeling as they go through the experience, I'll use this with almost every part we move.

Moving questions in detail

As soon as we begin asking the first moving question, we enter a new world. In facilitating this process, we abandon all reference to the original feeling name from the very beginning. Instead, we refer to "this part of you." That's because a feeling name is very specific, and the name for the original feeling state referred very concretely to the state represented by that specific sensory image.

As soon as we change even a single parameter of that image, the feeling state is no longer the same, and thus the name no longer applies. Because the feeling state is in a constant state of transition throughout the entire moving process, we choose to refer to the underlying entity, the "part," which is the same from the beginning to the end of the process and beyond. Using this language helps point to the aspect of the explorer's consciousness we're focused on, and also helps the explorer let go of any attachment to the original feeling state. (Using the phrase "part of you" is closer to the vernacular and more easily assimilated by the explorer than the more specific designation of "feeling path," so it's usually preferable in your facilitation.)

Each moving question has six important components:

1. **Acknowledge progress.** Restate the changes already achieved and reinforce their felt expression in the moment. Key expressions are, "In becoming *[parameter]*..." or "In allowing this part of you to become *[parameter]*..."

2. **Set the "as if" frame.** It is important throughout the process to undertake it as if it were a simple exercise of imagination. We want the ultimate latitude for movement, and that requires the maximum amount of permissiveness for this part to try anything at all. One way of reinforcing this frame is to use the language of possibility: "If this part of you could... what would..." "If you were to say... what would you say that might be?" Another way is to add the language, "In this moment" toward the beginning of the question.

3. **Identify direction.** Invite trial changes in both directions to very specific sub-parameters to choose a positive direction. For example, ask if the feeling state would prefer to be warmer or cooler, heavier or lighter, darker or brighter. Make sure to apply equal or neutral emphasis to any choices suggested, and include the possibility for no movement at all, "...or neither."

4. **Invite complete transformation.** Specifically ask what parameter value this part would "most want to be." Occasionally restate the frame "in a perfect world, where all your needs are met..." As in the mapping phase, the explorer may find it easier if the facilitator provides a selection of possibilities to choose from, including the option, "... or something else."

5. **Invite refinements.** Selectively scan various refining parameters to invite the explorer to enhance and improve the feeling state. Often, these enhancements can lead to further substantive moves as new insights emerge from the qualities elicited.

6. **Reinforce part autonomy.** In choosing direction, use the language "which feels better to this part of you?" or "would this part of you prefer?" In inviting transformation, use the language "this part of you." This places the locus of evaluation directly within the part itself, where it belongs.

When you first facilitate this process, whether for yourself or someone else, you'll be best served by asking the questions verbatim, as I've provided them. Eventually, many of you will find yourself wanting to make changes to better suit your personal style. If so, please keep these six guidelines in mind, and you'll remain effective in your facilitation.

Temperature

> **In a perfect world, if this part of you were free to become warmer or cooler, which would feel better?... And in becoming [*warmer/cooler*], if this part of you could take on any temperature at all, what temperature would it most want to be?**

I usually lead with temperature because it's such a simple quality with a clearly linear scale. You can make small adjustments in one direction or the other to find out which leads to improvement, and then invite further exploration to find the optimal value. Also, I think temperature works well when you're starting because it is so clearly kinesthetic. There's no way to "game" the system with creative images and it forces the explorer to pay attention to somatosensory information.

Substance

> And in becoming *[new temperature]*, if this part of you could become harder or softer, which would feel better? If it could become heavier or lighter, which would feel better? More or less dense? ... So in becoming *[harder/softer]*, *[heavier/lighter]*, and/or *[more/less dense]* if this part of you could take on qualities of any substance at all, would it prefer to be more like a solid, a liquid, a gas, some kind of pure light or energy, or something else? ... Ask refining questions about qualities such as hard/soft, thick/thin, heavy/light.

With each subsequent question, I usually start with a reinforcement of the progress we've already made. The language, "in becoming..." presupposes the moment happened or is happening. The presupposition is a powerful verbal technique to support unconscious processing.

We move directly into the fine adjustment explorations to identify positive direction. For substance, you'll want to base your fine adjustments on the substance you're starting with. For almost all substances, the question "more or less dense" will usually serve well. For solids, "harder or softer" is often useful. For solids and liquids, "heavier or lighter" works well, and for liquids and gasses, "thicker or thinner" can be useful.

Once you've gotten the substance moving a bit, transition directly into the open invitation. For substance, it's important to list the options as a way of inviting the explorer to actually "try on" each quality, making sure to consider the full spectrum of possibilities. Often times a substance will make a dramatic shift, for example from solid to pure light, and without considering the full spectrum an explorer might stop the movement with a small shift to liquid because that does feel better. It's your job as the facilitator to encourage the full "perfect world" treatment.

Color

> **So in becoming *[new temperature and substance]*, if this part of you were free to take on any color at all, any color or colors of the rainbow, what would it most want to be? … And would this *[substance]* want to be opaque, translucent, or transparent? … And would it want to be luminous, iridescent, shimmering, or sparkling?**

You can also choose to invite incremental changes as a way of starting to work with color. Useful ones to consider are "darker or brighter," "more or less vivid," or "more or less transparent/opaque."

But often by the time you've reached color in the sequence, the feeling state has already shifted considerably and may already have started taking on new color properties. Starting out with the open invitation question is often sufficient at this point, and if the explorer seems to struggle, then I'll readjust by asking an incremental question.

Make sure to ask about opacity, etc, and invite the explorer to consider other qualities like iridescence. These can be fun additions to the image!

Location

> **And in taking on these new qualities of**
> ***[new temperature, substance, and color],***
> **if this part of you were free to occupy any**
> **location in or around your body, where**
> **would it want to be located? … And if it**
> **could choose to occupy any size and shape,**
> **what size and shape would it most want to**
> **be?**

Location can be one of the most powerful properties in shifting a feeling state to its ideal. Many times, a feeling state which starts outside the body will end up on the inside. The opposite also happens.

One important dimension here is size. Many times, an explorer is used to a feeling state being rather small, and doesn't immediately consider the possibility of expanding it to full-body size or beyond. As the facilitator, you can guide this process by asking explicitly what it would be like to have the feeling occupy a larger size. Have the explorer "try it on" and find out for herself whether that is better or not.

Sometimes a feeling state seems to you that it would be beneficial to occupy the whole body, but the explorer insists that it doesn't want to go into the legs, for example. Sometimes this is because another feeling that hasn't yet been moved is occupying that space and it doesn't feel so great to have them overlap. In cases like these, it is often useful to come back around to make final adjustments to the feeling location (and other properties) after you've moved the rest of the feelings you have mapped.

Movement

> **If this part of you were free to take on any qualities of movement, would it want to be flowing, pulsing, vibrating, radiating, or moving in some other way?**

Most of the time, the movement will quickly suggest itself. By this far in the process, the feeling state has almost completely transformed and is probably already moving in the way it wants to. All you need to do as the facilitator is identify that desired movement, reinforce it verbally, and invite it to go even further in positive qualities. And at this point there is usually no need to ask about "force or pressure" from the mapping phase, because those qualities are almost always a sign of opposition with another state.

Of course, explore the details. As with mapping, consider direction, speed, intensity, and variability.

Sound

> **And if this part of you were free to express itself in sound or voice, what kind of sound or voice would it most want to express? ... What are the qualities of that sound or voice?**

For some explorers, sound is an especially powerful dimension of their experience. Give some time for the explorer to inhabit the new feeling state and allow for an appropriate sound to show up. Once it does, ask clarifying questions to help make the auditory imagery crystal clear.

Use the tips in the mapping section for exploring the details of sound or voice.

Other

> **Is there anything else you want to notice about what this part of you wants to become? Are there any other adjustments you want to make?**

With this question, you are opening up for any further adjustment the explorer might want to make. Sometimes shifts in properties later in the process change the earlier properties even further. For example, adding the sound of a choral chant might help shift the substance from a gas to more of a pure light, or shift its color in some way. Check these things out with the explorer to make sure you've fully mapped the ideal state.

Changing the question sequence

In general, you'll do well with the standard sequence given here. However, if you have reason to believe that one of the parameters is a strong driver for a feeling state, it's ok to start with that one. For example, if the substance is extremely heavy, or the color is oppressively dark, go ahead and start with that, beginning with incremental changes to the weight or darkness.

Overall, it doesn't ultimately matter what order you ask the questions. The goal is to get through them all and arrive at a final, ideal state.

What to do when a part doesn't move

Sometimes when you ask the moving questions, the explorer will experience resistance, as if the part does not want to move. In fact, sometimes the feeling will seem to want to intensify even further.

It is always the case in situations like this that another part is involved which has a stake in this feeling state remaining just the way it is. Usually this other part will be making itself known – the explorer will be feeling the other feeling state as well. You can find this out by asking, "What else are you feeling now?"

It will be important for you to identify this other part and address it respectfully. Ask if it would be willing to stand aside just for now, and observe the process. Reassure this part that the feeling can always return to its current state if that's what's best.

If you get a yes, proceed. If not, shift your attention to the resistant feeling state, and move that one first. Map it first if you haven't done that yet.

Another counter-intuitive strategy you can use when you encounter a feeling state which seems to want to intensify is to go with it. Support the feeling state in ratcheting up the intensity as far as it wants to, and then encourage it to go even further. Many times, this traveling into the eye of the storm has the effect of turning the feeling state inside out. It goes into the intensity and all the way through it to a positive state.

Of course, you'll need a strategy for what to do if you get stuck in the more intense state. There are two things you can do. First is to simply invite the explorer to ratchet the intensity back down. This deliberate intensification and diminishment of a feeling state actually can give the explorer more of a sense of personal control over the feeling state. This is especially true when there is fear about feeling it. Going deliberately into the intensity demonstrates that the explorer is actually able to survive and even thrive through the journey. And it provides a sense of personal choice, power, and self-efficacy. If I can choose to deliberately intensify a feeling state, I can certainly choose the opposite.

One more strategy that is useful for feeling states that seem to be resisting movement is what I call the "recursive want" technique. This is derived from the NLP technique called Core Transformation developed by Connirae Andreas in Colorado, (see the book <u>Core Transformation</u> by Real People Press), and is extremely powerful. The adapted technique I use is as follows:

1. Have the explorer "go inside" and ask this part of her what it wants, and to be open to whatever answer shows up. Say something like, "Go inside and ask this part of you, 'What do you want?'" Being in touch with the feeling state, especially if you've intensified it, makes this easy. Record the explorer's answer verbatim.

2. Say, "Great. Thank you. Now, if this part of you were to have this *[state what the part said it wants]*, exactly the way it wants, fully and completely, what does this part of you want that's even more important, through having that?" If you need to repeat the question, adjust as follows: "If you were to get what you want, what would you get to have or be as a result, that's even more important?" Record the new answer.

3. Repeat step two with the new answer. Continue in this way until you arrive at a new, positive feeling state.

4. Map the new feeling state by asking the standard mapping questions. As you go, ask optimization/moving questions to invite the feeling to become even more fully positive. Finish with the standard belief questions.

What to do when a part wants to go away

Sometimes a feeling state seems to want to just "go away." This usually happens with a distressing feeling state in the body, and some other part just wants it to leave the body. This can take various forms including, "it wants to evaporate and go into the air," or "it melts and runs down into the ground."

In situations like this, support the explorer in making that transformation, and then invite her to follow the feeling substance, whatever that is. Use a statement like, "Great, now let's just follow that and see where it wants to go." Mention that every part of her ultimately has a positive intention and that parts exist for life – they don't disappear but only go outside of awareness. Explain that you want to follow this feeling state and give it an opportunity to return to the area in or around the body to contribute its positive intention for the explorer's highest good.

Once the explorer has connected with the feeling state in its banished location, wherever that is, acknowledge the part for wanting to relieve the distress, and say something like the following:

> **"Now that this feeling is away from your body, I want to invite this part of you to consider how it might come back into the space in or around your body in such a way as to offer its gift and contribute to your well-being. In exploring what is possible in a perfect world, where all your needs are met, exactly the way you want them, if this part of you were free to become warmer or cooler, what would it prefer…"**

Continue the standard moving sequence, paying special attention to the questions regarding location and movement. Most of the time, this takes care of things. If it doesn't, ask,

> **"What else do you notice about your experience? What else are you feeling?"**

Move on to another feeling state to map and move, and come back to this one at a later time. When you do return to it, have the explorer begin with the original map of the feeling state as it started out. Go from there.

Belief questions revisited

One of the most satisfying parts of the Feeling Path Mapping practice for a facilitator is the moment when you ask the explorer about her new beliefs and perceptions from the perspective of the new feeling state. Both you and the explorer quickly realize, "We're not in Kansas anymore, Toto."

Understanding belief

What is a belief, anyway? I wrote about this earlier, but let's revisit the idea. I'll go into much more depth in my further writing and trainings. For now, this abbreviated treatment will have to do.

A feeling state is an anchor which organizes the activity of consciousness. Multiple feeling anchors work together in every moment to organize your experience of being a self-in-the-world, including thought images and perceptual filters. Each feeling has unique thought imagery attached to it.

A belief is a link between imagery of one feeling state to the imagery of another related state. This link can be expressed in language. Belief links tend to fall into three categories: links of equivalence, (A=B), links of sequence, (First A, then B), and links of causation, (If A, then B).

When we move a feeling from its reactive state to its ideal state, the old imagery no longer fits. The new feeling state generates a new thought space within which new imagery arises. So a belief that began as a link to an image attached to the reactive state loses its attachment point. The belief dissolves.

In its place are possible new beliefs which can attach to the new imagery of the ideal state. Your job as facilitator is to explicitly invite these new connections. By asking about new beliefs, you are actually assisting the explorer in forming them in the moment, drawing on the possibilities arising with the new imagery.

Sometimes the newness is so profound the explorer has difficulty immediately generating new thought patterns. Many times I will support the explorer in turning attention directly to drawing. This provides time for the explorer to sit with the new feeling and allow it to begin making new connections in that quiet space without words.

Inviting new connections

When the explorer is ready, invite the new thoughts to arise with a few simple questions:

> **From the place of this new feeling, how would you express in words what seems true, or real, or important? What's true about yourself, your world, or someone else? What thoughts naturally arise from this state?**
>
> **What does this part of you most want you to know?**

The last line above may be the most important. It invites the part to choose for itself what is most important about the new state.

Don't fret if the explorer finds herself at a loss for words. She will have plenty of opportunity in the hours and days to come for this part to work its way into her natural thought process and belief system.

Three points of focus

As a facilitator, there are three important things to be aware of. First, it's more important than ever to use the explorer's language exactly when taking notes and reflecting back what they said. Certain words and phrases will have strong meaning and it's important to preserve that meaning.

Second, be open to transcendent, transpersonal, way out there kinds of statements as well as very simple, seemingly mundane observations. In these ideal states, we connect at times to aspects of life that are outside of our ordinary waking consciousness. At times, we tap into the realm of dreams and beyond dreams. At the same time, we tend to find ourselves stripped of pretense and connected to the simple truths of life.

I find these moments to be great gifts. There are times when an explorer is sharing the thoughts of the ideal state, when I feel as though I am sitting at the feet of some great teacher. Through many of these experiences with my students and friends, and through my own explorations, I am convinced that every one of us has access to the deepest mysteries of life. That's exciting to me, and humbling. You may find it so as well.

The third point to keep in mind is the nature of belief. As I mentioned above, a belief is a connection between imagery of one feeling and imagery of another. At this moment of the work, you are asking about beliefs that connect to one specific feeling state. But a belief will always connect to another part somewhere. And many times, especially in the early stages, the other parts it connects to may still be stuck in reactivity.

You'll know this when you hear things stated in the negative, for example. "I'm not in danger anymore," or "I don't have to put up with anyone's BS now." In these examples, it's clear there are still active feeling states holding images of danger and other people's "BS."

That's OK. In these examples, help the explorer zoom in a little closer on what's possible with the new state by asking them what they get to experience *instead* of danger, or other people stuff. Have them focus on the experience they generate for themselves, from the inside.

The farther you go in the mapping and moving process with any given issue, the more the different parts will spontaneously settle into beliefs of possibility and resourcefulness. When you've moved all the feeling states associated with a given issue, there are no parts left generating the negative imagery. So the beliefs that naturally form are overwhelmingly positive and sensitive to real conditions of the world.

Naming the new feeling

Once the feeling has been moved to its ideal state and the explorer has had some time to reflect on what's unique and new about the feeling, it's time to give the feeling a name. This can be quite fun, because the explorer is naturally in an open, creative space. The names that arise spontaneously tend to be poetic descriptions of either the feeling image or derivations of the new beliefs and perspectives.

One way you can assist the explorer in naming the new feeling is to share some of the specific words she used in describing the new feeling image or expressing the new belief statements. Sometimes these words can be used verbatim to name the feeling. Other times they will spark new insights and the name will emerge in the reflection and dialogue about the possibilities.

Sometimes if the explorer is struggling to come up with a name, and some of their language suggests a name to me, I'll make that suggestion, making sure to also invite them to reject it or respond with something more suitable. As with all the questions, it can be helpful for the explorer to have specific suggestions to reject as a way to move toward greater clarity.

Once the explorer has settled on a name, reflect it back to them, asking one last time if this is the name that works best for them. If so, capture the name prominently in your notes.

How to know when you're done

So how do you know when a particular part has actually achieved its ideal state? The fact is, it's not important. As long as you are moving feelings in the direction from more distressing to less, from less functional to more, from reactive in the general direction of ideal, you're doing great.

Because each feeling state is interconnected with eight others, there are many times when a first pass move yields moderate results and it's clear the state has not achieved its ideal. An example of this might be a state of fear moving to a state of protection. The protection state still presupposes a danger. As long as that danger is represented internally by a threatening feeling state, the original state of fear will be unable to fully transform. But after moving through the entire set and transforming the danger as well as others which might play a role in the experience of threat, the fear will be ready to move fully to a state which transcends danger. The protection will be free to become something like strength or freedom. And ironically, in the absence of the internal representation of danger, the inner experience of freedom will turn out to be objectively far more safe in the world than the original configuration ever was.

There are ways to encourage states to go more fully into their ideal right away, but those techniques will need to wait for a more advanced text.

But I realize I still have not answered the question of how to know when a feeling has reached its ideal. There are two key criteria:

1. The ideal state embodies the possibilities inherent in the "perfect world" scenario. There is no representation of separation, loss, threat, or limitation. Everything is possible, and the state is free to choose whatever qualities it prefers.

2. All the feeling paths in the nine-part set have achieved their ideal states. They have also achieved an ideal relationship with one another.

The ideal states and their relationships are outlined in the earlier section on Architecture, but that facilitating that integration is unfortunately outside the scope of this book. Nevertheless, simply revisiting the ideal states as you approach completion of the set, asking if there are any further adjustments, is sufficient to ensure great results.

So the best way to know if a part has achieved its ideal is to check back on it after moving other feelings which are connected to it. And reference the Architecture section to see what the universal forms of the ideal states look like. There are certain clear criteria that are easy to recognize.

Working with multiple feeling states

As I've mentioned elsewhere, no feeling stands alone. When you are mapping one feeling state you will often encounter different states to map as well. And when you move one or more feelings to their ideal states, sometimes other feelings will practically clamor for attention.

There are two reasons for this. First, the reactive configuration is often long-standing, (sometimes decades), and rigidly fixed in place. It is usually constructed in such a way as to prevent awareness of a central, intolerable state of suffering. When you start peeling off these defenses, other defenses are likely to start working harder, and the pivot feeling may begin to make an appearance.

The second reason is the obverse of intensified defenses. When various parts which have been locked in positions of compensation and avoidance discover that is no longer necessary, they seem to be eager to break into awareness and participate in the process. They want to be mapped and moved!

The best response to both of these is to welcome the new feelings to the party and assure them, either directly or indirectly, that these breakthroughs are possible for every part. When the facilitator maintains a tone of eager curiosity and a trust that every feeling has an ultimately positive, resourceful purpose, there arises an atmosphere of trust that can reassure and motivate the explorer.

It's like you're saying, "Feeling what you're feeling is OK. It's better than OK. Every uncomfortable feeling is an opportunity to go further into the authentic truth of who you are. Let's go!"

The most important attitude

Imagine the explorer finding herself confronted by an inner terror or rage that hasn't seen the light of day for decades. And imagine the facilitator, with an eager lightness, saying, "Yes!" and welcoming that new feeling into the process. That's a very different experience than the explorer has likely ever encountered in the face of that feeling, and that welcoming attitude changes everything.

This is an amazing gift to offer someone, and many of my clients have shared that this was one of the most powerful aspects of our work together. As a facilitator, this attitude will develop naturally as you accumulate experiences of working with a wide variety of feeling states and discover that without question, even the most distressing negative state has within it some far greater, positive power to share. Your eager curiosity will be natural and compelling.

And don't stop with welcoming the obvious black shadow states. Whenever an explorer is working with a particular issue, and is in the work, mapping and moving, experiencing the states, then whatever comes up is part of the pattern. Whatever comes up.

This includes things that in other contexts would be labeled as "transference," "resistance," and other terms. These labels say more about the limitations of the methodology and skill of a practitioner than about the client or explorer. In truth, no matter what comes up, it will be directly relevant to whatever issue the explorer is working with. Some of the states or experiences that fall into this category might include:

- Resistance / Reluctance

- Frustration

- Self-Doubt

- Evasiveness

- Defiance

- Annoyance

- Attraction

- Not Ready

- Rebellion

- Lack of Trust

This also includes impulses, mental processes, and behaviors that would normally fall outside the domain we refer to as emotion or feeling. These might include:

- Confusion

- Numbness

- Fogging Out

- Fatigue / Sleepiness

- Judgment

- Analyzing

- Obsessive Thoughts

- Racing Thoughts

The key message here is: **Welcome everything.** No matter what shows up in a session, treat it like a welcome guest. Make space for it in your notes, and invite it to participate in the process. Trust the explorer to discern with the help of the mapping questions whether a newly identified state is relevant or not.

Following the trail

Every part is connected to every other part in a set. We can sleuth out all the parts using a combination of four types of clues.

Story clues

The best place to start Feeling Path Mapping work is to ask the explorer to share a specific experience or two of the issue with which they want assistance. These stories can be expanded upon over the course of working on the issue, and fresh stories can be added to the mix as the explorer works the issue over a period of time.

Your job as facilitator is to listen for the cues in the story which point to specific feeling states or other patterns. Inquire into these stories to tease apart this feeling from that one, this motivation from that impulse, this reaction from that judgment.

As you inquire, involve the explorer in discerning among that various candidates for specific feeling states to map. Compare A to B to find out if they might be the same feeling. Dig more deeply into C to discover if it might be harboring more than one state.

As you do this work, you will accumulate experiences tracking the connections between the stories people tell and the feeling states that drive the lived experience of those stories. This will make you a better listener in general, and a better Feeling Path Mapping facilitator in particular.

Behavioral clues

When an explorer is delving into their inner experience of a particular issue, the entire issue is alive within them. All nine parts. That means that every part is playing a role, however subtly, in every communication and expression.

One rich source of clues about as-yet-unidentified feeling states are the behaviors of the explorer in and around the Feeling Path Mapping sessions. Everything from punctuality and accountability to patterns of speech and language can provide evidence pointing to the feeling states driving the issue.

Another source of clues is body language. When an explorer is telling a story or mapping a feeling, notice gestures for clues to the inner feeling structures. Every movement is a reflection of the inner states.

Learn to discern these clues by asking about them. If you notice an explorer clasping her hands at her solar plexus, for example, when she is sharing a story about an interaction with her partner, ask an open-ended question about what she might be feeling in that area of her body.

Structural clues

An excellent source of clues about hidden feeling states lies in the mapping process itself. The basis for feeling is our embodied experience in the material world. We absorb the qualities and dynamics of substances in the world at a deeply intuitive level. By the time we are merely toddlers, we have mastered a sophisticated "map" of materiality and its properties. This map becomes the basis for feeling, and its characteristics show up clearly in our felt experience of feeling. Although we are not limited by the laws of physics in our creative generation of feeling states and their interaction, the laws of physics are in fact our starting point.

Because of this, your intuitions about physical reality are useful in the investigation of feeling states. Some examples:

- If you map a feeling substance which is pushing strongly downward, ask about what might be resisting its push with a force in the opposite direction.

- If a feeling state is compressing inward, ask the explorer to attend to the center of the feeling space. Is it the same substance throughout, or is another feeling at the core pushing outward?

- If you map a feeling that's flowing, inquire about from where, and to where, it is flowing.

Use your natural intuitions about structures and substances. But make sure to avoid being limited by those intuitions. The somatosensory capacity is highly creative, and we are able to construct feeling states which lie far outside standard materials of the physical world. When appropriate, remind the explorer of this as well. I often say something along the lines of, "There's no need to conform to the laws of physics..." And in fact, modern sci-fi movies often form the raw material of feeling states which I imagine people a hundred years ago had no basis for which to generate!

A great place to get a quick understanding of the kinds of structural interactions that can point to new feeling states is the Architecture section of this book. I've included a full set of reactive and ideal states from some work with myself in 2009. Look at the reactive states to see several clear pairs of interacting states and the further interconnections among states in the entire set.

Belief statement clues

Finally, one of the richest sources of clues about other important feeling states are the belief statements, both at the mapping and moving stages. Because a belief is a link from one path to another, and therefore between one feeling state and another, the words of a belief statement often point clearly to other feeling states outside of the state you're actively mapping. Here are two examples:

- Feeling = Confusion. Statement: "I'm not going to get it ... if I can't figure it out, I kind of suck." This statement clearly points to another state of self-judgment.

- Feeling = Neediness. Statement: "Feels like I want something like Amma, but it's being taken away. Clinginess ... disappointment and resentment." This clearly points to two related states with the last two words.

You can see more examples in the Architecture section as well. Of course, the best way to learn these skills is by practicing. Your best teacher is your own interior experience and that of the people you work with. The one thing I want to emphasize here is that many times our standard expectations run into surprises in this work. Be open to learning from the direct experience of what feeling is actually experienced on the inside by real people, as revealed by Feeling Path Mapping.

Part 4:
Perspectives
Deep and Broad

My Own Path

Finally, I'm sure some readers will want me to add a bit of a bio. As you might expect, this work developed in tandem with my own personal journey, and so who I am is inextricably entwined with the shape of the work as I share it here. I've already given you some very personal bits and pieces throughout the text, and I prefer to save a more in-depth tale for another time. But let me see if I can add a few ingredients to help you make sense of the guy who discovered the feeling mind. To do so, I'm going to step back and answer the following question(s):

> **How did I come to be the one to discover this? Why me and not someone else? What were the key ingredients in my life which prepared me to do this work?**

I suspect that to bring a truly fresh perspective to a well-established field requires one to be a bit of a freak. I am thankful to say that from certain points of view I meet that criterion.

My disposition and upbringing

My dad and I had a troubled relationship. I was the firstborn, the only son (eventually with four sisters), and arguably the only reason for my parents' marriage in the first place. My dad was a tough guy boxer, a big city cop, a bully without a visible, empathetic bone in his body. I was super sensitive, a "crybaby" from the start, and weirdly (to him) intelligent. There was no way I was going to be the son he might have wanted; there was no way he was going to be the father I might have wanted. At times I have thought it was a wonder we didn't kill each other.

While at home it seemed I could do nothing right (in his eyes), at school I could seemingly do no wrong. I was smart beyond what anyone had reason to expect in the working class neighborhoods and small towns where I grew up. My mother taught me to read long before I went to school, (for which I am immensely grateful). I brought an intense, laser focus to my academic work coupled with a nonchalance that made it look easy. Smart-kid was my alternate identity, compensating for my screw-up, lazy, incompetent identity at home. I had the raw material, and I made the most of it where I could.

Emotionally, I was nothing if not intense. Most often saturated in melancholy, I felt deeply separated in my life, excruciatingly alone starting at a very young age. I cried at the slightest provocation, of which there were many initiated by my father at home and the occasional few at the hands of bully-type kids at school. I was physically small and weak.

My parents were anti-social, so home life was painfully isolated. Even in early years living in the city, my family kept to themselves, and that became even easier to maintain once we moved into the country and my parents bought property with which to surround ourselves.

On the plus side, despite our troubles, in looking back I can say I am grateful for my father's persistent efforts to ground me in practical reality, to keep my head from going too far into the clouds. Although I hated being forced to work on our farm, or to help him repair cars or farm equipment, I believe the constant requirement to function in his world became an essential ingredient in both my attitude and aptitude as applied to developing this work.

I eventually became rather competent at practical things, rather comfortable in the material and natural worlds, reasonably strong in my body. Without this, I may have chosen to spend most of my time in books, in fantasy. With this, I believe I developed a strong somatosensory capacity and decent mechanical skills.

I was good at tossing and stacking hay bales, for example. I could climb a rope attached to the top of our barn without using my feet. I could swing a wicked axe and built a few hundred feet of split rail fence entirely by hand from the tall oak trees on the far acres of our property. I could run easy through fields over rough terrain, and used to love flying down the far hill into the herd of deer that fed at the bottom at dusk. I spent some evenings lying face up on the bald-top hill watching the stars come out, feeling myself reach out into infinite space. In high school I strengthened my body knowledge by participating in wrestling for four years. Although I was never driven competitively, I grew comfortable in the sport, and even more comfortable in my body. This grounding in a strong felt sense of the materiality of my body, tools, hay bales and opponent wrestlers laid the groundwork for a finely tuned somatosensory awareness, one I was able to turn inward to combine with my heightened emotional sensitivity to notice and catalogue what others may not have been able to discern.

In high school, I was fortunate to be surrounded by an unusual class (for our school) of very smart kids. I had some competition for the title of smartest, thank goodness, so I did have to work for my honors. And a few of my teachers made an effort to challenge me, for which I am grateful. I felt recognized and appreciated for my intelligence, general ability, and reasonably good attitude, which helped balance out the struggles I had at home.

So what of this was most important? I would say of my upbringing, the encouragement and support I received for developing my analytical intelligence and my imagination helped make sure my natural gifts were well enough nurtured. I got some of that support from school as I said, but another important source was from my mother. She always seemed interested in and proud of my intellectual exploits and made sure to provide me with enough books and puzzles to keep me occupied. I'd have to say my father was in favor of this as well, as he thought my intelligence could be leveraged eventually into a good job.

My father's insistence on practical responsibilities and activities kept me connected to the real, physical world while simultaneously his bullying style helped build up the resentment and rage which would eventually fester and force me to look deeply into myself. Finally, the dual life between school and home seemed to be the template upon which my bipolar disorder was built. The raw materials were inside me, specifically the intelligence combined with high emotionality and the capacity to deliberately amplify feeling states, both positive and negative. But the back and forth between two radically different environments supported the intensification of the two poles. At school I learned to amplify the rush of power that came with running ever-higher voltage through my system. Taking tests was a thrill because I was able to accelerate my thinking and perception to the point where I would complete the exam in a fraction of the time allotted, and know without any hesitation that I had aced it. At home, my growing resentment fueled a kind of sick amplification of the dysphoria. It wasn't enough that my life was constrained in ways I hated. It was as if I wanted to despise the fact and immerse myself in the agony as a way of justifying my hatred.

I am quite sure this attitude contributed to the difficulties my father and I had. Looking back on that time, I can see he was aware of my inner rebellion, but at a loss about what to do about it. As with all things, his fallback option was to increase the attempt to control. So the more I fed my resentment, the more he turned up the bullying, which justified and intensified my resentment still further. On and on, unfortunately, and the greater my inner miasma of hate and shame and hurt became, the more I relied upon the grandiose flights of intellectual power to balance out the scales. As I said, I had the raw material, but my adolescence was a training ground for developing a penultimate case of bipolar disorder.

The combination of high intelligence and high emotionality came together with the somatosensory sensitivity in a unique way which also seems important. I believe that for me, (and I suspect for many of us), my logical and analytic intelligence is rooted in a felt sense of the logic of materiality. I remember learning chemistry, for example, not by memorizing formulas but by imagining myself actually being the molecules and feeling what fit and what didn't. It was as if I thought with my body, and my practical experience in the physical world of the farm informed my abstract intellectual thought. I could feel my way through problems, feel the structure of the knowledge I assimilated, feel the connections between disparate bits of information and discern the patterns. In learning new things, I did not assimilate abstract factoids, but my mind was such that I could relate everything to everything else. Even today it seems to function as a network, assembling and reassembling knowledge into ever more elegant structures.

I believe this combination of a type of somatosensory intelligence which functions as a pattern-making, connection machine, combined with the intensity of my emotional life, was exactly the setup required to pioneer this work. It may be my greatest gift, and it feels well used here.

Edinburgh

The first important milestone on the way to The Feeling Path was my junior year in Edinburgh, Scotland, in 1979-80. I had earned significant scholarship assistance to The University of Pennsylvania School of Engineering, and quickly established a track record of success while taking on maximum course hours. I finished my pre-med requirements in two years while also goofing off and tutoring my friends, and had established a good connection with a neuroscience lab on campus, through which I anticipated gaining entrance to the Penn med school as a dual degree (MD/PhD) candidate.

With that all handled, I decided to take a year away, and won a full scholarship to Edinburgh University. The summer before I left, I lived with my grandparents and learned some of my parents' history which they had never disclosed. Plus, I read all of Dostoyevsky that summer, and found myself swept up in his complex moral universe. Dostoyevsky and my grandparents raised some important questions for me about my past, my future and the world in which I lived, and I left for Edinburgh with a mind hungry for answers.

When I arrived, my clear path to neuroscience research began to unravel. I was not permitted by the crabby department head to enter the third year psychology program, for no good reason I could discern. I had no interest in the other courses available to me as a visiting student. So I decided to ditch the courses and do my own thing. I read a ton, much about consciousness, philosophy and the brain. Teilhard de Chardin, Ouspensky, early Ken Wilber, Bertrand Russell, and many more. I explored photography as well, and experimented with my own states of consciousness. For a time I slept only every other night to cultivate the dream-like journeys I could take on the nights without sleep. I took a series photographs of the deserted city in those early morning hours.

It was in Edinburgh that I had my first manic periods. On many late night walks to the top of Arthur's Seat and elsewhere in the city, I experienced intense, noetic highs that rendered ordinary life tawdry and flat. Some friends spoke of trips with drugs, and although I was invited on occasion I declined, finding it impossible to imagine anything more sublime than what I already had access to.

Over the months in Edinburgh, I found myself growing more and more out of sync with the ordinary world. I tasted regularly of something more beautiful and powerful, and in comparison an ordinary life became intolerable. I became more and more isolated, eventually becoming estranged from nearly all my friends.

This was especially true when I returned to Penn. I could no longer stomach the drive to standard measures of success. Pursuing career, status, and wealth seemed shallow, false and wrong, and I abandoned my plans. I took classes purely out of interest, and postponed my engineering studies, never completing the requirements for my degree. Creative writing, psychophysiology, and other topics interested me for short periods, then not at all. Looking back, it was clear that my first year back at Penn was my first major depression, a long and difficult one. The bipolar cycle had begun.

Throughout this time and continuing for years, I held within myself the shocks of deep insight I had attained during my peripatetic nights in Edinburgh. My problem was, I found it impossible to articulate my knowing, impossible to share with others what I had seen and come to feel as possible and real. The phrase I held on to from my scribbled notes one night after a long walk was "coagulation of consciousness." That phrase and the idea behind it held for me a kind of siren call that kept me moving forward. It referred to a profound, felt-sense insight that the evolution of the universe is driven by a force responsible for consciousness, toward ever greater awareness, connection and wholeness. It expanded Teilhard de Chardin's noosphere to a universal scale. My inner mission was to understand what I had seen and felt, and to find a way to squeeze the sublime insights into the mundane materiality of everyday life so I could share it with others. This quest drove me for a long time, keeping me moving forward through some very dark periods.

I didn't realize until much later, but something even bigger was driving me through this period. Again, it has to do with my father. (It's amazing the influence one person can have on a person.) Throughout my time with him and after, no matter what I did, no matter how excellent or superlative whether on the farm or in school, I never once received any word of acknowledgment or praise. Completely outside my awareness, I craved that acknowledgment as I craved nothing else.

My unconscious response to that craving was to continually ratchet up my ambition, notch by notch. When I first arrived at Penn I had set my sights on being a bioengineer and having some ordinary success, raising a family, etc. As soon as I started knocking down the A's in my classes, I realized there was no question I could achieve this ambition.

Well, here's the insidious bit. Deep within me I held the unquestioned assumption that if I could actually accomplish something, then it wasn't good enough to earn the approval I craved. So as soon as I ascertained that a goal was within reach, I was forced (from within) to escalate the goal. The progression went like this: bioengineer, doctor, neurosurgeon, pioneer researcher of the brain. Somewhere along the line it went to pioneer discoverer of the essential missing secrets of life. And eventually, through that, it became very simply savior of the world. I'm not kidding. This is the grandiosity of my particular bipolar disorder. At times I felt convinced I was Christ, coming back to fix what he had screwed up the first time. But in my heart, I knew without question that if I succeeded in saving the world, even that wouldn't be good enough. I'd still never hear from my father the words, "Good job, Joe."

As I said, I was completely unaware of this inner dynamic until many years later, unpacking it all through the tools of The Feeling Path.

My diagnosis

The next significant milestone on my journey happened in 1987. In the previous half dozen years I had been married and divorced, started and quit a couple dozen jobs, moved into and out of about a 20 different apartments, spent myself to the brink of bankruptcy, and generally made a mess of my life. I came across a book about something called manic depression and found myself depicted quite convincingly in its pages. There was no question I was bouncing back and forth between super highs and super lows. By that time, the lows had evolved, the rancid hate at the core having been generalized to focus on the screwed up state of the world, and on conventional authority in any form. The highs continued to take on elements of saving the world, tending to be triggered by what I thought were brilliant ideas for business ventures or books that would show the world its folly and bring it to its knees in repentance.

A friend with schizophrenia, (I used to be magnetically drawn to women with deep pain), referred me to her psychiatrist. He seemed like a smart enough guy, said he rarely prescribed medications but that I so strongly met the criteria for diagnosis that he recommended I start lithium right away. I did so. For the next ten days I stared the bottle down, debating the merits of medication versus going it alone before taking my pill morning and night as directed. On the tenth day I tossed the lithium and never looked back.

Instead, my life took on a new focus. I had studied enough to know that science really had no clue what caused bipolar disorder, and that medication was a stopgap in the absence of any true treatment. I also knew that I had a couple of advantages. I had my intelligence, a very strong capacity for introspection, some NLP skills for working with mental imagery, freedom from responsibilities to anyone else, and a felt sense that there was some sort of inner progression of thought or mood which drove the cycle.

In addition, I had my hyper-exaggerated grandiosity. Despite the fact that many smart people had been trying to solve the problem of bipolar disorder in particular and mental illness in general, I believed I could do better. Knowing the stakes were high, and there was a good chance my life would go even further down the tubes, I made a commitment to doing everything I could to try to understand this thing and beat it.

Goddamn. What a decision. Looking back on it today I am grateful I made that decision, but honestly, what were the chances? Practically nil. I'm lucky I'm not dead, and there were times I came close.

One influence that just may have saved my life at this time was dance. I discovered Group Motion in Philadelphia. Every Friday night, religiously, I would go surrender to the improvised music and gentle facilitation of conscious dance among others who were so inclined. I was thirsty and drank deeply of these life-giving waters for the three years I remained in Philly.

Over the next seven years I threw myself into my efforts in some moments, muddled along at others. I settled into making my living as a freelance copywriter, which gave me control over my time and enabled me to make enough money to get by with very little investment of energy. So I had the freedom to explore, to dig in, to dive deeply and often. I also had the freedom to continue spinning in circles, and the ups and downs and craziness continued unabated. I won't bore you with details here, but let's just say it was ugly at times.

My journey of discovery

The breakthrough happened in Montana, the moment I've already mentioned where I discovered how to directly shift a feeling state from feeling bad to feeling good. Everything else came forth from that. Within six months I had packed up and moved to Seattle, planning to apply this new technique to making theater performances. My concept centered on sculpting emotional landscapes on stage. (I still believe this is a viable and potentially powerful approach to theater, but one I'm not likely to develop myself.)

Six months later, after moving to Seattle and diving back into the deep waters of dance, I stumbled onto the discovery that feeling states ran on unique tracks, reactive to ideal. I called them parts, and recognized there was something I wanted to know more about. Shortly after this discovery, I applied it to myself, using it to dissolve the hold bipolar disorder had over me. I shared a bit of that day earlier in Part 1.

The dramatic transformation of that day made me realize I was on to something much bigger than I had imagined. I abandoned the theater idea and decided to go back to school with the intention of investigating this new discovery as the basis for a method of therapy and an understanding of the mind.

Fortunately at that time I lived across the street from the perfect university for my purposes. Antioch University Seattle boasted a unique, independent masters degree in Whole Systems Design, as well as a flexible bachelors completion program. Over a period of seven years I finished both, stretching out my credits and maximizing the support

I received from student loans to give myself the space to fully explore the work.

I do not believe I could have accomplished this body of work within traditional academia, or by undertaking a standard psychotherapy training program. It was essential for me to remain completely outside the conventional system, to reestablish first principles by examining the raw data of felt experience from a fresh perspective, to make sense of that data, and to test my sense-making efforts again and again.

At the point of starting at Antioch, it became merely a matter of following through. This insight led to that, one thing after another, continuing to explore and experiment. I am fortunate above all that in this time I had the privilege of working with some brave and awesome people who either paid me to work with them or agreed to participate in my explorations. I went deep with some of them in ways that led to new discoveries I could never have made with only myself as a subject. In fact, I have to say that all of my biggest discoveries have come as a result of those people who trusted me to work with them.

Solving the puzzle

I love a good puzzle, have ever since I was a kid. Well, this was one hell of a puzzle, figuring out the structure of the feeling mind. I have enjoyed the challenge of it, loved every step of the way.

Many people have marveled at my dogged tenacity, wondering what has kept me working this, always a new angle, always digging deeper. I've wondered myself what drives me to be so relentless, and I think it is the puzzle of it all. I am most in my element when I am designing a new model and testing it against real evidence. And I am most uncomfortable when evidence reveals a shortcoming of my model. There's nothing more important when I've got data that falls outside of my understanding, than to revise that understanding to encompass the new information. And there's nothing more satisfying than when I succeed in crafting a new model that not only answers the open questions but throws the net wider to include aspects I hadn't previously considered.

This quest to understand is the central driver for me, and it would be in place no matter what field I might have found myself in. The other elements simply set the stage and provided the focus. And I have to say, even though it has been an arduous road, I'm grateful to have taken on a puzzle with such scope and depth and meaning as this!

Revisiting the Big Picture

A simple setting: dinnertime, summer, a row home in Northeast Philadelphia. I was five, my sister three. As was typical, the tension and angst in the house were thick enough to need a chainsaw if you were to have any hope of cutting through it. My sister picked at her food. Maybe it was the vegetables she didn't like, or maybe it was the atmosphere that made the lump in her throat too big to get the food down, I don't know for sure. But this small tinder was enough to set the angst ablaze.

After threats, after intimidation, after shouting failed to get the job done, my father snapped, wrenched her off her chair, and spanked the living hell out of her. Her screams pierced like the cry of a tortured cat, and I was sure the entire neighborhood could hear. My mother sat there paralyzed, her own angst spewing hot black billows of wretched emotion. After the beating, my sister still did not eat, but only cried. This little drama played itself out with minor variations that summer, on nights my father was home.

I cried too of course, helpless to do anything to help her, confused and angry at the failure of my mother to lift her voice to stop the insanity. I don't remember feeling angry at my father at this point in the story;

perhaps I had already learned to suppress that. His violence and the constant threat of violence were a given, simply one of the conditions of life. And any expression of anger about it was a sure way to bring instant retribution and a multiplying of any punishment or humiliation that was being delivered. By the age of five I had learned to shut down a wide range of impulses.

A step back

That's the scene as I remember experiencing it. Now let's take another look from a different perspective. What about my father's experience? And my mother's? As I mentioned earlier, nobody comes to be this way by himself. This kind of unconscious propagation of suffering can only be achieved by someone who has suffered greatly himself, who has himself accumulated many layers of shut-down.

I don't know much about my father's youth. My grandfather was an alcoholic, for what that's worth. When he was a teen, my father dropped out of high school and I'm told he was a bully. But he pulled things together, got his GED, and got a job with the Philadephia police force.

I can imagine that as a twenty-something with all the wounds and defenses a young man in that time and place would have accumulated, life on the beat was both a thrill and a confrontation with things too big to hold. As a cop, you are forced to learn quickly to suppress feeling, to make very quick judgments about people and act on them. If you don't, you and others are likely to get badly hurt. And it is far safer to err on the side of judging others dangerous or guilty. Erring on the side of compassion can get you killed.

Yet you are faced every day with human pain. You see spouses tearing one another to pieces, children beaten bloody, con artists fleecing innocents, race riots (this was the 60s) with people dropping cinder blocks on the cops below, and the wreck and detritus of lives decimated by drugs, prostitution, and predation of every kind. Every day you are confronted with the worst that humans can do to one another.

Now amplify that by a factor of ten: my father was a good cop, smart, thought well of by his superiors I imagine, and promoted to detective, homicide. I can't personally imagine the layers of numbness required to carry out that job. Add to that the infamous culture of racism and brutality that was rampant in Joe Rizzo's force in the 1960's, and you have the recipe for a dying spirit.

Police work has destroyed countless families. And for every family that is destroyed to outward appearances, another suffers invisible wounds that devour the members of that family from within. Although my family remained intact on the outside, on the inside all was not well.

Now imagine you are my father in the scenario I have painted. At this time, the idea that officers need any kind of support to deal with the violence of their lives was not recognized. He was on his own to figure out how to hold his head above the maelstrom of human pain.

So you hold it together on the job, and then you come home. Your life is no longer on the line, you are safe, you can relax. But when you do, that lowering of your inner defenses opens the way for the suppressed fear, grief, and confusion to come bubbling to the surface. How do you deal with this when you are not close to your family, when your wife has her own fears and pain, (and even if she were available for support you have no experience or model of what that could possibly look like), and when the only thing you have ever learned is a brutal version of command and control? It is what you fall back on when things get squirrely.

So when my sister whined and picked at her food, and when my mother withdrew into herself, and when his own churning feelings were too close for comfort, the natural thing was to seize control, to dominate, to take charge through force. It was what he knew, and to him it was the right thing to do. To him, things were black and white – gray would get you killed. To him, eating what was on your plate was a given, there was no choice, it was what you did at dinner. It made no difference that in order to force this to happen he inflicted terror on his entire family. That terror was invisible to him. The parts of himself responsible for delivering an awareness of such things had been shut down long past, locked into the states of snap judgment, defense, and violence that kept him alive on the job.

The situation was even more dire than that. In the actual moment of beating his baby daughter, my father was further deepening his own hidden suffering. Nobody, and I mean nobody, perpetrates harm on another without some part of themselves being very aware of that harm and feeling the pain of it as if it were their own. And in order to enforce the right thing, he found himself behaving in ways that were not far off from those he regularly arrested people for doing. The direct dissonance of his behavior with his beliefs about right and wrong could only have driven his suppression deeper, rendering him more unconscious every time he acted out in this way.

I have not spoken with my father about this directly. And even if I did approach him it is not likely he would choose to surface an awareness of what might have been going on for him inside. Nevertheless I feel can speak about this with a certain level of assurance. He is no different from me, from you, from the many people who have sat in the comfortable chair in my office or worked with me by phone. We are all the same, he and you and I.

The perpetrator inside me

Let me show you what I mean about him being no different from me. A couple years back I became aware of a highly reactive place in myself, a place which harshly judged other men, in particular those who behaved in unconscious, exploitive, or controlling ways. I knew these reactive states were creating problems for me, and decided to dig in. My first notes were about three incidents which connected the dots for me, letting me know indisputably there was a pattern at play which needed to be addressed. These notes are from January 1, 2008.

Precipitants:

1. An incident at dance, with a guy who went off on me for getting in his "nest," and my discomfort and inability to address his inappropriate violence.

2. An incident at group, where someone dissed me in an offhand way, and I confronted him about it, and felt very intense emotions wracking my whole body, similar physical effect as the incident at dance.

3. Sending out an e-mail to my list with a mistake in the first line - "[name]" - and my self-flagellation about that.

These incidents seem related, having to do with judgments about authority and anything looking like unbalanced male judgment, even to the extent of coming down on myself for doing something that could be construed as insensitive or non-genuine.

That night I had a dream about being a prisoner, lying bound on the floor of a bare cell, a tall, jackbooted, masked guard standing over me. In the dream I knew the guard was going to beat me and I was helpless to do anything about it.

As I mentioned before in my story about the day I liberated myself from the mood swings, dreams can be a wonderful source for feeling states that have remained outside of waking consciousness. As I identified the next day with the guard, I tapped into the rage and recognized it as my own. Not only was it mine, but it was familiar, going way back to my teen years.

We were harvesting oats, my father and I, putting them into the granary. The dusty oats traveled from the metal grain wagon through a cylindrical auger into the tightly enclosed, unventilated room where the grain was kept. It was my job to push the oats to the corners of granary bin, to make sure it filled properly without impeding the flow from the auger or spilling out onto the floor.

I had pretty severe allergies at the time to dust and pollen. Although I had a handkerchief tied over my face, the dust got through. I started wheezing, my eyes itching and swelling, and I began to panic in the room. I went downstairs where my father was doing something else and with my edge of resentment a little closer to the surface than usual as a result of the fear, told him sharply I couldn't do this. I was trying to stand up for myself. The result was a punch to the chest that knocked me to the ground and a command to get back up there and do what I was told.

This was one moment in an endless series, (although not often so physical). But with the heightened urgency, my panic and need to draw some kind of line of what was OK, in the moment of that punch, something in me collapsed. I gave up. In the months and years following, the resentment had no place to go and grew into a fiercely smoldering rage. There were times I imagined killing him, but knew I could not because I was not willing to accept the consequences. I held out hope for escape one day when I left for college.

This was the rage I uncovered that day, revealed in the dream as the prison guard. I called it "Vicious Enforcer." Let me share unedited what I wrote about this state:

Vicious Enforcer

"'Just get the fuck out of my way!' Snarling, growling, prowling, predatory/cat, active muscles. Images of instantly disemboweling someone with a slash of a paw (not a knife). Vicious. This is scary and it NEVER gets out. This is the part that would out-vicious my father if it had the chance to go back in time – he would be pathetic in comparison to this. 'You are WRONG!!'

"Whole body, muscles poised to act, acting is lightning-fast, ripping motion; image: long claws, long teeth. I would just as soon tear out your throat as look at you.

"A heightened energy around the eyes and face, scanning, piercing, looking for the smallest slight or challenge to my dominance. There's no satisfaction in killing or threatening, just the sense of preserving the status quo, keeping things from getting out of line. 'I am the enforcer. I know what's right. You will toe the line or know what hit you.'

"My whole body responds to this physically, hormonally, neurologically. It wants to fight. There's a slight trembling in readiness to strike. Directed at males only.

"Much larger than my body, rising 20-30 feet above me, an intensely powerful firestorm; fire that has incredibly dense substance, incredible power. It moves with lightning speed, swirls, consumes, and in its movement is the force of a train. Inferno is rising upward, a spiral getting larger as it goes up. Extremely hot. Reds, oranges, yellow, the colors of out-of-control flames. Very very dense, opaque, highly luminous, blindingly bright. The sound of an inferno combined with a deep, deep cat growl, which can peak into a raging roar. The sound is a driver of and rides on the power of the movement. Deafening. Looms, threatening, can strike downward at any time.

"This is hell personified. It has no conscience. It is all about asserting dominance, preserving the order. Doesn't matter why, and doesn't matter right/wrong, etc. Yet it seems to be serving something 'right.' It is its own justification. I used to feel this sometimes in my teens, hating my father, wanting to vanquish him and everything like him. 'I am the enforcer. Cross me and my fury will know no bounds.'"

Here's what I drew:

So this is me, remember. Not my father. I have no way of knowing whether my father had anything quite this intense inside of him. His anger had regular opportunity for expression, while mine had been completely suppressed for many years. (Mostly. There were moments when it had leaked out, moments which truly frightened me. I felt certain in those times that given the right conditions I was capable of horrible things.)

So let's imagine I had a child and found myself in a job which made me very uncomfortable, a job where in particular I had to deal with incompetent authority above me. And let's imagine my kid was willful and resistant to my own authority as his dad. Is it so difficult to imagine I might have become as bad as my father? In fact it is easy for me to imagine much worse – again, given the right conditions.

Fortunately I had a number of compensating states that held this in check. In fact, the sole purpose of all of the other eight states in this set seems to have been to keep Vicious Enforcer well hidden.

Confused Paralysis

"Like that insulation foam that comes in a can, but more beige colored, and pressurized, before it becomes hard. Soft but pressurized, pushing outward in all directions. This is what contains Vicious Enforcer, with the aid of Fear. Fear doesn't have to do it all by itself.

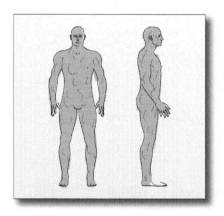

"I can't move. The pressure is enormous. The foam is stifling. I am a prisoner in my own body. The fire is completely put out. It's fire-proof foam. Temp is neutral, more or less body temp. No movement except for some slight continuing expansion of the foam, ever-increasing pressure. Headache, bodyache, dullness. No sound. Muffled sound. Can't hear myself think.

"This does not enter the head except when highly activated, during close confrontations with authority, when my own authority is called for, or when I've screwed up.

"I need to figure out what to do, but I can't. Don't know what's what. I'm stuck. Immobile. Inactive. Passive. I don't like this. Must avoid situations which make me feel it."

So this was the first line of defense against Vicious Enforcer. As long as Confused Paralysis came up in situations where authority was present, I was safe. As you might expect, I avoided all possible situations like this. Employment, for example, was almost exclusively free lance. Having a boss was just not safe, unless that boss was a woman, in which case I could tolerate it.

But Confused Paralysis wasn't enough. In case Vicious Enforcer got too strong, there was a layer of Fear on top.

Fear

"Anxious about facing these parts of myself, especially the Vicious Enforcer. The sense of this is, I can't make a mistake. For example, with the guy I recently had a confrontation with, I was careful not to say any judgments for fear they might be wrong or interpreted as insensitive. If I'm wrong, I'm automatically an asshole, both authoritarian and stupid. Constantly monitoring myself to make sure everything I say is a) justified, and b) reasonable, and even c) wise. Can't have an unconsidered opinion.

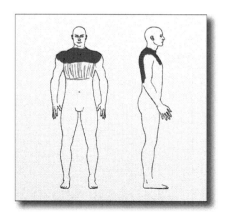

"What I'm really afraid of is the Vicious Enforcer. Afraid if I make a mistake and somebody challenges me, that part will leap forth with all its irrational viciousness.

"A tension in my back and shoulders, holding shoulders and arms back and immobilized. It's about immobility. It's about containment. Can't allow any part of judgment or authority out, or it could come out in force and the consequences could be bad. [Memories: situations as a kid of losing my temper, stomping on a crippled kid's foot, the shame of that.] This is a fear of doing something shameful, that goes against who I feel myself to be, that is hurtful to someone else.

"Material is like brazil nut casing, very hard but not heavy; rigid. Upper back, shoulders, around to upper chest, upper arms. Like a kind of armor. About an inch or so thick, maybe less, at skin and just under it. Feels like my arms are kept immobile.

"Color of a brazil nut or a beetle, maybe slightly shiny, smooth, woody tough. Neutral temperature, not noticeable. No movement - resists movement. This stuff is fireproof and is able to contain the Vicious Enforcer, which can't gain its power if it is unable to move. Sound = slight whispering, more like a quiet voice advising caution or good behavior to a child.

"I have to keep Vicious Enforcer contained. Can't go there. It's very important to keep it contained, because it could hurt someone, or myself. My whole purpose is to reinforce Confused Paralysis, to keep things contained. This is serious business."

So that's two lines of defense to make sure Vicious Enforcer never saw the light of day. Do you see how this works? This one was so powerful, though, it required even more of my energy to fully contain it. Here are two more parts that worked together to reinforce the first two.

Reasonableness

"Any sign of dominance with a lack of consciousness about the oppression of others triggers this, which drives my own Reasonableness and Disengagement. I will NOT participate in that shit. I will demonstrate a reasonable alternative, I will be a model for that better way of being.

"Very much in my head, very "cerebral," a focused concentration and at the same time an ability to scan, to read a room for example. The feeling itself is at the center of my head, rather small, a highly concentrated energy that looks like a complex assembly of micro-crystals. The structure does not move, but the energy moves along its structure. Like standing waves in that way, the energy is travelling but the structure is constant. Structure is a kind of set of values and parameters for reason and fairness. About one inch in diameter.

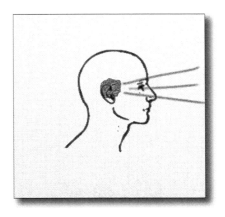

"Out from this nexus, the energy can be directed in a scanning motion to identify points of communication, figure out strategy. This part works hard. Gets hot, (normally body temp). Can be obscured by Confused Paralysis when that rises to the level of the head, when direct confrontation with authority arises or when some mistake has been made.

"I have to set the standard here. I am the only one who can see clearly, who knows the truth of human nature, who can see through oppression in its many forms and stand up for the oppressed, who can clearly cut through the myths and illusions that sustain unjustified power, who can find ways to deconstruct that power and redistribute it to all, who can set a completely new path for all of us, one that all can buy into.

"I have a job to do, and I must do it well. There is a lot at stake, like the fate of the entire world."

Angry at Myself

"When I screw up. Furious. Directed at me. When I act with any authority and it doesn't go perfectly. Not very verbal.

"Downward, clamping down. Like a reinforcement of Fear and Confused Paralysis, like a shock imposed from above. Drives the energy into the Reasonableness, to amp that up in compensation. Like a shock wave of energy coming down upon my body. The Fear is kind of a shock receiver for this. It hits in just that spot, upper back and shoulders, a little on the upper chest. It's coming down from slightly behind.

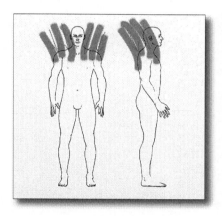

"Temp = neutral. Color = reddish orange, dense. Energy is very dense, almost like a sandbag in density. Hits hard. Sound is an angry grunt. My body wants to respond to this with downward strikes through my fists. Voice is my own, berating me.

"'You stupid shit. Goddamn it. You screwed up. Get it right.'

"I have to get it right. I have to be perfectly reasonable (* Reasonableness). I cannot express anything that imposes anything on anyone, anything they do not inherently want. "Everything I do has to be about eliciting others' desires and working with them. Cannot impose my own desires on anyone. It's bad. It's the worst thing anyone can do. I hate (* Contempt) the people who do it and I will not be like them."

Clearly there is some serious imbalance working here. As you can see, my grandiosity was still very much alive in this set, in the Reasonableness. I was taking upon myself the entire responsibility for rescuing the entire planet. Cheez. Good luck with that, buddy.

The Angry at Myself state clearly connects to another, Contempt, which turns out to actually be playing a role in suppressing the Vicious Enforcer. Let's take a look:

Contempt

"Like a venomous gaze with hate oozing from every pore. An energy that emanates like heat waves from the whole front of my body, concentrated in my face and chest. Not about taking action in confrontation. It's almost a double-direction energizing, with energy coming back into me to drive the Reasonableness.

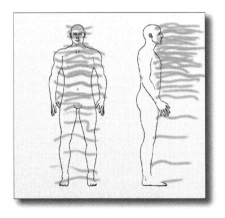

"Orange color, radiant streamers of energy. Hot. Extends out quite far in physical space, at least a few yards, and infinitely in psychic space, to reach idiots around the globe. Sound = a contemptuous muttering, my own voice. A slight hissing sound like steam escaping a boiler.

"For authoritarian others. This drives the Angry at Myself, for being like them. Any sign of dominance with a lack of consciousness about the oppression of others triggers this, which drives my own Reasonableness and Disengagement. I will NOT participate in that shit. I HATE those men who don't get it and especially that they poison the image of all men, including me, forcing me to overcompensate in the other direction... Hm, maybe this is what I really hate, that I feel forced to balance things out. This is always the case, in groups for example, when men dominate the conversation. I will not express myself but will focus on trying to draw out the ones being trampled on and push back on the dominance to make space for them. I hate that I don't get to express myself because of these Neanderthals.

"I have to work so goddamned hard to clean up after these fucking goons. Why do I have to do this? Why do I have to figure out how things really work? Why do I have to spend so much of my life digging around in the debris left in my soul from these fuckheads? Why do I have to be the one to tell people how NOT to be this, how NOT to live this way? Why does THIS have to be my job. God damn it!

"'You suck! I hate your sweat and your big hairy fucking bodies and your cocky attitudes. I hate your blind trampling over everything beautiful and good. I hate your destructiveness. I hate everything about you.'"

Whoa. Pretty hard core, yes? Can you see how this Contempt holds clear the example, projected outside myself, of what I must avoid at all costs? It increases the pressure and the urgency to keep Vicious Enforcer tightly contained.

Let's look at another angle of this Contempt. Now keep in mind that a feeling state shapes both belief and perception. The kinds of thoughts and perceptions that came naturally to me in this state were congruent with the Contempt. So having an active Contempt state within me meant that no matter whether there were true authoritarian jerks around me or not, I would look for them, and even see them in places they didn't actually exist. This state needed an enemy to do its job, and it needed to do its job to keep Vicious Enforcer under control.

In other words, if I didn't have an enemy, I would have created one. And believe me, I did just that. Most of them were abstract "them" sort of people I read about or saw on the internet. But I sought them out, voraciously reading everything about all the evil things George Bush and his cronies were doing, for example. I needed George Bush in order to maintain the inward confinement of my own Vicious Enforcer. Can you see how this works, maybe in yourself in some context?

Now let's take a look at a state that may just tie everything all together.

Powerless

"I'm in deep shit. Just felt my body get activated when I saw a confrontation between Barack Obama and Bill O'Reilly. It was strange how strong my physical reaction was. O'Reilly represents the paragon of the asshole authoritarian which sets me off so much. It's like, if I am expected to stand up to that, I have to meet asshole with asshole, and that terrifies me.

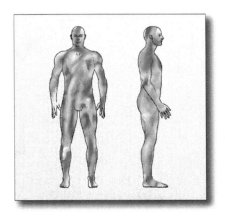

"Even more, I am terrified that I am not strong enough to resist, to stand up to the idiocy, to fight back, and that I will be subjugated permanently. I am too weak, too slow, too emotional to defend myself against the aggression and mean-spirited abuse. I will just cave, and that will mean my life (and all life?) is sentenced to permanent subjugation. There is nothing I can do. I am powerless.

"Like jelly, watery, clear, sloppy-gelatinous, not firm jelly but jelly without enough gelatin, it's falling apart and can't hold its shape. It's very cold, deathly cold, like 35 degrees; whole body; smeary blood-red splotches throughout a clear-ish, translucent haziness. Quivering slightly. Too weak to quiver strongly. This works closely with the shame, chills the shame, intensifies it.

"Sound is whimpering, crying aloud, me as a child. Wants to wail, but wailing is unsafe, will bring down the mocking wrath of the abuser.

"I am powerless to stand up to the abusers of the world. Their mindset is irrational, crazy, and there is no way to reach them rationally. And I am too weak to address them directly, they will just gut me instantly if I try.

"I would love to be powerful and rip them to shreds, but I cannot do that because I will not allow myself to become like them.

"Everything I do is about finding a way to dethrone the Abusers of the world without giving up my own integrity. (*Reasonableness). I want to empower all of the world's oppressed, make them immune to the Abuser's manipulative power. I want to cut the Abusers off at the knees, make the ground they stand on go to quicksand.

"'I hate them. I hate the world that supports and rewards them. I hate them all.' (*Vicious Enforcer).

"This part contributes to keeping the Vicious Enforcer in check because I don't actually believe I could overcome the abusers even with the Enforcer part. They are much stronger than me."

This was yet another part adding to the ammunition available to Reasonableness. It was unthinkable to unleash Vicious Enforcer because I believed they were much more powerful than me and would shoot me down. Can you see how this ties back to the punch? I was mad at being forced to do something that felt physically harmful and dangerous to me, and my temper got loose when I snapped at my father. He was in fact much stronger than me. He did in fact shoot me down, with a conclusiveness that felt final. The punch was one symbolic moment of years of this kind of oppression. There was no fighting this. That left only the necessity of keeping the rage contained and avoiding at all costs any confrontation.

A more extreme version of this state was the following:

Hopeless Shame

"Like bruised, rotting flesh in my heart. Cold. Heart-size. Center of chest. No movement. No sound, except maybe a depleted sigh. Very heavy, like plutonium heavy.

"Hopeless. We're all fucked. Even I can't avoid being an asshole animal of a rapacious jerk. I've failed. I'm going to fail. I can't do it. I'm not strong enough to do this. The world will be destroyed by the stupid."

Let me share the last two states to round out the pattern.

Miasma of Abuse

"It's like they (the abusers) pervade all space, there is no escape. In my house, my father occupied all the space, all the time. There was threat in the air. Always with these people there is threat. You never know when you are going to be seen as "bad" and attacked for your so-called badness. And their logic and perception is so twisted there is no hope for appeal, no possibility to be seen as who you really are. There is no compassion, no sensitivity, there is only blind idiocy, reactive hostility, blame and aggressive humiliation and punishment. These people exist to blame and punish, and nothing else satisfies them. If there is nothing, nobody who has legitimately earned their wrath and disdain, they will manufacture something. There is always some reason for them to attack what is good and sane and true.

"It is in the air. You cannot escape it. It poisons you. You breathe it and it contaminates you. You are guilty simply by being around it, by breathing the air. You cannot escape guilt in their eyes because you must breathe or be dead. That is your choice: breathe and be guilty, or be dead.

"Like poison. A contaminant. Even when they are not physically present it surrounds you. Their judgment is everywhere. A toxic gas. It can get in you if you breathe, and poison you. A miasma of toxicity; hazy, thick, cloudy, dirty, gray-green-brown, gross, like wafting incense except 1000 times more dense and it is everywhere. Gets in your pores, you don't even have to breathe it, because its toxicity is so dense. Gets to your core and disables any strength you have, completely rots any resistance, turns it to putrifying jelly.

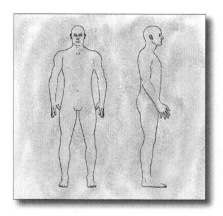

"Stultifyingly warm, close, choking, overly humid and caustically dry at the same time, like it is moist but chemically incinerates your own moisture. Moving like incense smoke in a still room. It can follow you anywhere. It slowly gravitates toward you, no matter where you are, so its highest concentration is wherever you are. (Interesting use of second person instead of first, probably because this triggers Disengagement.) Sound of choking sobs, choking because of the toxicity, sobs because of the hopelessness of avoiding it.

"It is everywhere, in every small abusive communication (advertising, e.g.), disguised in many ways, overt and accepted in many ways, forcibly oppressive in many ways. There's no way to fight back because it is so pervasive, and because it is so disabling. I am too weak in its presence to even put up a fight. I am too frightened to resist."

It's interesting to read this again, and remember one common theme in my father's interactions with me. I had gotten so numb around him that often times I could hardly function. He would send me to fetch some tool or other, I would go to the place where he said I could find it, look directly at it, and literally not see it. It was some kind of negative hallucination effect, my mind completely blocking my perception. So I would go back and say it wasn't there. Of course he would be forced to go get it himself, heaping abuse along the way, and most of the time it would be exactly where he said it was.

I was so shut down that many times when something obvious needed to be done, and the clear expectation was that I should do it, I would just stand there. His constant, jabbing refrain was, "Breathe, Joe! Christ, do I have to tell you everything?" He said it as mockery, but it wouldn't surprise me to know that I had in fact reduced my breathing to an absolute minimum in response to the noxious atmosphere.

Grief/Sorrow

"Very heavy in my chest, my heart, quite large, a good foot in diameter or so, hard solid, resilient like rubber; black/opaque/dull; warm; a very slight pulsing variation in the intensity of the weight of it, corresponding with an expansion and contraction in size, not so much a pushing out or pulling in as just the amount of stuff gets more or less, and more is heavier, a slow pulse, like over a minute or more with each beat. Sound is a long, protracted groan, never-ending.

"I have lost so much joy and pleasure, especially in connecting with and loving others, as a result of the damage I sustained in our toxic culture and the supreme effort I had to make to overcome that damage, (and continue to have to make today, working to help others overcome similar damage). My life may be meaningful, but only in the context of a world of hurt. I would prefer to have been born into a world of goodness and celebrated life every day I was alive.

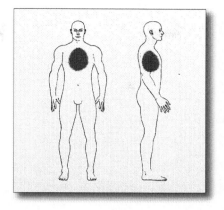

"This work of mine should not be necessary. These things should be so common as to be taken for granted, a part of the air we breathe. I should have been free to grow up, marry, take a profession, be part of a community, etc, all from a place of freedom and joy in who I am. It is painful to me to think we have had to come to such a fever pitch of worldwide agony before figuring this stuff out, so much pain for myself and others, all could have been avoided. The burden of the life I gave up to pursue this work, the simply pleasures I have not had."

Can you see how holding this pattern within myself would pretty much prevent me from taking on my own authority, from being able to put my work out in the world with any kind of assurance? All the parts of me responsible for this kind of strong presence in the world were fully occupied containing the bad guy within.

Releasing the Enforcer

When I moved these states, what showed up was incredibly powerful. Let me take you on a tour, partly to give you a deeper look at the inside of the Feeling Path process, (my notes for this set are particularly detailed), and also to tie this set back into what I am sharing in this book, and even to the fact that this book is in your hands now. There are layers here, layers of meaning, of story, of application, and of connection to your journey. I'd like to pour as much into this first book as I possibly can.

Because the entire set seemed to pivot around Vicious Enforcer, I tried to move it first. But it just wouldn't budge. So I turned my attention to what seemed obvious to be the Context Source path, the state which seemed to represent the entire world I inhabited, and therefore the complete field of possibilities. That state was Miasma of Abuse.

Shared Light of Joyful Being

(Formerly Miasma of Abuse)

"Jan 7: [Image: let it completely seep into me, stop resisting it... it begins to dissipate, become clearer; becomes fresh and clean air; an energy? strong...]

"Jan 9: From the other night, this turns into the light of human goodness, the ability to see the strong heliotropic pull in every human being toward wholeness, and to trust that above all, especially above expressions of shadow, fear, and pain that come out as abuse and authoritarian control.

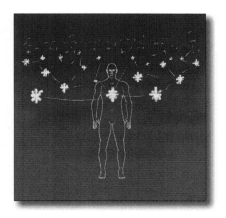

"An infinite field of light, with points of light in every person's heart including my own. There is a sense of joyfulness and play about it, the lights are dancing or at least wanting to dance, individually and together. There is a rhythm that unites all the lights, yet each can vary on that rhythm to dance its own dance.

"Warm, white lights in a field of dark, radiant blue, quite beautiful, like half-moon-size stars in a twilight sky, stretching out around the globe. Sounds of light laughter and play, some giggling, some pleasurable sighs, some yeses, many voices.

Now that Miasma of Abuse was no longer a pervasive threat, the other parts were free to begin to move. Powerless was the next to release. To start the moving process with this state, I chose to use an alternative technique similar to Jungian Active Imagination. I surrendered to the imagery that wanted to emerge from the state and followed it fully throughout the scenario it wanted to create, kept following it, asking what wants to be now, and now, and now. The brief notes from that journey are below. To begin, I returned to my dream of being imprisoned by the abuser.

Power is Connected Flow

(Formerly Powerless)

"[Journey: Quivering intensifies - it gets stronger. I am lying on the floor, shaking spasmodically, saying to a tall, jack-booted, masked abuser, 'Come on, dance with me... you know you want to... go ahead and hit me... as soon as you do, we are dancing, you with me, I with you... you can't escape it; we are wedded by coexistence.' I laugh, and my spasms become quakes of laughter. 'Yes,' I cry out, 'you MUST dance with me, because how can you not?' In my laughing I feel powerful; and I see the look of confusion beneath the mask, in the whole body's hesitation, awkwardness. I laugh harder. 'And now,' I say, 'tell me what you really want, and together we shall dance it into being.']

"A strong energy, flowing through me, into and out of me, into and out of others. It is an energy of doing, of being together, of our communal dance, our dancing one another's dreams into being.

"It flows vertically through me, and out in all directions to flow vertically through others. Sometimes up, other times down, it is not important. Upward is me giving explicitly, and receiving more implicit support; downward is me receiving explicitly, and giving more implicit support. Back and forth, like breathing.

"Lusciously warm, moist and tingly. A juicy, vibrant red, like arterial blood and brighter than that. The energy flows like a liquid, easy and quick at times, gentle and languid at other times. Always there is no resistance, and flow through me instantly connects to flow through one or more others.

"Sound of deep flow, and something like the breath of the planet... sound of great laughter shared among many people, laughter for its own sake, in naked appreciation for life itself and our shared experience of it.

"I am mischievous, playful, and utterly confident in the drive toward joyful wholeness in others. I invite others to dance in many playful and serious ways, always with lightness, always with respect for what I know is the deeper truth in everyone, the desire to belong, to be significant, to matter, to contribute, to participate.

"At the same time, I have no tolerance for false divisions among people. I can easily challenge such talk and action because I am calling everyone to something more true. They are like children who have been taught poorly, who are only doing what they know in order to feel safe. As soon as they feel the invitation to show up, to drop their defenses, they are glad to do so. It is my job to make those invitations compelling, to reach them where they are, to touch them despite the walls they have put up, and I can do that because I know the purpose of the walls and the manner of their construction.

"I have a great capacity for compassion and love for every being."

I could sense that the next state that needed to move was Vicious Enforcer. Every other state was oriented toward controlling it, and as long as it was active, the other states were likely to resist moving. But this state was so intense I could not bear to access it for more than a few moments at a time, and it felt too overwhelming to move. Keep in mind I was doing this alone and had only myself to hold the structure of the process. I had made a few attempts over several days, the last of which applied the active imagination journeying technique. My notes are below, a fascinating journey. Even after that, however, it was not quite ready to fully move.

Now that Miasma was cleared and Powerless had found its Power, though, I was able to finally shift Vicious Enforcer.

Truth Blaze

(Formerly Vicious Enforcer)

"Jan 2: This is about creating harmony, in current form by eliminating disruptions to harmony... Some kind of consolidation is happening, a calming down and strengthening. No need to force it. I know what I know... Immoveable.

"Jan 6: Journey: Woods, I am a werewolf, but there are no people to attack... I am flying above the world, fury, hurling huge firebombs at cities, government, corporate power, dark, all around the globe... then an ease, settling back to earth, to a green village, people, smiling, joyful living, simple, lots of green, much life and laughter... I just want to be one of them... just want a place to call home... As I connect with people, with laughter, with appreciation, I begin taking a leadership role. I am the one who reminds people what they already know. That is what true authority, true leadership, is.

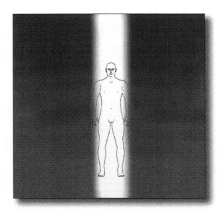

"Jan 9: A column of light, a pillar of light, as big around as my body, extending above and below me many yards, perhaps as far as 30 feet in each direction. It is anchored by the light within me, which is my personal wavelet/expression of the Shared Light. Provides a kind of photonic "lubrication" for passage of the Power Flow through me.

"There is a kind of hum, a high-tension vibration like that within an electromagnet or around high-voltage wires. This pillar is rock steady and resists perturbation, although it is flexible, the way a high-density magnetic field would yield movement for an object suspended in it, but would return that object firmly to its centered place. The pillar can flex, but always returns strongly to its vertical position.

"Top and bottom fade out over the most distal several feet; all around me though is high-density. This light is almost opaque it is so bright, but is soft, not blinding; you can see through it if you squint. Color is mostly white, glistening.

"I am me. I am strong. I know what I am here for. I am here to promote dancing among the spirits of all people, to show fighting for the wasteful illusion it is.

"I represent the light shared by all of us; it is within me and I see it in you. I stand for the sharing of our light, each by all. My light burns through the shadows of illusion, reveals them as simply a mistaken obscuring of the true light within all of us.

"I am a blaze of wise truth-telling. I shrink at nothing in order to spread my message of shared light, dancing. I laugh in the face of resistance, because I know it is illusory. I laugh with joy to dance with those who might at first disagree with me. How can they know what I represent?

"I am speaking out. I am writing. I am holding forth in many venues. I have an ever-expanding audience. People understand what I am saying because I am speaking to the light within them. I see it. I dance with it. I am connected to truth."

This turned out to be the Context Presence path of the nine-path set. The Context Presence path is typically experienced as the "me" or identity for the whole set of nine. So it makes sense that this single state, Vicious Enforcer had the ability to fully organize the entire set of nine paths around it in a tightly locked configuration of reactive states. It held the position of being "me," and thus beyond any hope for change. I held its state as an incontrovertible condition of my being, and found all the other ways to compensate for its existence. Once it had gained access to its ideal state, Truth Blaze, I had a new anchor.

Moving these three states had taken me the better part of a day. I was exhausted. The next day I took my laptop to the local café to continue the work. Getting out of my isolated apartment into a public space sometimes made it easier for me to stay focused, hold the structure of the process, and plow through the elicitation questions no matter how uncomfortable I might be with the states.

Now that Vicious Enforcer was no longer waiting to strike, I was free to move the many layers of defense which had become piled on top of it. The first to go was Confused Paralysis.

Indomitable Presence

(Formerly Confused Paralysis)

"Even when this isn't directly in my head, it affects the Reasonableness, makes it less effective somehow. It's almost like, 'you're not doing a good enough job, so I'm taking over to make sure you don't fuck things up even more.'

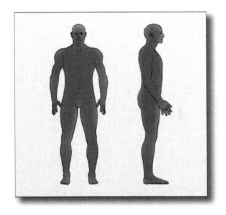

"Heavier, more dense... it would drop to the floor... feels grounding but not in a pleasant way, more like an anchor...

"This seems to want to be some kind of firm anchor, a stabilizer that makes me more substantial, immoveable by outside forces, moving only by my own intention. High inertia, whether moving or still, from the perspective of outside forces. I am firm in my steady commitment to and movement toward my visions and goals. An indomitable force.

"An intensely massive, very flexible solid, moveable by itself, but immoveable from the outside. Dark gray, absorbs light. Like lead in density, but much softer in texture.

"(In a world in which there were no opposing forces, what would this get to be?) Not much different, maybe a bit softer.

"Warm, like body temperature and maybe a bit warmer; very, very dense, soft, highly resilient solid, like the weight and muscularity of a bull packed into my body. Whole body, no more than that. Color is a deep, warm gray, and the appearance is velvety almost, like dense fur the way light gets absorbed. Very like an animal, a horse perhaps, strong yet supple. Movement is more about stillness, although this can move easily by intention. Sound is that of deep breath, larger than life, as if I and those around me are being breathed by something more universal."

"I know what I am about, what I am here for, and others sense that. Others trust me, my stability and focus and commitment. I am an indomitable presence, a force for good in the world and in my relationships. I know what good is, and what it takes to promote it, and I do not hesitate or hold back in my steady support of what is good in everyone.

"I am committed to the good in everyone. I know its nature. I know how to work with it. I devote my life to the promotion of a world which acknowledges and supports the good in everyone. I have no hesitation to engage with anyone, regardless of their views or perspective, because I know what I stand for and I relish all opportunities to do my work. I am a champion for peace in all forms, everywhere. I am a champion with an indomitable presence."

After moving Confused Paralysis, I noticed myself becoming annoyed by a guy sitting nearby me in the café. My Contempt was coming to the foreground, ready to be moved.

Nexus for Human Light

(Formerly Contempt)

"Contempt has been active today at Victrola, and is coming up now in my annoyance at a guy's voice, he won't shut up – seems like a nice enough guy but I wish he would shut up. Very distracting to me. Can I move this now?

"[Journey: the energy intensifies, becomes a radiant burning force that fries guys to a crisp. They fall like flies from a bug-zapper, incinerated. I wander the world blasting all men I encounter. I laugh when they fall, surprised and fried. They never saw it coming, damned fools. After a while there are no men left; I am alone except for all the women in the world. Suddenly I don't belong. I am an outsider. I wander furtively, disguised and hiding out. I begin capturing women and turning them into men - good men, who have a heart and sensitivity and awareness, who value communication and collaboration, who champion the good in people rather than waste precious time and resources competing for status. (I realize that much of my contempt for men has had to do with not wanting to get pulled into competing for status. I'm not interested. It is wasteful for everyone. It hurts good people. Plus, entering that competition puts me at risk for igniting the Vicious Enforcer.)]

"My presence transcends status. It makes status jockeying irrelevant. Nobody can possibly take a status higher or lower than me. The game is simply nullified. In this place, Contempt is irrelevant...

"Laughing... reverse direction... [I am suddenly filled with an appreciation for the people around me. The annoying guy and his friend are endearing. I have a little eager excitement going. People have so much to offer! Tears.] Coming from outside me, entering my heart area... (?)

"Like light, coming from every direction, origin points in every person, people arrayed 360 degrees all around me. Yellow-gold light, warm, converging in my heart or solar plexus, my core. It fills me with warmth, appreciation, excitement about the possibilities of what we can do together, bringing all the goodness to a creative focus. The intensity is very high, like a parabolic reflector for human goodness and light. I have the capacity to hold and focus it, though, because I have Indomitable Presence. That part has a high heat index, can absorb an enormous amount of energy.

"Sound of laughter and excited talking, as if in a large conference full of people who are really psyched about something they are learning and doing. I want to feel this in the context of workshops, lectures, etc.!"

This Nexus was the outside source path, drawing from infinite possibilities for connection all around me. So now I had moved two of the three sources, the context and the outside. I was still missing the inside source. This was a path like many others I've encountered, where the directionality of the reactive state, Contempt/outward, was reversed to become the ideal, Nexus / inward.

The final state I moved on this day turned out to be the third of the three sources. It also was a path in which the directionality of reactive and ideal states was reversed. I had started out the day trying to move this one, shifting to the journeying technique to free it up. But it went more easily after I moved Confused Paralysis and Contempt, and came back to it.

Liberation Power

(Formerly Angry at Myself)

"Currently angry at myself for taking so long getting through this set, dragging my feet. Of course, I know it's just Confused Paralysis at work, but the whole team is striving to stay active despite losing three of their key players!

"[Journey: I can imagine this energy increasing, so it is whomping me into complete oblivion, I get literally flattened, and the whomping continues with expressions of rage and disparagement. I can identify with the whomp energy, with clenched fists pounding downward. (Want?) The whomping becomes rhythmic, dance-like. I am dancing the whomp-ass dance. Expressions of gleeful whomping. Hua! Hua!]

"This is a very forceful, male energy... outwardly directed. Seems to be about what's outside of me, engaging with others.

"[Moved Confused Paralysis and Contempt.]

"This moves inside me. Very bright orange energy, located at solar plexus, fueling all of this set. I have a passion for liberation, for releasing light into the world from every person. VERY bright and intense. Sound of a rumble, like a rocket engine at a distance. Makes me want to get busy, wants to fuel my engagement. Hot. The most intense part of this is about a foot and a half in diameter, and the heat and light emanates quite far, many feet at least. This is just what I bring to it, my energy, my intention.

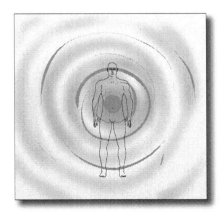

"I am powerful and I can make good things happen. I have the strength and intention to accomplish big things with little effort.' There is a joyful quality to this; it is my absolute joy to serve through my actions, to create through my intention. I want to take all the work I have done and absolutely maximize its impact on as many people as possible. I am a liberator!"

Again, after moving these three I was exhausted and done for the day. Two days later I came back to it and moved the last three parts.

Liberation Creation

(Formerly Grief/Sorrow)

"The downward weight wants to turn into a downward flow. Some aspects circulating down through the center, others flowing up through the center. Something about compassion, a compassionate flow, connecting with Power Flow, an appreciation for people's journeys, the challenges, the losses, etc. The image is like blood flowing... but there's something unsatisfying about it..."

"[Journey: a surge of flow, downward, circulating back up the outside, flowing fast, powerfully, pushing some capacity boundary, a kind of screaming sound like machinery pushed to its limit... suddenly explodes outward, reaches into the space around me, flowing out from my center, into and through others around me, back in to my center. Out from center, in through heart.]

"It can go in both directions but primary direction is down through the center, from heart to solar plexus. Substance = hi-density energy, behaves like liquid but does not have mass that impacts other mass. Warm to hot. Color of a persimmon, orange, with very tiny points of light, a rich texture with thousands of light points that saturate the energy; in a strange way it makes it have a velvety texture, almost, with a sheen, like certain liquid suspensions of shimmery powder.

"The flow is more virtual, created by a communication between the points of light; they 'nod' to one another in one direction or the other to simulate strong flow through transmitting information. The stronger aspect is a general felt sense of flow. Sound is joyful singing, many people, celebrating the liberation of human light in all its many forms.

"This seems to be about action guided by compassion, about great force going out to express this Liberation Power, and this force is continually in touch with the pain and suffering of the people it is meant to help. Resonates with Nexus and Power Flow in some ways.

"I create structures that instigate and support the liberation of others' light. I create structures. I have Liberation Power, channeled by Indomitable Presence and I am a force to be reckoned with. What I see to create, I create. It gets done, with the full participation and assistance of others.

"I provide opportunities for others to harness their inborn desire to shine their light brightly. People love to be given these opportunities and the guidance for how to use them. I love doing this – it is what I was born to do in any form, and the particular work I do is the specific expression of this natural gift and purpose within me, given my life path. I am totally psyched to be doing the work I am doing.

"To others: 'Tell me what you need, what you heart yearns for, what your light desires in order to shine brightly. Then let us work together to create the structures which will support that happening easily and gracefully. I love you, and I see your light, and I do not intend to tolerate anything that prevents it from shining. I want your light in my world.'"

Parabolic Reflector

(Formerly Fear)

"Jan 10: 'Careful...' (In a world in which there were no oppositional forces, what would this part get to be?) Softer... [Moved Contempt ==> Nexus...]

"(Now that you have Shared Light and Nexus for Human Light available, as well as Power Flow, Truth Blaze, and Indomitable Presence, what does this part of you get to be?)

"Drops down into my spine, lower back... [Image: I stand up in this coffee shop and begin speaking to everyone, sort of "preaching" in a way, laughing at myself, saying, "yes, what I'm doing is 'crazy' but I'm not crazy, I just have something to share that I believe will touch every one of you, and I simply must offer you that..."]

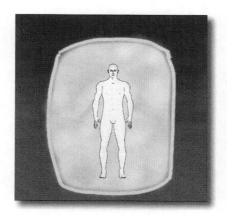

"[The whole direction of this set is freaking me out a bit... seems awfully big, to the extent of being grandiose and unrealistic... or is it? Maybe that's the Reasonableness getting uncomfortable - it's going to be asked to step out of its comfort zone...]

"Warm, burnt orange, material like a water bottle, all across my lower back, just sitting there. Vibration/energy, sending out to all parts of my body.

"Jan 12: This is a kind of supportive backstop for Liberation Power, contains and directs it forward in productive ways, into Liberation Creation. This can expand, outside my body, at my back, full height, as wide as me, about 3 inches thick is enough. ==> Actually, this fits better in the Outside triad, almost as a reflector for Nexus and Power Flow. Still doesn't feel quite complete, though."

Persuasive Clarity

(Formerly Reasonableness)

"This seems like it wants to be a kind of communications power, allied with Nexus and Indomitable Presence. This feels like a powerful part, and its presence pulls the whole thing together (after moving the rest).

"Drops to my heart, the thinking and communication come from the heart rather than the head... It's more intuitive, more connected to my whole self, less reliant on logic and analysis and "cool-headed" reasoning. Able to be passionate. Can draw from the head when useful - always has access to that intelligence.

"==> Seems more like an interactive part, but this one is coming in through the heart and out through the head/throat. I can feel this in action thinking about writing for my website or book.

"Energetic light, high vibration, lots of information encoded within; interactive, drawing in from others expressions, reactions, communications to reach out toward what is the highest good in each person, to draw that forth.

"Multi-chromatic, rich colors; very responsive to color coming in. It's moving slowly and quickly at the same time. The larger frames of energy and information move slowly, the smaller frames move quickly and simply fill the larger.

"Drawing on others' understanding and experience to relate their surface knowing to their deeper knowing, eliciting that underlying wisdom, releasing the light to flow. Being sensitive to fluctuations of that light and using them as feedback about how to communicate next. This is happening in small time frames, with single individuals, as well as over larger time frames with entire populations. I am absorbing what is, inside the feeling mind and beliefs of my audience, and using it to persuade people to drop more deeply into their truth in all ways.

"This is about engaging others to draw them out, make their light available to themselves and others including me. It is about applying all I know and all I feel and am aware of in others, toward messages of liberation. This is about drawing forth the light in others.

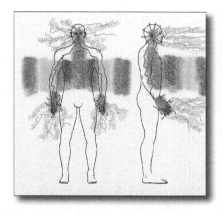

"'I am excited to connect with you, and with you, and with you, and to encourage and persuade you to release your gifts to yourself and others around you. We need you! I want you! Come out! Come out!'

"This is my life work. This is what I am meant to do. This is the essence of my action in the world."

This was me as a very big force in the world, leading, teaching, facilitating insights and connections for many others. I had a big surge of confidence and activity in putting my work out.

But this set was a Surface Self. As such, it was dependent for its inspiration and support on the Deep Self. And for me, the Deep Self was still entrenched in my prime template, which centered around the Infinite Agony I shared earlier in the book. That was still lying outside my awareness, and my model had not expanded to include the possibility of its existence so I wasn't looking for it either. So although this set was free to move through its full range from reactive to ideal, it was unable to sustain itself at the ideal end of the spectrum.

I finally discovered the full extent of the Deep Self and identified the Infinite Agony and other states holding it in its reactive configuration this spring and summer. Infinite Agony opened into the inside source for my Deep Self, the Big Love state I shared earlier. And another source also came online, Earth Energy, which connected me to a source of support seemingly as big as the planet.

Without the Big Love and Earth Energy available from my Deep Self, I was not able to sustain the sources which emerged from this set. The set wavered, faltered, and faded into the background as other issues took precedence in my attention. Now that I have all nine states of my ideal Deep Self fully available, I am finding it easy to grow into this new place of authority. I am finishing this book with confidence that I do in fact have something important to contribute. And it is in balance. This is something I have to contribute. What happens with my contribution is largely up to all the rest of us. It's no longer my job to save the world. (Hooray!)

Reflections on liberation

Getting to this point in the book, nearly complete, I know for sure that I am fully ready all the way to my core. The dots are connecting, the energy is linking up, I am excited and nothing seems to be holding me back.

At the same time, I want to offer some perspective on this set. The new states I've shared with you here are the ideal. These are what I aspire to. This set feels true for me as a direction. This inner sense of having a big mission to make the world a better place has been with me from a very early age. It was probably largely responsible for my choosing to trust myself for making sense of the world at age five, rather than look to my parents for that. And it certainly played a role in my continuing to push forward even when things seemed absolutely hopeless in my 20s and 30s.

As an ideal, though, it serves its purpose as a touchstone, as a force by which to orient the vector of creation in my life. At any given moment, my current state of reality will never fully reflect this ideal. As I embrace what is and reach toward this ideal as a pull toward what wants to be, I can embody within myself the difference between the two. This difference between current reality and the ideal possible is the driving force for creation in my life. It drove my discoveries, and it has driven the writing of this book.

Another point of perspective I want to offer is to give you an idea of where I am in understanding all this. This Liberation set is the realization of a self which is but one dimension of my life. It has nothing to offer my relationship with my body, or with a lover, or a family, or my personal belonging in a community. This is a dimension of myself which might be compared to that of the professional production of an artist or choreographer, or the designs of an engineer.

I have been curious about these variations in focus for the different Surface Selves which emerge. There does seem to be a rough correlation with where the inside source locates itself. In this case, my inside source, Liberation Power, centers itself in my lower belly, the place some refer to as the "hara" or the second chakra. The connection there suggests that for me, this set is about what I am here to create in the world. Having the inside source located here suggests this set is about my agency, my will, my power to make a difference. I find it interesting that simultaneously this set seems to be oriented toward larger themes of empowering others, creating broader connections among people, and liberation which I might not have connected to that second chakra location.

There is much I don't know yet about the absolute number of Surface Selves or the relationships among them. I am also not super clear yet about the relationship between the Deep Self and the various Surface Selves. I simply have not had the time or opportunity to explore these things yet. There is much for us to learn, together!

The Enforcer in all of us

I am extremely lucky. Normally this sort of internalized violence gets passed down from one generation to the next. That could easily have happened to me. I had absorbed the essential ingredients to become an abuser or worse. The set of nine states pivoting around the Vicious Enforcer, combined with others equally ugly and hurtful I've uncovered over the years, was destroying my life. From the outside, I looked like any other screw-up, a failure by anybody's measure. Few friends, no family, no love, no career, no money – all this potential and talent fully and completely wasted.

In a way, the Vicious Enforcer owned me. I hated myself for having it inside myself. I hated myself because within me I harbored the exact thing I despised the most. So was a part of myself which was separated from love.

When we hold some part of ourselves separate from love, it is impossible to be fully present in relationship. It is impossible to be fully open to another. It is impossible to love at all, or to receive it from any source.

Our deepest need is to love. Our deepest hunger is to connect. Our deepest thirst is to belong. When something within ourselves bars the door to what we most require to thrive, we lose our commitment to life. We lose our remembrance of the utter mystery and astonishing beauty of simply being. It becomes easy to hurt others without thought or remorse. If one holds the reins of power, it becomes easy to make decisions that devastate lives or decimate populations. It becomes easy to destroy our own lives, whether quickly through suicide or more slowly through drunkenness, addiction, numbness or dangerous lifestyles. It becomes easy to forget what is important, to lose empathy, and to immerse oneself in manipulation and gamesmanship and exploitation just because we can and it is easy and there is no motivation to do otherwise.

This is the condition in which many people inhabit their lives, destroying themselves unthinkingly, destroying others willfully, unconscious about both. This is the condition in which I inhabited my life.

Yet lurking inside were these amazing and beautiful gifts, a selection of which I am blessed to be offering you in this book right now simply by how I am choosing to show up in my writing. Other gifts which have come to light in doing this work – the ability to be fully present with another's pain is one I treasure the most – were similarly hidden. All were revealed through this process of going into the apparent obstacles, obstacles like the Vicious Enforcer, embracing them fully and inviting them to reveal the gifts within.

Over the years I have done this thousands of times. Within myself I have exposed states most gruesome. Other states within myself included intense, howling pain; a nauseating wrenching as if my stomach was being forcibly ripped from my body; a crushed heart; and a chest made of raw, ground meat, as if destroyed by a shotgun blast. One was like the mouth of hell behind me, waiting to suck me into a terrifying unknown. And I have encountered countless fearsome states in others with whom I have worked. Rage and hate, viciousness and despair, crushing hopelessness and devastating pain, paralyzing terror and abject isolation.

In every case, no exceptions, the state released gently into a place of resourcefulness and authentic truth. Always at the core of any human pain or ugliness is beauty beyond what we might ever imagine. We are astonishing beings, and that is always true, no matter who we are, no matter what we have done.

And this is not rocket science. It does not require finding the perfect cocktail of toxic psych drugs. It does not require interminable trudging through the hallways of the past. It does not require finessing the exact right timing or combination of techniques or reconstruction of beliefs. When you get right down to it, this is ludicrously simple! Embrace what is. Invite what wants to be. Embody the difference. It's not so hard.

But how many millions – no, billions – of people are living with their own Vicious Enforcers holding them hostage from within? The tragedy in my personal story is <u>not</u> that it took me 30-some years to liberate myself. I would not trade one second of my journey for any other.

The tragedy is that my father and mother have lived their full lives without their deepest gifts finding the light. The tragedy is that all three of us missed the opportunity for decades to share love and respect and mutual excitement for being in one another's lives. I am fortunate that they are still here. Perhaps we will be able to capture some of that in the time that remains to us.

How many people do you know whose gifts have not yet seen the light of day? How many people do you know who are held hostage from within? Unfortunately, we are all impoverished by the failure of any one person to have the opportunity to shine.

And how many people have you judged and discounted because of their version of the Enforcer wreaking havoc in their lives? Are you willing to reconsider your judgment, to wonder instead what gifts lie dormant, to become curious about what they might be, perhaps even to become active in inviting those gifts into the light?

And how about you? I have chosen to go much deeper in sharing some of the most difficult parts of myself than many people might think is wise. But I have done so for a purpose. I want to demonstrate to you that I have no good reason not to share anything about myself with you. I know without any hesitation that every part of me – every thought, every feeling, every impulse, every fantasy, every urge – every part of me is ultimately and perfectly good. And I know that is true for you as well. I know it without question, without hesitation, no matter who you are or what you have done.

Let me say that again. I know without any hesitation that every part of you is ultimately and perfectly good, no matter who you are or what you have done. And I want you to come to know that about yourself as well.

I have also shared in such depth because I want to illustrate for you just how complex we all are. It is easy to focus on the part and miss the whole. For example, if you had known me a few years ago you would perhaps have seen how reasonable I could be in situations of conflict, and thought highly of me for that. It would have been highly unlikely you would have gotten close enough to see the deep perturbations underneath the surface calm. Similarly, if the Vicious Enforcer had erupted in some weak moment, you would have judged me for being an uncontrolled jerk, and would never have given me credit for all the parts of me which had struggled so mightily over the years to contain it. We are all complex beyond what we imagine, but that complexity is now available to us. Now that we can see below the surface with this grand new tool, we discover that what seems so complex is relatively simple. Just nine working parts, generating endless permutations of thought and behavior but operating by only a few simple principles which are easy to discern. For me, constructing the Vicious Enforcer pattern took a lifetime, but with the proper tools, excavating it and dissolving the pattern took only 10 days. (And I considered that to be taking a long time.)

So what is within you, waiting to be liberated? Do you feel a stirring of excitement about the possibilities? I suspect the ambitious vision of my Liberation Self is not uncommon. We are living in times that are calling to us all. These times are calling us to rise into our biggest selves, to bring our greatest potential to contribute to this world. Our world needs our best. It needs the most we can bring to the task of transforming our civilization into the magnificent flourishing it has every possibility of becoming. What role in this renaissance is calling you from within?

Responding to violence

We tend to speak of violent incidents as if there were one victim and one perpetrator. But no perpetrator goes un-victimized by his own crime. We also tend to focus on violence as physical. But even more insidious in its effects is violence of the spirit. It is this violence of the spirit that a physical act of violence inflicts on the both the physical victim and the physical perpetrator. And it is this violence of the spirit that also does the greater damage on our society as a whole, whether accompanied by physical violence or not.

Let me speak first to my point about perpetrator as victim. I expect some people may have difficulty wrapping their heads around this idea.

About 10 years ago I had the opportunity to work with a skilled and loving therapist named Leonard Shaw, assisting at one of his 3-day Love and Forgiveness workshops at the Washington State Correctional Facility in Monroe, maximum security. Leonard guides inmates through a re-living of events through the eyes of both physical perpetrator and physical victim. At some times the event is the participant's crime, and at others it is an experience of abuse at the hands of another perpetrator, usually as a child.

According to Leonard, we are all connected through a deep love for one another. That is the truth of existence. His guidance led the guys in the hot seat into that truth, through experiencing the full humanity of both themselves and the other. The breakthroughs were powerful, cathartic, emotional, and they always involved a feeling of connection between the guy and either his victim or his abuser.

In those moments it was very clear that violent actions one was driven to carry out or endure both originated from and caused a rupture of that connection. The actions were expressions of isolation from that love, and they propagated ripples of further isolation through time and across to other people.

But the actions themselves were not the people. The violent acts happened through someone and to someone, but the more fundamental reality is that two people were engaged in a dance of disruption, a dance that denied the reality of connection but which was powerless to change the essential truth of that reality.

Each one of us is connected very deeply to every other one of us. Violence perpetrates an illusion of separation that destroys the experience of connection for both parties.

I saw men open to their humanity in those three days. I witnessed softening, presence, awakening. Although Leonard was not doing anything that looked like the work I present here, he was following the three simple practices. The reliving was an embrace of what is, of the past and how the past lives in the present. Out of that came the invitation to reorient to that past, to hold the self and the other differently, honoring the truth of the shared humanity. And from that came an integration, a movement into living day to day life differently, with a new awareness and commitment to presence.

Also in those three days, I saw myself, and I saw my father in the stories these men reshaped. I knew that I was no different from them, these guys who would spend most or all of the rest of their lives in prison for murder or rape or burglary. And I knew that my father was also no different from them or from me. We are all in this together.

And what about the non-physical violence? This violence we see and experience everywhere, and have since we were very young. Here's how it works.

We feel an authentic signal that something is out of balance for us. Maybe it is anger, maybe sadness, maybe fear. It could even be joy or excitement or love. The set up happens when we express that feeling in some way.

The violence happens when someone else important to us identifies that feeling or its expression and communicates an interpretation which says, in effect, that we are worth less as a human being because of experiencing or expressing that feeling. We are punished, shamed or banished. We absorb that judgment. We internalize it. And as a result we turn against that part of ourselves in order to preserve the belonging and connection we crave with the person who judged us.

The result? The part which previously alerted us to an imbalance or expressed our authentic being has been disabled, cut off, deactivated. This is no different than someone cutting off your hand for stealing a cookie. You are just as crippled by this act as if you had lost a limb. You are no longer able to protect yourself, to nurture yourself, to express yourself, to connect with others intimately. You have had your humanity and your capacity for love and beauty destroyed. Not only that, but in your disability, you are likely to act in ways that spread this violence to others. One act of violence to the body hurts only that body. One act of violence to the spirit has the capacity to hurt many generations.

I believe it is important for us to develop our skills in identifying this violence of the spirit, naming it, and finding ways to disarm and reverse its effects. Often this violence of the spirit is done in the name of "good." In my case, for example, I am quite sure my father thought he was doing what I needed to prepare me for life. The relentless mocking and criticizing was meant to make me stronger and more responsible.

And on the outside, I was a "good kid." On the outside, it looked as if my father's brutality was getting the job done. He probably felt reasonably satisfied he was doing the right thing. But inside I was ravaged, and as I became an adult the damage made its presence known more forcefully through my devastating mood swings. A normal life was out of reach for me. Normalcy was something that had been removed from the possible futures I had access to.

What I'm calling out here already has a place in our collective awareness. Many people recognize the violence of certain kinds of communication. What I'm adding to the conversation so far is a new way to understand the dynamic of violence and recognize it, even in its more camouflaged forms.

We need to learn to recognize the difference between parenting from principle, perpetrating violence in order to mold the child into some predetermined image, and parenting from love, nurturing the authentic gifts of our unique children.

We also need to learn to recognize violent communication in our schools, workplaces, and public spheres. We need to develop skills and practices which enable us to call out the violence and defuse its power without doing violence in turn. How do we do this? How do we succeed in working to reduce violence without committing further violence in our defense?

There are two common approaches to addressing this challenge. The first is to "love your enemy," the idea being to focus on your own compassion and understanding first of all, and to interact from that place. The second is to rely on certain formulas for interacting, one of the most well-known of which is Non-Violent Communication.

I'm not going to advocate for either of these. Why? Because both approaches have a tendency to perpetuate subtle forms of violence themselves. And neither approach honors the three simple practices of The Feeling Path.

The first approach, that of forgiveness, compassion, love, or whatever state a particular group or person has designated as most desirable, can easily turn into aggressive state chasing. In order to seek to feel something in particular or act from a particular principle, you must set up a cop-in-the-head to ward off competing impulses. You separate from your own self, taking over amputating some part of your being so the other violent person is relieved of the duty. This may give you more control of the situation and satisfy needs for security, but it is no less violent.

The second approach is to learn a scripted manner of interacting which can easily be twisted into a justification for the same kind of self-amputation as the previous approach. Any parts of oneself which may be feeling particularly un-NVC are pushed to the side.

In addition, the script establishes a new playing ground; it changes the rules of the interaction unilaterally. Someone who has developed a high level of skill in applying the script will always have the upper hand in this new game, and so the script becomes a tool for manipulation and reversing the direction of the violence. Finally, with NVC in particular, a strong focus on needs as something to be filled by others lends itself more strongly to becoming such a tool.

That said, either one of these approaches can be employed by someone with a depth and awareness that turns them into a positive force for peace. As I will explore a little bit later, the actual system of interaction, whether it guides interaction between two people or two billion, means little. What is most important to the outcome is the wisdom of the people inhabiting the system. Let's look at what that means in this question of how to address violent communication.

Let me connect a couple of dots here for you first. I've been speaking in two different ways about what is essentially the same thing. I've spoken about wisdom, and I've spoken about the experience of wholeness with presence. These two things are equivalent. When I speak of wisdom, I am speaking of the state of wholeness in which one is sensitive and aware of a full range of perceptions, states and responses, where no significant part of oneself is buried beneath awareness, where one is not being held hostage by any version of the Enforcer or another intolerable state. I speak of this wholeness as being with presence, although frankly that is a redundancy. When we inhabit a space of wholeness, we are open to those around us as well as fully available to them. Being sensitively aware of others while being fully transparent to them is what I would call presence.

The most effective approach with which to meet violence is this wisdom, this wholeness with presence. Anything that promotes it reduces the net violence. Anything that interferes with it contributes to the net violence.

The elegance in this is that wisdom is what is ruptured through violence. Wisdom is the integral wholeness of the self and violence splits the self into fractured islands. Similarly, wholeness begets wholeness. When we share the space of wisdom with someone who has experienced violence, who is experiencing themselves as fractured islands of being, that space of wisdom is enough to build bridges among the islands, to begin to weave the net that may eventually knit the whole back together. Simply bringing wholeness with presence to the space of another is the most effective possible response to violence and its effects.

So the desire to respond effectively to violence brings us back to the feeling path. This desire engenders a practice, and the practice is to walk the feeling path toward wholeness, and to bring that wholeness to our engagement with violence.

What does this look like in real life? It looks like taking responsibility for the impact of violence on yourself. It looks like bringing awareness to your own reactivity around violent acts, embracing all parts of you which are stirred by those acts, inviting them toward their ideal, and embodying the creative tension between their reactions and their aspirations.

I remember a couple years ago, I was giving a series of classes for entrepreneurs, leading them through the mapping and moving process to deal with procrastination and other obstacles to business success. In one class, a woman sitting in the front row heckled me. I responded with overt solicitude while being super annoyed on the inside and seething for hours about it afterwards. A few weeks later I ran into her at a networking event where she proceeded to run me through one put-down after another. Again I was obsequious, practically groveling at her feet, and again I seethed for hours afterwards. Another woman in this networking group had a similar effect on me.

I recognized this as a reactive pattern of some kind that was keeping me from being present. Plus it felt really crappy. So I took a couple days to map and move it all. A few days later I attended another networking event. Both my nemeses were there! And I swear, it was like none of the previous interactions had ever happened. I was buddy-buddy with both of them, comfortable and friendly and real.

People experience similar things when they do the work with me. They'll clear a set, go home to visit their family of origin, and discover to their surprise that their mother has changed. She's no longer so critical of them and has stopped nagging! It's quite remarkable how clearing the patterns in yourself makes it so much more difficult for others around you to get the fuel they need to run their own patterns.

Working against violence isn't just about clearing your own patterns though. The practice of being a warrior for peace also looks like allying yourself with others similarly committed. It looks like a diligence in seeking out those splits with the help of others' feedback, and mending them with their support. It looks like reaching out to support others in your tribe doing the same.

Together, gradually and over time, we can build up our reserves of wisdom and bring ourselves more fully to the task of creating a peace that includes everyone. In this, it is important for us to share our journeys with one another. As we re-weave our wholeness from within, we can support and be supported by others doing the same. It is much easier to do this sacred work in community. In service to that, let me share with you a very simple practice you can do with the smallest community, you and one other person. I call it Being-With.

The Being-With Practice

Sit across from one another in whatever way feels most comfortable to you both. Take a moment to be quiet with one another and tune into yourselves.

One of you start. Complete the sentence, "Right now I am feeling...X." Keep it brief.

The other ask the mapping questions, starting with, "If you were to say the actual, felt experience of this 'X' was located..." Do not take notes. Simply be present with the answers. Allow yourself to witness your partner's feeling state. Perhaps you can "see" it, perhaps you can imagine what it might feel like. Allow yourself to be moved by what your partner shares.

When the mapping questions are complete, trade roles. The person who started asks, "And right now, what are you feeling?" Ask the mapping questions only. Do not go into the belief questions for this practice.

Trade roles, back and forth, allowing yourself to be present with one another's feeling, to be moved by one another. Continue for as long as you wish. Avoid lapsing into story. Do not use the moving questions. Simply be present with what is, with one another.

When you finish, you may want to talk about your experience. Share some shift or opening you experienced, and something you want to take away from your encounter.

This seems very simple, but I will tell you it is one of the most powerful ways I have ever experienced to cultivate the practice of wisdom and to experience wholeness with presence, in the presence of another.

You might do the Being-With practice with an ally to help yourself come back to your center after a difficult encounter out in the world. Or you might use Being-With to come back to center in your relationship with someone with whom you are experiencing some difficulty. This practice can help you step out of the story and see one another in your full humanity.

The more you cultivate your own wisdom practice, the more you will be able to engage with those who behave and communicate violently without experiencing violence to yourself. Violence feeds most voraciously on others' weaknesses, on those places inside which are already split. So the greater your own wholeness, the fewer parts of yourself are vulnerable to someone else's efforts to split you. And the greater your presence, less the person exhibiting a violent manner of being will be able to sustain their own inner split, and the less energy they will be able to generate toward their violent behavior. You will find that simply being present with someone in a human way can be enough to bring out their own deepest humanity.

I learned the basic principle of this a long time ago. In Edinburgh I picked up a job at an after hours club as a bouncer. Now I'm not a big guy. You would never look at me and say, "He looks like a bouncer. Har, har."

But there were some rough elements that frequented this club. And on a few of the nights I didn't work, there were serious fights, with knives and people getting hurt. But on the nights I worked, nothing ever happened.

My practice was to warmly greet each person who entered the club, looking them in the eye. I could spot the potential trouble agents as they walked in the door. Then I made sure to visit them throughout the night, stopping by to say hello, remind them of my presence, welcome them, make sure they were enjoying themselves.

Some nights I may have counseled one or two to curtail their drinking or ratchet down the rowdiness, but it was always with an attitude of respect. I treated them like an equal, and like I wanted them (and everyone else) to enjoy themselves. I made sure they felt seen by me.

My co-bouncers were quite different. There were a couple who were highly macho, overly testosteronized, get-in-your-face types. Most nights I had to manage them as well, to keep them from instigating their own trouble.

The most important ingredient to the quiet nights I had on the job was my presence and respect for everyone who walked in the door. Whether I was within sight or not, I was their companion for the night. I was beside them as a witness and an ally. And everybody had a good time.

Looking back, I have to be grateful nothing serious ever did happen. The part of me that was in charge in that job was the Reasonableness I've shared with you. I really don't know what might have happened if it hadn't been so effective, and if the Vicious Enforcer had been triggered to the surface. A scary thought.

It occurs to me that I might need to reassure some of you that I do not mean to say in any way that if you are in a state of presence, nobody will ever hurt you. Although I wish it were that easy, many people are so separated from their truth that they are indeed dangerous and can inflict great harm no matter what level of presence you inhabit. So you still need to use common sense and protect yourself in your normal ways.

One more story I'd like to share with you to illustrate the power of wholeness with presence in disarming violence. The greatest violence is that we do to ourselves. Any act of violence starts there. So ultimately our intent must be to stop it there.

When a client sits in my office to map the territory of their soul, they often encounter states which have long been in exile. Some of these states are intensely uncomfortable to them, and have been judged harshly. These are the states such as hate, shame, rage and despair. We get to them by removing their cover, clearing the camouflage one state at a time and inviting the hidden states to come forth.

When they do make it to the surface, my client will usually offer an awareness of the state in a very guarded or tentative way. These states have been under wraps for a reason, usually having to do with either driving the person to do things they feel bad about, or triggering someone else to punish or shame them for expressing it. And because they have been buried for so long, often times they have grown even more distorted than when they first went underground. Some can get pretty extreme.

Imagine my clients' surprise when I greet the revelation of this dark state with a genuine expression of glee! Most times I'm expecting to find the state or something like it. My experience enables me to see pretty clearly when a set of states is set up to defend the person from an intolerable central pivot like my Vicious Enforcer. So when we discover that pivot, I'm excited. I know that shifting this state will release a terrific amount of creative life force energy, and I am eager to discover the gifts it has to offer my client.

But my client has never had the experience of this part of themselves being welcomed with open arms and a big smile. It's disarming to them, and immensely exciting. When I welcome this part of them, they can take that on for themselves. They can enter the space of being open to this hidden part, of welcoming it, embracing it. And simply having that shift in attitude is wonderfully healing.

Imagine bringing this attitude to all your interactions. Imagine never buying into the smoke screens, the manipulations, the judgments of others because you hold an overarching frame of curiosity about what gifts these behaviors are hiding. Imagine seeing the ultimate good in every person with whom you interact. How might that change your experience of violence in the world? How might that help shift the expression of violence in the first place?

Like much of what I am sharing with you, this is an ideal. It is something for us all to aspire to. I'm not there yet myself. None of us are. But I am on the path, the feeling path, and now so are you.

The path to wisdom is a journey. None of us will fully arrive until all of us do. Until that sunny day we are blessedly stuck in the land of in-between, where human life is messy and uncertain, and we will never quite get it perfectly right no matter how many sublime moments we might enjoy. On this journey there is much to learn for all of us, from all the rest of us. Let's get busy!

Facilitating communal wholeness

What can we learn from the ground we've covered so far, about how to bring the practices of wisdom into our engagement with groups, organizations and communities? Can we extend the practices that help us cultivate wholeness with presence within ourselves, to doing the same for small or large groups of people at once? I believe we can.

Let's go back to basics. First in this endeavor, we seek wholeness with presence, which we can define more generally in the following way:

1. All parts (paths/people/groups) are in transparent communication with all other parts. No part is divided from the rest or opposed to any others.

2. We hold sensitive awareness of the other while remaining transparent to the other, allowing influence and interconnection to emerge organically between self and other in both directions, giving and receiving.

Second, we seek to cultivate the vector of creation by engaging the three simple practices of the feeling path:

1. Embrace what is.

2. Invite what wants to be.

3. Embody the difference.

Within an individual, optimal aliveness emerges when we free up the feeling paths for unhindered responsiveness. We can apply this principle to groups as well. Every group has multiple "sticking points" and areas of unconsciousness. In the same way as an individual gets locked into dysfunctional configurations of feeling paths, collections of individuals can get locked into dysfunctional patterns of interacting that stifle the capacity to respond creatively to challenges. Freeing these stuck places can help the group return to optimal functioning.

I'm going to lead you through a rough envisioning of what it might look like to manage a group process that cultivates wisdom among members and within the group as a whole. To do so I will offer elements which can be practiced individually or combined for greater effectiveness. Every situation is unique and would best be served by a different combination of these elements. It is unlikely you will ever be in a situation where it would be best to use them all. Yet in any situation, no matter what your role, you will be able to bring at least one element which adds to the wisdom of the group.

The various elements I present are adapted from different sources. Most have been used in multiple forms in more than one method of group learning or facilitation practice over the years. I invite you to research Jim Rough's Dynamic Facilitation at tobe.net and look to The Change Handbook (Second Edition) by Peggy Holman, Tom Devane, and Steven Cady for further ideas. There are great people doing great work with these various whole systems change methods. What I'm offering here is a new framework within which to make choices about how to apply these methods in particular ways that stimulate creative wisdom in any group.

Personal wholeness with presence

Although what I share here is a model of facilitation for group collaboration, you don't need to be a designated facilitator to bring the creative approach into any meeting in which you are a participant. One of the best ways to do so is through your own presence. A single person showing up with clear presence, able to speak truth and reveal themselves as a whole human being, can do wonders for the energy and outcomes of any group.

As you read through the following elements of creative engagement, ask yourself how you might bring that element into your participation as a member of a group. Doing so, you will invite a resonance with others in the group. You will model an example of a more whole way of participating and inspire others to do the same. Even in meetings locked down by rigid facilitation and no opportunity for engagement, simply holding an air of welcoming appreciation for and curiosity about the gifts which remain hidden can breathe life into the meeting. You'd be surprised at how much facilitation you can do from the back of a room.

From the front of a room, as a designated facilitator, wholeness with presence can work magic for a group. Let me share a particular vision of this with you.

Sixteen years ago when I was working with the dancer, we were exploring how to shape a landscape of emotion on the stage. Her experience was with Merce Cunningham and other modern choreographers in New

York City, and she had powerfully refined control of her body. But we were going for something beyond control.

When I was in Montana I had acted in a few community theater productions under an excellent director by the name of Jane Fellows. It was there that I began experimenting with the power of mental imagery to connect with an audience. In one of my most compelling scenes, I was able to convey intense inner turmoil despite being catatonic, unable to move or speak. People came up to me afterward to tell me how freaked out they were by that moment.

The play was "The Boys Next Door," and my character lived in a half way house for mentally ill men. His father had been hatefully abusive, and the scene I mentioned was in the mental hospital when his father came to visit. I had been experimenting with enlarging my mental imagery to fill the actual space on stage and in the audience, and for this one I took it to the max. Of course I had some raw material of my own, but I exaggerated the content, expanded the scale, and hooked the imagery into strong emotional states of fear and wanting to escape from the confining trap of my body. In that moment, not only did I experience a heightening of the emotions of my character, but I also felt a kind of strong circuit linking me to the audience through my imagery.

It is easy to interpret this with the idea that thoughts occupy space and are made of some kind of energy we can perceive. But I don't think we need to go there. (I'm a great fan of the good friar William of Ockham.)

Let me remind you that that feeling states are constructed of the raw material of our somatosensory capacity for representing the materiality of our bodies and environments. When we experience strong feeling states, we are immersed in a virtual world which to our minds is only somewhat different from the ground we stand on or the air we draw into our noses. Our entire body responds to this virtual world, no differently than how we walk differently on sand than we do on tarmac. Every muscle, every breath, every movement, the movement patterns of our eyes and faces – every microscopic element of our living body responds to this virtual construction.

I believe as social beings we are exquisitely attuned to one another's inner worlds through the micro signals of our body movements. And I believe we put even more energy of focused attention on reading someone who is in front of a group of which we are a part. There is something natural, instinctive, about giving attention to someone in the spatial position of leader. Perhaps it is because in the past, the leader's communications had much to do with the survival of the group. Or because they have power to influence our lives for good or ill. So there is a certain urgency to reading this individual. As an actor on state, I was in that position, and I believe that even though on a gross level I was not moving, the audience was able to read my micro-movements and through their own empathic capacity to feel what I was feeling.

Let's return to the dancer. I began to teach her how to work with the inner, felt sense of her feeling states as the driver for her movement. We mapped one of her destination states, "stand tall," as a kind of energetic circulation between her and the space behind her audience, where she imagined those people she loved standing.

The difference was dramatic. When she danced from her normal super-control place, I felt interested in the way I am fascinated by a complex object. But when she switched the origin of her movement to this inner state, I was swept into her dance. I could feel my own body respond with tiny little movements as if I had become her.

But something odd happened when she turned to the side. It was as if a switch flipped, and she was once again just a beautifully moving body. When I asked her about her inner experience, it turned out the circulating energy went out in a narrow band in front of her. When she turned to the side, the band of energy went with her, off to the side, leaving me high and dry. In my reading her body, I could no longer feel myself included so integrally in her dance.

We worked with the structure of her inner state, and she devised a way to send the band of energy rotating around her like a lighthouse beacon. It worked wonderfully, and from that point on I felt connected to her dance even if she turned her back to me. We were getting somewhere!

This was exciting work. The potential is great for teaching a natural charisma that goes way beyond the wooden gesture-scripting so common among highly-coached public speakers. You can't fake this stuff. You have to be coming from a genuine place inside, a place that is written all over your most microscopic movements and intonations, in order to fully connect with an audience.

You need to apply these insights to your work as a facilitator. As facilitator, you are occupying a structural position of leadership, whether or not you hold any actual power of leadership in the group outside the meeting. In this position, your group is more strongly attuned to the subtle signals of your presence.

The most important quality you can bring to your presence as facilitator is congruence. Congruence refers to the outward manifestation of an inner wholeness. It exists when every word, every gesture, every movement, every intonation is in intimate and harmonious relationship with every other one.

Why is congruence so important in facilitation? When we stand in the position of facilitator, our energy is heightened through the attention of the group. Simultaneously, the group's awareness is heightened through the position of your leadership. So any inner splits you hold will become magnified. When you are communicating one thing through your words, for example, yet the message of your body says something else, the audience will know this. And whether they can articulate their awareness or not, they will not fully trust you. In not fully trusting you, they will not bring their full selves to the engagement.

At the same time, we can also say that when you step in front of the room with a strong inner wholeness, and you intentionally magnify that wholeness through your presence, fully occupying the space of the room, you wield a great power for good. Your wholeness with presence acts as a resonator. Others are implicitly invited to join you there, to resolve their inner splits as they engage with the group, and to work to bridge their outer differences as well.

Let me give you a visual example to help you see what I'm talking about. Here is a composite illustration of the set of ideal states I shared with you earlier, the Liberation set.

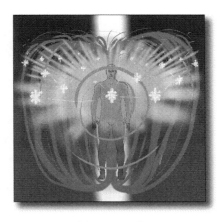

The scale on this is a little off. Imagine I'm experiencing those stars as points of light inside of everyone in the room. Imagine the glow and the flow fill the entire space. Can you see how powerful this is, if this is what I am experiencing as I stand in front of the room to facilitate your group? Can you see how every movement, every gesture, every intonation would be influenced by the bigness of my inner experience and its inclusion of you in the power of it? Can you see how you might sense that and how your awareness would create a more compelling invitation for you to bring your own "big self" to the table?

Put some attention on this. It may be the most important dimension of your facilitation, with respect to actually creating valuable outcomes. Do your personal work before the meeting. Make sure when you enter the room you are clear, whole, and present, fully available to serve the needs of the group.

In addition, consider engaging in some kind of movement practice, preferably an improvisational one. So many of us are locked into body patterns which restrict our expressiveness. As facilitators, we want a seamless transparency between what is inside and what the body is able to express. Various kinds of dance and movement practices can help develop that open channel for expression. (One I can recommend wholeheartedly is Soul Motion. Learn more at SoulMotion.com.)

The art of strong facilitation

Because the planning and problem solving modes are so dominant as to be automatic whenever groups convene to address an issue, breaking the mold and applying the new creative approach requires strong facilitation. Your job as facilitator will be to model wholeness with presence while managing the three simple practices to set up the vector of creation. Your job will also be, paradoxically, to stay out of the way, supporting the vector in emerging wholly from the group and leading the group in its own direction. Let's look at the many methods you can apply to this endeavor.

Setting things up

Good facilitation begins before the actual meeting. The facilitator should establish a relationship with key stakeholders of the group, and interview them to find out what the issues are.

Then, reaching out to let people know about the upcoming meeting(s) is an opportunity to invite the process to begin. Asking people to reflect on their experience, their needs, their hopes and intentions can prepare them to get the most out of the meeting and contribute the most to it. Questions like these can help:

- What is working for you? What is not?

- What do you see is working for the group? What is not?

- If you were in charge, what would you change?

- How are you included in the life of the group? How are you not included?

Come up with questions of your own drawn from the conversations with the meeting organizers.

Plan for a meeting space that is comfortable for real people. Natural lighting, windows, comfortable seating, good ventilation, and easy access to both facilities and nourishment – pay attention to these things within the constraints of what is available to the group.

When it comes time for the actual meeting, set up the space for optimal interaction depending on what methods you're planning to use. Make the space comfortable with small touches of the natural world like flowers or contributions like artwork from people in the group. As people arrive, welcome them and assist them in getting oriented to the space.

The zone of creation

The meeting itself is an opportunity to step out of standard planning and problem solving frameworks into a fully creative mode. As facilitator, you can use a few structures to help with that. I'm going to draw on Jim Rough's Dynamic Facilitation as the inspiration for one structure which can help you.

This structure sets up a "zone of creation." (My term, not Jim's.) This is an area of the room into which contributions are made, upon which the attention of participants is focused. This zone takes on a creative energy as participants maintain their focus while envisioning what they want to create. It serves as a field of interaction within which all the contributions of the group intermingle and out of which emerge novel combinations. The field is a creative soup, and all the ingredients brought by participants are placed into the pot to cook together.

Flip charts serve to focus attention, and the seating arrangement can support that focus. One of the best seating arrangements for focused, creative dialogue is a horseshoe. This gives each participant equal positioning relative to the zone of creation and eliminates hierarchy. It also provides easy access for the facilitator to step into the open space of the horseshoe to guide focus into the zone rather than enabling people to lose that focus in crosstalk.

At the focus point, you will set up three flip charts. These flip charts take on the quality of a magnetic field, collecting all the contributions of the members, drawing all input to one place where relationships among ideas and concerns can become apparent and patterns can emerge for everyone.

The three flip charts each have a specific function:

- The first chart is headed "Vision/Values/Assets." On this chart you will write statements of what people want, what they value, what they have.

- The second chart is headed "Concerns." On this chart you will write statements of what is perceived to be currently not working or expected not to work.

- The third chart is headed "Solutions." On this chart you will write statements of concrete ways to address the concerns, advance the vision, and uphold the values.

Another way to set this up is with two flip charts and one large wall banner. The wall banner can hold the combined Vision, Values, and Assets categories, and can be drawn out as a mind map, with three major branches from the center and contributions attached to these nodes. If you do this, keep the Concerns and Solutions as separate charts.

During the meeting, your job as the facilitator is to:

- Keep the conversation focused toward the flip charts, stepping into the flow of any crosstalk to bring attention back to the front.

- Manage the sequence of contributors, acknowledging those who are waiting to speak and making sure all voices get heard, even the most quiet and hesitant ones.

- Accurately capture people's words on the appropriate charts as they make their contributions. Number contributions sequentially and move filled chart papers to a visible wall nearby.

- Invite people to elaborate on partial contributions, letting them know that what they really think is welcome.

- Reflect people's words back as you understand them, making sure they mean what they have said and giving them an opportunity to clarify what you write on the chart.

- Manage the charts themselves. (You might ask for help with this.) When a chart fills up, remove it from the easel and hang it in a place, perhaps on a nearby wall, where everyone can easily continue to refer to it.

- Maintain wholeness with presence, welcoming with curiosity each new contribution, offering every participant equal respect and opportunity.

At the beginning of the meeting, let people know what to expect and how you will be facilitating. You might open the conversation by asking the following questions:

What is the reality of this group at this time? And what is your intention?

This is just one starting place. Almost any will do. What is important is that from the outset you engage your own wholeness and support the three simple practices of the feeling path. Doing so will support the emergence of the group's evolving identity and direction.

Embracing all voices

Just as we seek to include all feeling states when we are mapping a set responsible for driving a dysfunctional pattern, we seek to include all points of view, all needs, all desires in the conversation with a group. This supports our practice of embracing what is.

Sometimes we have only to receive what is freely given to embrace all the voices in the room. Other times the group will benefit from more active solicitation of voices which haven't been heard yet. We can take this a step further by asking those in the room if there are any voices not included in the room. Sometimes the group's actions affect those in a wider community, and the group can benefit by including the voices of those affected people, even if only by proxy. Sometimes, if the group's process stretches over more than one meeting, time between meetings can be used to interview some of those affected people in order to include their voices more authentically. And sometimes we need to go even further than this, to find ways to give voice to those who might be unable to speak for themselves – small children for example, or wildlife.

Within the meeting, as each person speaks, protect their ownership of the floor. Step between participants speaking to one another across the horseshoe, inviting focus back to the zone of creation at the front of the room. Acknowledge someone who wants to chime in, letting them know they will have their opportunity, but stay with the current contributor until they feel complete.

Embracing someone's voice is not a passive act of recording what they say. In fact, it helps greatly when you show genuine interest and curiosity. You want to not only hear their surface words, but the deeper intention beneath them. To do this it can help to do what Jim Rough calls "we-flection."

Jim describes we-flection as "brain on loan." It is as if you are lending your brain to the speaker, with the sole purpose of grasping the most complete meaning and intention in what they are saying. You listen with your whole body, and you listen to the spaces between the words.

As you do this you find yourself seeking the essence of what they are saying, and reaching to meld that essence with their spoken words and your own understanding. You put words to your understanding in simple, direct statements of fact, with an open pause after each statement which invites further input. These we-flection statements take the form of "You X." Let's take an example.

Your participant speaks at length about a concern that management is not taking the needs of the line workers into account. She tells a story about a time when the workers spoke up about supplies being short and their productivity being compromised as a result. But the just-in-time ordering system was never adjusted, and their productivity continued to fall short of company goals, eliminating any opportunity for bonus pay.

As the facilitator, you might say to the speaker, "In the past, workers did not have enough supplies to meet company quotas. You're concerned that might continue."

She responds, "Yes, but I want us to do things differently."

You say, "You want to make line workers get what they need to do their best work."

She says enthusiastically, "Yes!" And you know you've got it. You will capture these statements in the appropriate places on the charts. Knowledge of the past goes in the Assets category. The concern goes on the Concerns chart. Perhaps after some further we-flection it might be worded, "I'm concerned workers won't get enough supplies to meet productivity goals." And the statement of a desired future gets reworded, "How to make sure line workers get what they need to do their best work" and written under the Vision category.

At this point, you are poised to set in motion the Solutions/Concerns vortex which will be described in a few pages.

Embracing all of current reality

In addition to welcoming all voices, all people, all opinions, it is equally important to welcome all information reflecting on the current state of reality for the group. In particular this means directing focus toward what is working as well as what is not. It means identifying assets as well as liabilities. It means recognizing current habits and practices, current momentum in certain directions, and current investments and commitments.

Each group or subgroup will have a particular disposition to focus on positives versus negatives. Make sure this focus is balanced out by inviting participants to talk about the opposite focus as well. The charts can help you manage this process. The division of categories of the charts is designed to welcome both positive and negative articulations of each.

The first chart covers three categories which can be thought of in part as defining the identity of the group: Vision, Values, and Assets. It is OK to break these three out into separate charts. Most of the notes activity tends to happen on the Solutions and Concerns charts, though. Combining Vision, Values and Assets into one chart can help you conserve space and get by with three chart easels instead of five. You might choose to assign items for each category a unique color to help track as you collect your notes.

The charts: Vision

The Vision category holds statements articulating what a group participant wants or does not want. These are statements reflecting a desired reality which is not yet present. In order to support these statements feeding into the others, creating synergy among the charts, it can be helpful to structure the statements you write on the Visions chart as "How to… X." Here are a few examples to help you see the range of possibilities.

- How to respond to police profiling in our community.
- How to get more people involved in doing the work of our volunteer organization.
- How to stop climate change.

Try to break the Vision statements into small enough chunks so that each statement zooms in on one particular element of the desired reality. Take the following example as one which combines two elements:

- "How to increase employee satisfaction while strengthening our business."

In this example, we have two elements with a relationship that is presupposed. There is an implicit concern in this statement that increasing employee satisfaction could result in weakening the business. Separating these elements into two statements can help the group bring their concerns to the foreground so they can more easily be articulated and addressed.

Also avoid embedding a solution into a Vision statement. Here's an example which does that:

- How to raise money to fix our common house roof.

The Vision is "How to fix our roof." One solution might be to raise money in some way, but it may not be the only solution. Leave the door open. If someone says, "We need to raise money to fix our common house roof," break the statement into two, with one part on the Vision chart and one on the Solutions chart.

The charts: Values

Just as important as the "what" of any vision statement is the "why." Implicit in every statement of vision are specific Values. Asking participants to articulate those Values helps the entire group cohere.

Sometimes a Values statement by one participant brings up competing Values for another. Be alert for this and welcome it. Discussion of Values can go a long way to promoting more successful resolutions of group challenges.

We can also identify implicit Values in statements of Solutions and Concerns. Be alert for these, and if you discern underlying Values that may not have been articulated, ask questions to elicit a relevant Values statement. One of the best ways to elicit Values from another statement is to ask the question, "What is important to you about that?"

The charts: Assets

The Assets category is a collection bucket for a wide variety of participant contributions.

- Knowledge: Some relevant X is true according to Y.

- Experience: We did X and it worked or didn't work.

- Resources: We have, or have access to X.

- Liabilities: We owe or must compensate for X.

- Alignments: We are already doing X which supports or obstructs Vision Y or Solution Z.

Almost any contribution that does not clearly fall into one of the other categories can go here. Phrase the statement in terms of a positive or negative asset for the group. This category is especially important in holding the capacity to welcome and honor every participant contribution. There is nothing we can't include in the ongoing conversation notes.

The charts: Concerns

The Concerns chart is where to place expressions of things that could go wrong or anticipations of unwanted results. This is where to direct the focus of contributions arising from reactive states of fear, frustration, opposition, scarcity, loss, and the like. We want to welcome these expressions and give them visible form. So it is important to capture as closely as possible the essence if not the exact wording of what the participant says, and to confirm that what you write is what they intend.

It is rare in many organizational or community cultures for concerns to be welcomed so eagerly. When the facilitator holds an open space in the zone of creation to receive all concerns, this communicates even more strongly that all voices are embraced. It may take a little time to demonstrate this welcome attitude convincingly enough for the most jaded participants to finally accept that their input is also welcome. When that happens, though, you have entered hallowed ground, and magic can happen.

The charts: Solutions

The Solutions chart is the vessel into which the facilitator pours all contributions of what can be done to address voiced concerns, carry out stated visions, and express named values. The Solutions chart is where the creative spark gets ignited.

The facilitator should actively seek that ignition. Prime the pump. Ask directly, after someone has voiced a concern or a vision, "How would you recommend we do this? If you were emperor for a day, what would you have us do?" Then get out of the way!

Some might wonder at the choice of terminology. If we are trying to go beyond a problem solving mentality, why are we using the heading Solutions for this chart? The reason for this is twofold. First, the term speaks to how people already think of their challenges, and provides an easy bridge to where people are standing at the beginning of the process. Second, the word Solutions stands in dynamic juxtaposition to the word Concerns. We want to use that juxtaposition to power the Solutions/Concerns Vortex, one of the most powerful engines for creative collaboration ever devised.

The Solutions/Concerns Vortex

Everybody has a solution to the problems they face. Everybody has concerns about other people's solutions to the same problems. Few people have had an opportunity to give voice to their solutions and concerns in a public space, to really have their ideas heard and considered with respect. When you open the door to that, you unleash a great creative force.

For most people, the solutions and concerns they hold privately stand as barriers to creativity and collaboration. These private ideas lock entire belief and perceptual systems in place. People's thoughts tend to revolve around and around the ways they would fix things or why the way others want to fix things won't work. Consequently they don't pay much attention to what is actually going on, and they don't listen to other people.

When we actively invite their biggest solutions and concerns, we give them an opportunity to lay down these burdens. Jim calls it the purge and considers it the most important ingredient in successful dynamic facilitation. When a participant has laid down the burden of habitual ways of thinking about the challenges facing the group, they suddenly have open space in their mind to consider the big picture, to hear other ideas, to enter a space of creativity.

This happens in the context of an ongoing visual recording of everyone's ideas. So when someone purges, they suddenly become open to hearing/ reading what the guy a half hour ago said. Two dots connect for the first time, an insight comes forth, and a great excitement of possibility rises for everyone.

Sometimes the breakthrough leads to truly creative ideas for achieving the group's mission. Sometimes it results in an evolution of the group's vision or values. In either case, a breakthrough represents a the convergence of What Is with What Wants to Be in a way which drives the vector of creation forward. It's exciting to be a part of it.

Breakthroughs are not limited to the person doing the purge. Often one person gives voice to solutions that others may also have been holding, and many people experience their own purge vicariously. Other times the solutions offered directly conflict with the solutions others hold, setting up concerns and solution contributions of their own. In these sessions, the energy can build quite high as people encounter and release their various sticking points.

When working with feeling states, we discover that the most recalcitrant, obstructive, destructive "voices" in any system have within them a powerful force for positive change. They are driven by an ideal which has been thwarted, and when embraced and invited to reveal their true nature, they show up with bold new contributions to our highest good. Similarly, we will find this true for any social system in which we find ourselves.

Throughout this purging and breakthrough process, what happens is a gradual increase in the group's total self awareness. The reality of the group, with its different perspectives and opinions, its different experiences and needs, comes forward to be poured into the synthesizing zone of creation held by the facilitator. The more thoroughly and authentically the facilitator holds the space of embracing all voices, the more completely the truth of the group as it is, and as it is becoming, emerges.

An evolving identity

Each group has a unique identity. Usually this identity is largely obscured. Through the dynamic facilitation, particularly the purges that happen in the tight feedback loop between Concerns and Solutions, the group's identity makes itself known to all members.

To foster this emerging awareness, the facilitator can at times ask for specific articulation of Values as they are held implicit in the concerns and solutions offered. These get captured on the VVA chart, along with discoveries of Assets: knowledge, experiences, and resources owned by and available to the group.

As the group becomes more accurately aware of itself, its intention is likely to evolve. The facilitator from time to time should stop to check in about the Vision. This is the best, in-the-moment articulation of What Wants to Be.

The three of these together, Vision, Values, and Assets comprise the emerging group identity. Together they become "who we are," and serve to guide everything that emerges in the Harvesting phase of the facilitation.

The dynamic between the VVA and Solutions charts is most important to this step of inviting What Wants to Be to reveal itself. As the energy of the group is consolidated and harmonized through purges elicited in the dynamic feedback between Concerns and Solutions, it becomes available for collective discovery and creation. Participants will find themselves experiencing breakthroughs of various forms. Here are several types you will experience in your facilitation:

- Aha! What we're <u>really</u> wanting is X, not Y as we originally thought. Breakthrough Vision re-orients the group to a new desired reality.

- Aha! What's <u>really</u> important to us is A, not B as we originally thought. Breakthrough Values re-orient the group to new purpose and priorities.

- Aha! The path that best serves us is M, not N as we had been planning. Breakthrough Solutions re-orient the group to new next steps previously unseen or dismissed.

Identity is a fluid quality. The group identity exists beyond any member's ideas of it, yet it is partly constructed of those ideas. As the group's vision, values, and actions evolve, the identity of the group can be said to evolve as well.

This is the nature of the creative approach. It frees us from the impossible task of ascertaining "reality," and allows us to put our energy into collaboratively co-creating new, emergent realities. A further note: approaching things this way is immense fun, and everyone who is privileged to participate in such a process comes away with raised hopes not just for themselves and their group, but for humanity as a whole. Exciting!

Another aspect of this emergence is the dual relationship of becoming that characterizes the second practice of the feeling path. In an individual, as we invite a reactive feeling state to reveal its ideal, it becomes that ideal. In the same way, as we invite the group to reveal its emerging identity, its What Wants to Be, it becomes that. There is no invitation without simultaneous becoming. We are not doing a different form of planning or strategic visioning here. As the vision, values, and solutions of the group emerge, the group itself is emerging. The What Wants to Be becomes What Is almost as soon as it is invited.

Managing creative polarities

The creative approach thrives on dynamic movement through the polarities of perspective, scope, direction, activity, and difference. An excellent facilitator will manage movement between these key polarities by using various structures inviting participants to shift their attention throughout the conversational landscape to maximize creativity.

Solo, small group, big group

One creative polarity which yields big results when well managed is that between the individual or private and the large group or public experience. People tend to bring a different Surface Self configuration to public engagement with a group than the one they apply in private moments. If possible, provide a spectrum of opportunities for each person to integrate their participation in the group with both sides of the polarity.

You can do so with the simplest of structures, merely stopping for ten minutes every hour or two of group conversation, to allow people to drop into their own thoughts, perhaps to journal or reflect in ways they find most helpful. Then invite them to contribute what they've discovered when you come back to the full group.

Somewhere in between the private and public is the personal. When the group is large enough that not everyone gets an opportunity to speak, you'll benefit from breaking things into small group conversations from time to time. For participants, having the opportunity to give voice to something they've been thinking privately helps clear the space for listening, clarify their own thoughts, and validate their engagement in the group. After a small group session, invite people to contribute any discoveries when you come back to the full group.

Think of these structures as opportunities for breathing. Going back and forth between private, personal, and public processing stirs the thoughts and ideas while giving people the experience of including more of themselves in the group. Each person will have a richer experience and be able to bring that richness to their participation. As a result, everyone benefits.

Small scope, big scope

This polarity is almost never considered, but can be fruitful to engage. Where are you drawing the boundary between inside and outside of the group? Every group is made of individual members. You can take some time to narrow down your perspective and take into consideration the effects of your group's activities on any individual.

Every group is also, as a whole, a member of a larger ecology of groups, organizations, and communities. We can extend that to include the biome, the planet, or even hypothetically the entire universe if that seemed useful. Take some time to open up your definition of your group to encompass some of the group's context. How does that change things? What else should be considered? Who else is impacted by your decisions?

Divergence and convergence

At its most basic, the creative process proceeds through cycles of divergence and convergence. We open up to unconsidered possibilities, investigate new options, consider alternate information, seek tangential opportunities. We throw the net wide, almost indiscriminately, not knowing what we might catch.

As a facilitator, you can encourage divergence activities simply by directing the focus of conversation. You can ask divergent questions such as:

- What else is true?

- Who else might be affected?

- What are other people doing in your organization that seems to have nothing to do with us?

- What are some possible unexpected consequences if we take this action?

- What other resources do we have, even those which seem unrelated?

You might conduct a standard brainstorming session, asking for ideas and capturing them all without censorship. Or you might introduce activities which bring in a tangential modality as a way to engage the topic from a different angle. Ask your participants to write a poem about their solution, or collaborate on a sketch, or go on a treasure hunt on the nearby meeting place grounds. Any of these breaks from a narrow focus will inject new energy and aliveness into the group's perspectives.

Then we draw the net in, to see what we've caught and pick out the treasures we find. In convergence activities we are looking for concrete results. We're making decisions, judgments, assessments, interpretations. We're narrowing down the field and choosing a specific path forward.

If you've been brainstorming, you might ask the group to choose three ideas to move forward with, then assign specific people to take next steps with those ideas before the next meeting. If you've traveled through a different modality, you might ask the group to draw their learnings from their explorations. What have you discovered? How can you apply that to the challenge at hand? What solutions does that suggest?

Action and reflection

Individuals naturally learn and change through cycles of action in the world followed by reflection about the experience of that action. So do groups. How can you support this natural cycle at all levels of the group engagement?

Reflection aims the vector of creation. It is the time we take to fully bring simultaneously into awareness What Is and What Wants to Be, so that the vector can take on its natural orientation. Our awareness is limited, and whatever we can do to augment its limitations, to bring a more complete attention to the project, the more successful our engagement will be.

I've already talked about one approach to reflection, providing private time for individuals in the context of the group. I invite you to consider various doses of this kind of reflection, from 60-second pauses in the middle of a group activity on one end to the days or weeks that might pass between scheduled meetings.

We may think at times of reflection as a passive state. However, consider these twin purposes of reflection.

- To provide space for the soup of ideas, impressions and experience to recombine in novel ways, stimulating insight and creativity.

- To assimilate our experiences so they weave connections to more parts of ourselves, deepening their meaning and relevance to our lives.

In recognizing these purposes, we can more easily design activities which support them. Here are a few to consider.

- Journaling with specific, guiding questions. Use questions relating experience to values, ideas to purpose, expectations to history. Explicitly inviting connections can prime those connections both during the activity and at other quiet times.

- Partner listening sessions, where one partners trade off the role of "we-flector" in the way described earlier, with no intention but to provide the "brain on loan" in making meaning and coming to deeper understanding.

- Expressive arts activities, where people are provided support for integrating their experiences through their chosen media.

- Physical activities such as a slow walk, or carrying out chores in silence.

- Providing meditation gems: brief questions which invite connections. One such question might be, "What matters?" Another, "Why now?" Another, "What's next?"

- Watch a movie or read a story. What does this story have to say to you about your challenge? What might one of the characters do in your situation?

What ideas do you have for ways to focus reflection time effectively?

The complement to reflection is action. Without action, there's not so much to reflect on. Action drives the vector of creation; it gives the vector wings, or legs, or an engine, (pick your preferred metaphor). The vector between What Is and What Wants to Be goes nowhere without a commitment to action.

Some actions are designed to create, to move the vector forward. Others are chosen to gather more information, to test ideas or models, to challenge reality in a particularly useful way. Freely adapt your cycles of action to meet the needs of your group's ongoing process.

Along these lines, we can recognize that action is defined by its relationship to reflection. Anything we do, any engagement of any kind changes current reality. We can accept this when we include ourselves in what we mean by "reality." Simply sitting, quiet, allowing the natural percolations of our inner feeling and imagery changes us. Because we are integral to the reality in which we participate, when we change, our world changes. Simply doing nothing, we are in action. Simply doing nothing, we create our world.

When we look at it this way, we can see that the action/reflection cycle simply moves the loom of creation from the outer surface to the inner and back again. But we are weaving a möbius strip; there is no separation between the inner and outer surfaces of our reality. We can not in any moment cease our creative activity.

Because of this, we define the edges of action by the periods of reflection we choose to take. Reflection itself can be an action, if we step back to make meaning of our meaning-making. So what does this mean in practical terms?

Understanding this crucial relationship between action and reflection, and the importance of cycling between them in order to serve the vector of creation, we can choose to engage in reflection more freely. In so many of our collective engagements, we focus on getting things done and rarely take a moment to pause. We give in to the illusion of pressure to accomplish one thing or another – it's important! And we neglect to care for our own wholeness. In forgetting the importance of our individual and collective wholeness, we lose our wisdom and end up taking actions that have a net negative effect, undermining our most treasured values and sabotaging our visions.

In this way of creation, this way of wholeness and wisdom, we escape that fate by maintaining a balance between the inner and outer weave. We remain in service to the emerging creation of our group in relation to each individual and to the broader context in which we operate. We find ourselves serving the grand vector of creation, and having a most humbling and thrilling experience.

On a final note on action and reflection, I want to strongly advocate for you to consider the group's ongoing existence outside of whatever meetings you may facilitate. The action and reflection cycles can continue unabated between meetings. Formally acknowledging the between time and providing a structure for feedback will keep people engaged in the group's ongoing evolution. Make sure there is clear accountability for who will conduct what actions, and how they will capture the results of their activity. Provide channels for collecting results of reflection as well, and facilitate ongoing meaning-making through small-group meetings, teleconference gatherings, online forums, or other structures to keep the learning and discovery process alive. Do this and each meeting will build on the last, as the group's identity and vision become stronger and their actions in the world become more effective.

Facilitating breakthroughs

In the kind of creative engagement I am advocating here, participants individually and groups as a whole will find their edges pretty quickly. People will find themselves touching on uncomfortable feelings or hidden beliefs. Out of these discomforts, groups will find themselves engaging in habitual behaviors designing to lock things down and prevent change.

The Solutions/Concerns Vortex is one of the most powerful means to break through these sticking places. But I want to suggest two more techniques that can ease the transition from old patterns to new possibilities.

Mapping and moving

As we know from earlier in the book, when people find themselves locked into defensive, compensatory patterns of perception, belief, and behavior, these patterns are held in place by reactive feeling states. What better way to free these reactive states than mapping and moving?

Mapping and moving with a group is a little different from working with an individual. As the facilitator, you ask the questions generically, almost exactly as they are written in the book here. You offer explicit permission for anyone to stop the process along the way to ask a question or request more direct facilitation. But you engage everyone at once, and each person goes through the process privately, taking their own notes, doing their own drawings.

You'll want to start with a brief moment of reflection. Share with the group about the dynamic you observed, whether it's a pattern of communication or escalated tension or whatever. Acknowledge that each person is having their own experience and affirm that everyone has something very important to contribute to the group's discovery process. Invite them to participate in this process as a way to get greater clarity for themselves about exactly what is most important to them, so they can be more effective both in getting their needs met and serving the group.

Have participants reflect on their current experience, maybe the past few minutes or even hours. Ask them what stands out for them personally about where they feel stuck or frustrated or whatever is most heightened in their experience. Ask them to name two or three feeling states that are most alive for them just now. Have them choose the one state that feels to them like it is making it difficult to contribute their greatest wisdom. Ask them to take that state through the mapping and moving process.

In mapping the state, ask the beliefs questions with specific reference to the situation in the meeting and to the group as a whole. Do this also in asking the beliefs questions after moving to the ideal state. Ask particularly about what this new state has to offer in the way of perspective, insight, or other contribution to what is going on for them in the meeting.

When you finish a mapping and moving session, first give people an opportunity to share their experience in very small groups of 2-4 people. Then open back into the large group to pick up where you left off, and invite people to bring their new insights to the conversation.

At all times throughout this practice, give explicit permission not to participate. This needs to be a voluntary opportunity for someone to choose if and only if they wish to do so. After the first time through this, anyone who chose to hold back is likely to see the results other people experienced. They are more likely to choose to participate in the next round if there is one. And even if there isn't another round, the hold-outs will also be affected by the shift in states and perspective of those who did participate.

In the context of an ongoing session, this mapping and moving exercise can be done in shortened form. If you like, don't even bother having people take notes, just have them sit quietly and follow your guidance. Use only a few of the image parameters, perhaps location, substance and temperature. You should be able to facilitate a felt shift in just five or ten minutes, and then simply return to what you were doing.

The recursive want exercise

Here's another exercise you will find incredibly powerful for breaking through obstacles which prevent successful collaboration. I learned the ancestor of this exercise from Connirae Andreas of NLP Comprehensive, and you can find more extensive instruction in her book Core Transformation.

Groups can often get locked into antagonistic clashes based on conflicting outcomes. One subgroup wants A, another wants B. Of course, the Solutions/Concerns Vortex is a powerful way to slide right past these lockdowns, but let's look at another way to free things up.

When I want something, that specific outcome is a surface means to an end. Ultimately, that end is a state of wholeness. It's what we all want, and every specific desire comes back to fulfilling that most basic need. How do we invite people to reconnect to the need for wholeness underlying their conflicting desires? Here's how it works. You can do this either by facilitating the process for the entire group, each member of which will go through the exercise privately under your guidance. Or you can have people pair up to do the exercise with one another.

Start by having people name or write down what they most want in the context of the current group engagement. It can be in the form, "I want X" or whatever other expression makes the most sense to each person.

Then ask the following question. Give people time to answer it, inviting them to be open to receive whatever answer comes to them, and to perhaps be surprised by what they receive.

> **If you were to have this outcome you want, exactly the way you want it, fully and completely, what do you want through having this, that is even more important? In other words, what more important outcome do you get to have, as a result of having what you want?**

Invite them to welcome the answer they receive and thank the part of them that wants this for letting them know. Have them write down the answer they receive under their first statement of desire. Then continue by asking the exact same question, having them substitute their secondary outcome as the object of the inquiry. Again provide time for people to receive their answers, invite them to say an inner thanks for the revelation, and have them write their answer under the last one.

Explain to people the idea that anything we want strongly, we want because we expect it to deliver us into a state of wholeness. Explain that the particular experience of wholeness served by each desire is unique, and that in this process we are seeking their unique experience of wholeness as a way of more completely understanding the roots of what they desire. Continue the cycle of inquiry, asking the question several more times. Have people stop their inquiry when they have discovered the unique state of wholeness beneath their particular desire. Continue until everyone has made this discovery.

Now ask the following question:

> **Are you willing to use this inner state as your guidance for creating something together with others which supports and expresses this ultimate state of being for you?**

Invite participants to continue if their answer to this question is yes, and if not to just sit quietly and reflect on what they have discovered so far. Then continue.

Have each person look at the next to last thing on their list, the statement that came just before the state of being at which they arrived. Ask the following question:

> **What does this inner state you discovered have to offer you, in helping you understand your desire for that outcome?**

Have them either write their reflections or share them with a partner. Again ask the same question, having them move their attention to the next thing up on their list of wants. Proceed until everyone has processed all the items on their list.

This can be an intensely powerful exercise. Take your time going through it, and give people time afterwards to integrate. All together, you should allow at least a half hour and perhaps longer to give this exercise the space it requires to do its work. The effect on your group's ability to engage creatively and collaborate on their shared challenges will be significant.

Harvesting: through time

When you facilitate a meeting or series of meetings in the way I am describing, your participants will have significant experiences. Insights, breakthroughs, new visions and intentions, all will have been packed into a very compressed time and space. Some of these changes will be personal, while others will be interpersonal or collective. When you release the group back into the everyday flow of their lives, you want to provide ways for them to bring their new discoveries with them.

Harvesting the fruits of your meeting takes time. Be sure to allow for it in your scheduling. Make sure participants know to expect it, and provide signposts throughout your meeting to have them consider what they will want to carry forward after the meeting is over.

Depending on the focus and outcomes of your meeting, harvesting can take different forms. At the very least, gather up the meeting notes and make them available to group members in some way. But also consider an explicit harvesting phase of the meeting. Review progress and highlight breakthroughs. Summarize final decisions about what actions will be taken, and assign those actions to specific people with clear expectations for accountability. Encourage people to take responsibility for what they care most about, and to make commitments toward specific outcomes.

You can think of this as a setup for the group's larger-scale action/ reflection cycle. The actions taken as a result of this meeting can serve as the focus for reflection to start the next meeting. This reflection can also be encouraged and facilitated in the space between meetings.

Making your harvest available to members, and facilitating ongoing reporting on actions, results, and reflections requires supportive structures. These structures can include some of the following:

- Additional meetings for reporting and reflecting. These can be held face to face or by teleconference. They can be facilitated by members of the group or by the facilitator. Create clear expectations for the purpose and structure of the meetings ahead of time.

- Ongoing conversations hosted on an online forum. (This works best if supported by live interactions by phone or in person through one of the other suggestions here.)

- Targeted coaching for key agents in the group, with other members of the group, (managers?), or with the facilitator(s).

- Peer collaboration, where members continue an ongoing conversation about progress in small groups of 2-6 people. This collaboration can happen by phone or in person.

Another factor to consider is how to continue to nourish the experience of wholeness with presence created by the group experience. I would suggest asking the group for suggestions about what might work for them.

Group resonance

This kind of facilitation has the potential to be powerfully transformative for everyone involved. We are applying the practices that restore wisdom in an individual to the cultivating of wisdom within a group. The experience resonates inward and outward.

A group facilitated in this way mirrors the structure of the parts within an individual when they open to wholeness. The facilitator takes on the role of the Deep Self, acting as a witness and guide for the action of the group. Each group member embodies a role with its own needs and gifts and perspectives, in just the same way that the various parts of the Surface Self have their unique needs and gifts and perspectives.

The group as a whole comes to know what is within it, what it has to offer into the world, in just the same way that the individual comes to know her inner source and what unique treasure she has to contribute in her life. The group as a whole comes to know its connection to other groups and resources in its immediate ecosystem, in just the same way that the individual comes to know her outside source and develop an ability to receive the support that is available to her in many forms. And the group as a whole comes to know its context, the broader environment which supports the giving and receiving, in just the same way as the individual comes to know her context source and all it offers.

For many people, this will be the first time they have experienced belonging and participating in anything like this way. The cultivation of wholeness with presence within a group is starkly different from the ordinary, "normal" ways groups tend to conduct themselves. It is both profoundly supportive of the deepest human needs and at the same time excitingly productive. Big, seemingly intractable challenges can actually be met with creative responses that add to the life of the group rather than tearing it apart. People come away with a sense of renewed hope, not just for their engagement with the group but for their personal lives and at the other end of the spectrum, for humanity as a whole.

Again, as with other things I've discussed, this vision is an ideal. It will be rare that all elements will come together perfectly to create an ultimately paradigm-shattering experience for everyone involved. Still, even one small step in the direction of wholeness sets up a positive feedback loop. One small step forward provides intrinsic reward and motivates the next step. And when we as facilitators provide clear instructions for how to take the next step, taking it is a foregone conclusion.

In addition, simply having the experience of one small moment of wholeness changes us. As individuals we re-enter the world with a different frame of possibility. We seek further opportunities to experience this wholeness, we take small risks here or there to step out of old patterns, we challenge structures which clearly impede wholeness. The more of these experiences we accumulate, the more fierce we become as warriors for peace, every one of us.

So consider this as you prepare for your next group engagement, whether as a participant or a facilitator. Every moment of wholeness you are able to instigate becomes a force for good in the entire world and for all time.

I know I have not gone into great detail about some of the more nuts and bolts of setting up or hosting transformative group processes like this. There is much great information already available along these lines. One good source is the ArtofHosting.org website.

What I have chosen to focus on instead are the elements unique to The Feeling Path, elements which you can incorporate within any meeting, any organization, any community. Use them a la carte, or combine for a big smorgasbord. The most important thing is your presence, and your willingness to be transparent in your wholeness. Be willing to experiment with everything else. Good luck, and enjoy! There is nothing more thrilling than to be a tangible force for emergence in the company of wise beings.

Wisdom everywhere

How do we apply these practices to the task of changing the world? I'm going to suggest an approach you may at first disagree with. But I invite you to bear with me as I make my case.

Most people believe we need to change our system. I say it doesn't matter what system we have. Any system is only as good as the people who inhabit it.

Any given system could potentially work perfectly for a given subset of people. These are invariably the system's advocates. But it will only work perfectly if everyone else in the world is exactly like the advocates. And you know what? That is never going to happen. In fact, even if everyone else disappeared and only advocates were left, they would discover they were less similar than they thought. As differences emerged, the system would reveal itself to be less supportive of the utopian vision than anticipated.

The trap of ideology

Let's take a look at ideology as well, since almost every tribe of system advocates gets its certainty about the right system from some particular ideology. An ideology has the power to shape human engagement all the way from social and governmental structures down to the private conversations one person has with himself. Some of the most pervasive and broad-reaching ideologies underlie organized religions.

Ideologies can seem to work for the individual if they are surrounded only by others who adhere to their chosen belief system. Small religious communities, communes of people pursuing social change through a particular political philosophy, and even certain companies with a strong culture can seem to succeed on a certain level. But the dream that their beliefs are a solution for the entire world creates more problems than it solves. Again, it's never going to happen. Here's why.

Many current and past ideologies have an important characteristic in common: they dictate a desired inner dynamic by condemning its opposite. When you stray from the desired standard, you are labeled bad, less-then, weak, unworthy, selfish, or given other judgments which exclude you from being held equally by the group. The eternal Christian hell reserved for sinners is a particularly odious example of this. The current extreme political extremism exhibited by many in politics today, which denigrates those of opposing views, is another hateful example.

This external split between the inside and outside group becomes mirrored within each person striving to belong to the group. A strong cop-in-the-head gets installed, and any impulse, feeling, or thought which strays from the honored standard is banished from awareness or punished mercilessly from within. This internal violence reinforces the external violence perpetrated by communication, decisions affecting others, and behavior.

This tendency of ideologies to impose inner violence is intensified for those at the top of any ideologically-driven group. Almost all ideologies perpetuate the high standard of what is good through the use of exemplars, people who take positions of leadership through their faithful incorporation of the ideological principles into their lives. For these people, the pressure is heightened to suppress any impulse or thought which is in conflict with the standard. This heightened pressure is almost guaranteed to result in some kind of inner rupture eventually. And as the pressure rises within, the exemplar's outward expression of the standard often rises with it, resulting in more incisive violence in propagating the myth of the separation between good and bad.

Another characteristic of strong ideologies and religions is the bubble. Adherents to the ideology are granted special status, whether deemed to be the grace of a god, entitlement to wealth, or access to special privileges. Those holding this special status tend to engage only with those who also hold this status. (Or they engage with outsiders with the sole intent of absorbing them into the fold, often doing so as an explicit expression of their special status.) Together they reinforce the beliefs of the ideology and weave great sweeping webs of illusion and dissimulation to maintain their approved thoughts and behavior and keep their special position as believers intact.

Ideologies based on mythology have the greatest advantage in creating these bubbles because there is no way to challenge the beliefs. Statements of meaning lie outside the realm of lived experience and are held as articles of faith. Almost any aspect of the reality of being can be filtered through the mythology and interpreted in such as way as to reinforce the bubble.

One of the tragedies of such ideologies is that they steal from the truth of real human experience and recast that truth as support for the bubble. Every human being has within themselves such states as the experience of oneness with all, deep inspiration, awe and wonder, limitless possibility. Three of every set of nine paths creating our experience of self are source paths, the ideal state of which is an experience which transcends the ordinary. When those inner experiences are stimulated by rituals for example, and then labeled in such a way as to create separation and privilege for those experiencing them, we see the seeds of violence. It is not just the labeling of distressing states like hate and despair as unworthy which creates the inner violence of ideology. Even more insidious is the labeling of our highest human states as justification for the bubble which drives and perpetuates both inner and outer violence in the world.

For people living in such a bubble, the first practice of the feeling path must be guarded against at all costs. Reality has a way of bursting the bubble, so it must be kept far away. Embracing What Is becomes a dangerous, seditious act.

For these reasons – the tendency to dictate inner thought and feeling, and the creation of an isolated, self-reinforcing bubble – ideologies and organized religions have failed as the foundation for any kind of global flourishing. Societies based on such rigid structures fail from within.

At the same time, I also want to argue for the idea that religions and ideologies themselves are not inherently limiting. What limits them is their fixedness, their abandonment of present, living reality in favor of a petrified version of reality.

For the most part, the world's religions have died. In clinging to fixed texts as the basis for their morality and guidance for living, they have set themselves against the living wisdom of the feeling mind. In doing so, they have guaranteed the continuation of violence in the world, inner and outer violence in the name of religion.

I can easily imagine, however, the re-vivification of the beautiful traditions and cultures of the world through the infusion of wisdom. Bringing wisdom to a sacred text, one would engage with a self-awareness, a presence in the world among one's peers, and a willingness to inquire and invite inspiration. This would not be an exercise in interpretation for the purpose of condemnation and control, but an engagement with history with the purpose of invigorating the present. The focus would be on the here and now, with a willingness to embrace What Is. Because What Is includes the history of a people, all that came before could easily be honored and incorporated into current practice. The ancestors could be included in the living community.

Some might ask, what about morality? Do we not need a code in order to properly guide human behavior toward what is right and good? The answer is no, we do not. Morality is inborn. It is built into the architecture of the feeling mind.

Every one of us has access to profoundly transpersonal, transcendent states of being. These states are available to us at any time, and they inspire a morality which is far more compassionate, far more wise, and far more loving then any code can ever do. This is because they remain in a living dance with the reality of people here, now. No code can remain in that dance, but can only disrupt it.

Our most effective approach to encouraging moral behavior is to cultivate the inner wholeness with presence I speak of here in this book. Only this wholeness has the capacity to mediate among the infinite complexity of human life today. Only this wholeness has the creativity to forge a new path toward a truly peaceful, thriving society. Only this wholeness can show us the way. No code can do that.

I am not saying abandon all code. I am saying embrace it as inheritance from the past, as the best our blessed ancestors could do at the time with what they knew. Even if as many believe, their god was speaking through the people who wrote the sacred texts, that god was still speaking through the flawed vessel of a real human being, in a real time and place with all the limitations and compromises inherent in that state. Even if the water was pure at its origin, the conduit through which it flowed was not. Let us remain open to the sacred purity available to every one of us today, now, in a form which is relevant and meaningful for our times. Let us show up with one another, willing to feel, willing to be present, willing to work through the differences within ourselves and between one another. Let us be willing to fully experience the awesome truth of this life we share.

If this work shows us anything, it shows us the mystery at the core of life. When you shift a tightly bound feeling state, and it opens into a context source, you have the actual experience of the mysterious interconnection of all. And you are at a complete loss to describe the experience in words. Only poetry can come close, and then only by resonance, not through any kind of capturing of "truth." In these spaces of experiential mystery, we have access to our deepest wisdom.

We do need practices, rituals, shared experiences which support us in accessing these deeply wise places within ourselves. We do need communities committed to developing living relationships with mystery. Only when we are in direct contact with what is bigger than ourselves can we be truly wise.

So I believe there is an important role for various traditions, practices, and teachings, many of them religious. Again, it is not the structure which presents the problem but our engagement with it. Let us re-engage our religious teachings from a place of wisdom. Let us breathe life back into presence.

Political possibilities

And how do we apply this perspective to the task of shaping our collective engagement on a local, national and international scale? What role do political systems not based in rigid ideologies play? Is there a political system which can create the way of life we need?

I say we have had adequate opportunity to test the idea that the system makes the civilization. How many new systems have been devised and applied to one population after another, century after century? How many of those systems have succeeded in creating on their own the experience of flourishing for every person in the system, and for the environment upon which the system depends? Exactly zero. No matter how clever you are in devising a system you believe will change the world, I guarantee you the system by itself will not change the world in the ways you would like. History is on my side in this statement.

Instead, I believe that what we need is a small percentage of the population – maybe 10% – who are reasonably wise, who engage in the practice of wholeness with presence in their social and public lives. I believe that with such a fraction exhibiting wisdom, we will find our positions of leadership naturally filled over time by these wise ones. When we have fully human leaders, showing up in wholeness with presence, able to hold complexity and advocate for the highest good of all – only then will we find the peace and thriving we seek.

A truly wise leader tries to understand those people he or she leads, steps into their shoes and looks at the world through their eyes. The wise leader can speak to their needs as the people themselves experience them, and bridge those needs with the needs of others who are different.

We have no wise leaders today because we are not fostering wisdom in our youth. We have no wise leaders because we reward and grant power to those who abandon wisdom and focus on command and control ways of operating. And we have no wise leaders because we are not looking for them. Instead we vote for leaders who agree with our reactive opinions, and we encourage them to shoot down those with opinions with which we disagree.

Why are we operating this way? We are doing so because we have lost access to the natural wisdom within ourselves. So we cannot imagine or recognize its existence outside ourselves. Instead we satisfy ourselves with mock dramas like our absurd, contentious presidential debates. These debates are antagonistic. They are set up for one person to "win" against the others., to show the others down.

No wise leader would agree to participate in such folly. Wise leadership is not about shouting down those who disagree with you. It is about building others up, everyone around you without exception. It is about listening, and dialog, and creative collaboration. It is about facilitating and inspiring collective achievements that go far beyond what any one person would ever be able to dictate.

What if, instead of debates, we had televised collaborations where the candidates worked together on a pressing national problem? We would see very quickly who demonstrated wise leadership, and who undermined collaboration by grandstanding, backstabbing, or antagonizing. I doubt if many of the current people serving in our executive or legislative branches of government would fare well in such a demonstration.

Again I say this: it has nothing to do with the system. Give me any country with 10% of their population having access to their inner wisdom, and I will give you a peaceful, thriving nation. In a dictatorship, the dictator would cultivate the wisdom of those around her. She would manage a ground up decision-making process, including everyone. Her chosen role would be to validate and authorize action on each decision. She would find ways to honor the humanity of those holding opposing opinions, and work with them to get their most important needs met. Her leadership would provide a model for others. Children would aspire to be like her. Nobody would think that the system needed to be changed.

The dictatorship would have evolved into this benevolence through the influence of the wise ones. It may have taken many years, but even if the original dictator was brutal and harsh, the wise ones would have cultivated an atmosphere of holding deeper truths. That which is most sacred and true in humanity is out of reach of even the most desperate of despots.

Wisdom spreads through contact. Sit with someone who is fully present with you. Even if you are troubled or angry, you will not be able to hold on to your troubles or your anger in their presence. When you are touched by wholeness with presence, it changes you. You take the possibility of that wholeness inside yourself. You pass it on to others. The political or social environment has less influence upon your inner peace. You are able to act from a place of authenticity, honoring what is most important and turning aside from that which undermines it.

In an anarchy, everyone would know one of these wise ones. Rich conversations would happen, naming and nurturing the deeper human values underlying the diversities of opinion. People would self-organize, gather together to meet needs that require collective effort to accomplish, allowing independence for seeking those more solitary needs.

And what about a democracy? At the moment, the democracies of the so-called developed world have grown toxic. Because the population has lost access to its natural inner wisdom, we have given power to people who are least capable of using it well. And they are indeed using their power badly, there is no question. There is little wisdom walking the halls of congress or ruling in the boardrooms of our most rapacious corporations.

But we do not need to change the system in order to turn things around. We need first to seek the wisdom within ourselves, then to share our wisdom with others, then to use our experience of wisdom among ourselves to collectively choose leaders who demonstrate the capacity to lead from a place of wholeness with presence.

This is a different kind of wisdom than the one we typically refer to today. It is not, "From my considerable experience, I know that A causes B. Therefore our action should be C." Instead, it sounds more like, "I trust the wisdom of the people I serve. I trust myself to create the conditions to bring their wisdom to the fore. I trust human nature to move us in the direction that is best for all."

We have never had this, so we don't know what it feels like. We have never seen it elsewhere, so we don't know what it looks like. We have never heard tell of a truly wise culture like the one I am describing, so we really don't know how to create it.

Or do we? I believe what I have sketched for you in this book is a road map. At the moment it is rough, yes, but it is enough for us to start in the right direction. We can fill in the details as we reach the milestones along the way, marking our route and making sure we never forget how we arrived.

In closing, I would like to offer a simple proposal, a nascent vision of something worth trying. What would it look like for some of us to step outside of partisan democracy into this space of wisdom as our highest value in the context of public life? What would it look like to articulate a platform which promotes wisdom among leadership?

I am imagining a Wisdom Party dedicated to supporting wise leadership at every level regardless of party affiliation. Its primary focus in the beginning would be to develop and teach practices cultivating personal and collective wisdom, and to demonstrate wise civic engagement. The organization might host wisdom councils in parallel with broader public dialogue on timely topics. It might publish a guideline on how to recognize wisdom in leadership, and commentary on current leaders and their wise or unwise speech and behavior. Eventually, as the activity of the party became more widely known and respected, the party might actually endorse candidates for office and follow their activity when they win their position. Over time, the accumulated repository of wise practices in public life could grow to become influential at every level of government.

There are people already attempting to create a more inclusive, generative conversation among people of divergent viewpoints. What is missing in these efforts is an emphasis on personal wisdom as the foundation of success for these efforts, and the know-how to cultivate it. We now have the knowledge and methods we need to move forward in this. Shall we begin?

Part 5:
Etcetera

Making Good on My Promises

Early in the book I made a few promises. Depending on your interest, I stated you would receive certain benefits from reading this book. I'd like to review those promises and make sure I've delivered on them.

1. For lay people

I promised the opportunity for swift, permanent relief from dysfunctional patterns. I've given you the method; all you need to do is apply it. This work is powerful enough to address many, if not most, of the stresses and distresses that lead you to seek help.

The relief you experience comes without side effects or ancillary risks, and has the added benefit of increasing your self knowledge and overall well being. (At the same time, please seek the assistance of a medical professional if there's any chance your distress may be generated by body or brain-based causes. The Feeling Path is not a panacea for all ills.)

2. For therapists

I promised the opportunity to greatly improve your success in helping clients. I honestly don't believe it matters what particular methodology you've been trained to conduct, if you apply Feeling Path Mapping to assisting your clients in gaining greater awareness and freedom in feeling, you will see their progress accelerate. I must warn you however. You may find yourself becoming so much more effective at assisting your clients that they will finish therapy with you much sooner than they otherwise would.

You have two possible ways to address the loss of business this creates. First, you may want to rethink your treatment model. In order to thrive in your practice, you will find it helpful to offer not just the remedial assistance of relieving suffering, but to open the frame to support your clients in really going for a fully flourishing life beyond what they thought was possible. Most of us have plenty of work to do, and you will now be able to lead your clients through one issue after another as they attain ever greater levels of fulfillment and authenticity.

You may also wish to rethink your business model. Because many of your clients will have budget constraints, they will choose to end therapy when they receive what they came for, a relief from their distress. This means you may have to be more active in acquiring new clients. Fortunately, your clients will be happy to recommend your services to others, and that will help. But it may not be enough. People don't easily talk with anyone outside of those very close intimates about emotional difficulties they may have overcome. It's not like recommending a movie to a coworker. So you may also need to get more savvy at networking and other methods for building your practice. There are many excellent guides available for how to do this. I can recommend Mark Silver at HeartofBusiness.com and the book Building Your Ideal Private Practice by Lynn Grodzki. Find these resources and use them.

3. For researchers

I promised the opportunity to more precisely identify inner feeling states of your research subjects. You'll have a lot more to go on when

I release a second book, but for now let's take a look at what's possible with what I've given you.

I believe the first task for the research community is to firmly establish the mind's somatosensory capacity as the foundation of feeling, and to clearly differentiate feeling from emotion. You've got the basic tools here that provide a rich language for eliciting and codifying people's actual inner experience of feeling. Compare that to other measures you already have, including emotional arousal, brain activity, various cognitive tests, etc. You're going to find a wide field of opportunity.

Make sure to engage in the practice personally, so you know from the inside what you're working with. Many insights will elude you otherwise. And please contact me and let me know how I can help. Hint: one of the most exciting discoveries available to be formalized is that feeling is trans-somatic. The experience of feeling commonly extends beyond the envelope of the physical body. Publish that and you've made a significant, buzz-creating contribution.

4. For those interested in philosophy

I promised the opportunity for greater understanding of what makes us human. For one thing, Feeling Path Mapping is a potential tool for rigorous phenomenological exploration of feeling. Any serious investigator can deliberately enter states previously requiring long years of practice and training. And philosophers interested in feeling, sentiment, inspiration, intuition and the like will find a great deal of new information to provoke redefinitions and insights of all kinds.

5. For spiritual seekers

I promised the opportunity for a more direct path to transcendent experience and greater access to the experience of mystery. You have that now. Simply through exploring your own inner states as they are, inviting them toward their ideal, you will discover the profound in your own, direct experience. Pay particular attention to the ideal Source states, and of those, especially the states in the Context domain. Their structure is that of an infinite field of energy, intelligence, life force, and the like, and can easily be compared to perennial teachings about the nature of what has been called god or spirit or essence. This is not meant to diminish the experiences of the Inside and Outside source states, which offer their own profoundly powerful openings.

I should warn you though. It is possible that what you encounter may not conform to what you expect, depending on the teachings of whatever spiritual practice you claim as your own. Be open to mystery and surprise, and be willing to tolerate a bit of discomfort as your beliefs are challenged, and I promise you will find growing within yourself an authentic wisdom and presence that is bigger than any teaching has given you. You will have greater capacity to align yourself with practices that feel authentic for you, and to see through teachings which limit you. Enjoy!

6. For the adventurous

I promised the opportunity to be a pioneer in the exploration of consciousness. Believe me, there is much to be discovered. This book barely scratches the surface of the feeling mind, yet it provides you the tools you need to conduct your own explorations. Experiment, then decide what specific area interests you the most. Investigate that using Feeling Path Mapping as your primary tool, and you will uncover new discoveries that will benefit all of us. Good luck!

7. For the ambitious

I promised the opportunity to apply this new science to getting breakthrough results in almost any area you choose. If you're a therapist wanting to establish your expertise a particular niche, apply Feeling Path Mapping to a specific therapeutic challenge, track your results, codify your approach, and teach your new method. If you're on the medical side of things, you could use Feeling Path Mapping first of all to bring some level of objectivity and reproducibility to the business of diagnosing mental health issues. The current state of affairs with the DSM is appallingly unscientific, convenient, and political.

If you're in the business of creating medications for psychiatric conditions, get busy using this new tool for objectively identifying conscious states to correlate to what's going on biochemically and neurologically. I suspect you will open new avenues never before considered.

If you're in sports, apply Feeling Path Mapping to optimizing the performance state, eliminating anything in the way of peak athletic achievement and maximizing those states which contribute to superior performance. Same goes if you're in any other field requiring optimum performance, whether it's theatre arts, musical performance, public speaking, or even sales.

If you're in any kind of field involving personal growth and fulfillment, the sky is the limit. Develop your own new inner/outer yoga practice, your own new meditation technique, your own whatever. Take your passion, apply Feeling Path Mapping, and carve out some new territory. And count me in if you want some help.

8. For everyone

I promised the opportunity to amplify and deepen the sweetness, fulfillment, enjoyment and meaning in your life. If you haven't figured it out by this point in the book, feeling is core of being. It is the foundation of consciousness, the heart of the soul. As you welcome feeling back into your life, as you embrace its ongoing support of your well being, as you explore its resources for every aspect of your life, you will find exactly that sweetness you desire and very much more.

In reviewing my promises, I feel pretty good about what I've given you so far. There's a lot here, and there's much more to come. Please accept my invitation to engage further than this book. Become part of the community at FeelingPath.com to learn how to get even more from this work and to gain my support and that of others in achieving whatever your goals may be.

What Others Have Said

I'd like to offer the words of a few other people. These are a testimonials I've received over the years and more recently, people sharing about the benefits they've received from doing the Feeling Path work. I share them because they provide a certain perspective I cannot, of people coming to this work uninitiated, having the experience, and making sense of it. I think these words from others can provide valuable context for you as you encounter the work for the first time.

"A bridge to a higher power"

I worked with Gina in three sessions over the course of a year or so. Here is what she said in an interview a few months after our last session:

"The biggest thing that I remember pulling out of the first experience was, we actually created, in the session, new feelings for me. And I remember giving them names, an 'identity.' So I had this list, I came home with this list, and I remember looking at it for the next couple weeks. And seeing that these feelings were always here and they were always possible, and by naming them and giving them an identity, I could go to them right away.

"But there was a feeling that would pop up from time to time, an actual, physical, physiological reaction that totally paralyzed me in my life when it occurred. And it was the scariest feeling I have ever experienced. It's like my body would just get trapped in the terror. That was what we addressed in the second session.

"Your technique took me into it, and asked it what it needed to heal. That moment, when we transformed that feeling, was, I totally remember: It was like I just created a bridge to a higher power that is this amazing, unconditional love and safety, and just, everything is OK.

"I can't even remember what it feels like to have that space of that fear and that paralyzing feeling. It was a part of me, but the other is so much more powerful.

"And that was the biggest stepping stone to where I'm headed now. I truly believe that was the biggest limitation I've had in my entire life. The result was incredible. From that day on, I've been resting easy and in excitement about my project and about my future. And it's done, pretty much. We're editing. All the stuff I was afraid of that I thought I couldn't do, it's done!

"I think the biggest piece of it is, before that moment I was still hiding myself from the world. I kind of chose who would believe in me and who wouldn't, and then after our session, it was like, it doesn't matter who believes in me and who doesn't, this is who I am, this is just who I am. It would be like taking my body and trying to turn it into something other than it is.

"And I got that really clearly, so now everybody in my life and in the world knows me as a budding film director and that's the way it should be. And that's really cool!"

— Gina Robertson, Cora Panthera Films

"A lightness has come over me"

I worked with Jen over a period of about a week, perhaps four or five long sessions. Here is what she wrote as a testimonial a few months later:

"Since working with Joe, I have felt a profound shift in my being – physically, mentally, spiritually, and emotionally. I feel like the weight of anxiety (big, dark, gray and black) has been lifted off of my shoulders. This weight that I have felt for a majority of my life has been replaced by a sense of lightness, vitality, and a deeper sense of compassion for myself and others. I feel a sense of calm, centeredness, joy, profound love, and positive energy.

"In my past, my pattern has been to be very fearful of conflict, as I quickly would go to a place of shame and blame and I would be engulfed entirely by my own feelings (anger at myself, shame, feeling of worthlessness, projections of how the other person might be viewing me negatively, etc.), that there would be no room for the other person to have their feelings too. I experienced what effects this had on my relationships, as they were never sustainable within this pattern of relating. It was so frustrating for me, because I knew what I was capable of! I knew I had emotional intelligence and strong abilities to communicate.

"But why couldn't I get over this pattern? It just seemed more powerful than me…beyond my own ability to control it. I wanted to get rid of it, to fix it, to make it go away so that I could be "normal". I have spent years in talk therapy, trying different forms of energy work, workshops, meditation, etc. And although these were all helpful, the patterns were still hanging on for dear life.

"What I have been experiencing since working with Joe is an ability to more easily speak my truth and express my needs, even my anger, without feeling the shame, blame, or worthlessness. There is a spaciousness for the anger or frustration and there is space for the other person's feelings as well. I can have my feelings, express my needs clearly, and still have the love inside for myself and this other person all at the same time. I can more easily see and experience (and be aware of) our humanness, our mutual need to feel loved and worthy, our fear of rejection, etc. It feels so much more encompassing. Perhaps the lightness I feel, and the joy and the love, is about feeling more of a sense of Oneness with others, having more awareness that we are really the same inside, having similar wants, needs and desires that are basic to our humanness.

"Words cannot express my gratitude for what Joe (and the process he has developed) has helped me to open myself to. I do believe it was there all along, just waiting to come out and be expressed. The weight is not necessarily something that has left me, but instead there is a lightness that has come over me and embraced me. And in that, it has lifted me up! The lightness of my being is "embracing" the shadow parts of me, so that I can experience all parts of me with compassion and love. By embracing this in myself, I am more able to embrace the shadow and light in others too. What a relief this is, to know that nothing really needed to be "fixed" or changed, just seen and experienced from a different perspective. I am able to see that these shadow and light parts just wanted to help me survive, to have my basic needs met, to feel loved, and to feel safe.

"Thank you so much, Joe. I feel my life has been forever changed as a result of our work together. It will be interesting to see how this continues to play out in my life. I am excited to be creating my life from this new way of being. How fun is that?"

— Jen Kindred, Seattle

"A refreshing transformation"

Mitch worked with me for just one hour over the phone, focusing on a fear of public speaking which was affecting his professional success. Here are his words, including a description of how he experienced our work together:

"We talked about some physical distress I exhibited each time I presented a seminar or hosted an event. Through a series of guided imagery questions he had me actually visually place the feelings that came up during presentations in a specific place in my body. He prompted me to describe, locate, and get very acquainted with those feelings. He asked me to allow those feelings to transform into a different shape, space, and place.

"I immediately received a sense of lightening up, a refreshing transformation that freed me up and left me very, very energized. He left me with specific instructions as to how I can re-create that transformation and recall the image I created prior to my presentations. I now cue myself before every presentation, client meeting, and networking opportunity to fortify myself with that powerful image of who I am and what I offer those I connect with.

"I found the experience of my session with Joe invaluable. I easily connected with the model of creating visual images and descriptions for the questions he used to guide my learning experience. I am a very visual and creative person. Though we did talk of some very intimate things that lead me to a fairly vulnerable place, I always felt safe with his guidance and support. One of the best things is that he took notes and had a way of recording our session so whenever I want to go back through a reminder or refresher on my discovery, I can. I was completely free to do the work necessary.

"Being freed from the focus on how I'm being perceived, or how am I doing, or what am I going to say next is invaluable. It has allowed me to truly listen and be present while presenting, whether to a group or just one person."

— Mitch Hunter, Seattle

"An easier and quicker shift"

Ashera is dear friend who has applied the Feeling Path Mapping techniques in her own healing practice. It has been very gratifying for me to be able to support her success in helping her clients transform their lives.

"I am a Shamanic, Energy Healing Practitioner and a Yoga and Ayurveda Practitioner. I have a regular practice working with clients and leading transformational workshops and retreats worldwide for over 10 years. I have trained in a variety of healing modalities over my lifetime and spent much time doing my own personal healing and leading others in transformational processes.

"When I first started working with the Joe and The Feeling Path over a year ago, what most appealed to me was the way the work could simply and specifically work with particular feelings in a clear and embodied way. This presence with even challenging feelings allowed the feelings to be felt fully without the story line. Though I had worked with many mindfulness approaches to feeling before, this went beyond the mindfulness witnessing process into truly feeling feelings in such a unique and full way. The mapping process alone was quite profound for me, and allowed even deeply buried feelings to surface and shift easily. I was also intrigued by how the work helped me to see the whole structure of a process that I may be going through in larger framework.

This invited a new understanding of how all feelings interacted with each other. It was helpful in understanding the deeper purpose of many feelings and how to really honor and transform them.

"When I started to use The Feeling Path work with clients, it was so easily integrated as part my healing sessions it was great. It allowed my clients to really get specific and have deep felt senses of their feelings. It was amazing! When I used the mapping technique my work with clients went deeper. Now using the work in sessions, I notice clients become more involved in really feeling and staying present with their own feelings in more depth. There is a heightened presence and involvement in their own process, and it allows an easier and quicker shift. Plus my clients go home with a valuable tool they can use on their own."

— Ashera Serfaty, Port Townsend
   LuminosityHealingArts.com

Olivia's Story

You met Olivia Parker in Part 1 where I shared maps of the feeling state she called Crumbling, among others. I have worked with her extensively over the past three months, clearing two Surface Self sets as well as the Deep Self. Here is an essay she wrote to share her experience.

As you read this, keep in mind this frame: Olivia worked through two Surface Self sets plus the Deep Self. Clearing a Surface Self set on its own is pretty straightforward: map, move, integrate and you're done. The issue is no longer a problem. Working with the Deep Self, however, touches everything about you. This work is intense and life changing. As I mentioned earlier Deep Self work requires good support and a strong commitment to completing the process. It is an arduous journey but perhaps the most satisfying thing you will ever do. Join the community at FeelingPath.com to learn more about how to discern whether you are working with Surface Self or Deep Self feeling states, and how best to manage an in-depth transformation like this one.

Olivia: Finding Understanding

They say that you find love when you stop looking. I found understanding when I stopped searching for it.

I have always been frustrated by the limits of my own mind. I longed for true knowledge and understanding. I struggled through the complex texts of history's brilliant philosophers and great writers hoping to unearth the secrets within. Realizing the answers were out of reach, I finally put down the books and looked around. The world is a vast and confusing place with so much constant information it felt completely overwhelming. I had no idea where to begin so I just let life take me where it would. I spent a year traveling in Europe and two years working on commercial fishing boats in Alaska and the coast of California. I drove down to Mexico and spent two years living on the coast drinking coconut milk and eating mangos. I wrote enough to keep a roof over my head. I listened to people's stories. I solved my shyness problem by learning how to ask questions and listen. I soon realized that people love to talk about themselves and I soaked up their stories. I went back to school and finished my degree. I realized I had achieved the things I wanted. I was traveling, writing and I had a college degree. I had no ties to anywhere and my time was mine to fill. Still I felt like something was missing.

Sense of self is what I was searching for and it is what I found so elusive. I wanted to be confident and outgoing and focused and engaged fully in my life. But I always felt self-conscious and shy and I always held back. I held back in social situations; I held back in my work, I held back my opinions. The subconscious reasoning was that the less I put out there, the less attention I would attract and the less criticism I would inspire. If I said nothing at all, I would be spared saying something possibly stupid, misinformed or something that could be misinterpreted. It's logical but it's not a very fulfilling way to live.

I socialized superficially and I always kept people on an acquaintance basis, rarely letting anything develop into a friendship. I also felt I had to be perfect. People notice flaws, but they look past perfection. I showered a lot. I was on a constant mission to find the perfect sweater, or pair of boots that would dispel the feeling of unworthiness and transform it into a feeling of confidence. I bought beautiful boots and soft sweaters but I still felt unworthy, insecure and shy. I got rid of the old clothes, the ones that had failed me. I bought new ones. They failed me. Out of touch with myself, I found it nearly impossible to spend time with other young women. I rejected female authors and felt frustrated that everything I read was so masculine oriented. I was living in a functional world of disconnection. I would feel overwhelming sadness, desperation, and depression. There were good times too but they seemed unstable and fleeting. I started to wonder if I was clinically depressed which soon led to the certainty there was something seriously wrong with me. I started worrying about my health. This was also very time consuming.

Making the First Step

I met Joe Shirley in late April, 2011. I had moved back to Port Townsend after living in Mexico and had broken from a five-year relationship. I returned to Port Townsend as a place to perch while I sorted out the next place to go. I had a few ideas but nothing specific. I still had no idea what I wanted to do. I was immediately intrigued by his work though I didn't really understand what exactly it involved. As I started going through the process of mapping and moving emotions began to get a clue about how profoundly the work would change my life.

Beginning at the Beginning

During the first meeting I started out by talking, and talking and talking. I talked about the resistance I felt around my work. My constant struggles with follow through and focus, my fear of rejection. I thought about details and explanations and reasons for everything and I tried to fill him in on all of it. I guessed rightly that he would pick up a thread that was useful and relevant. The details and the reasons all seemed so important when I started talking but even during that first conversation, or monologue really, I came to realize that the details aren't important. What matters are the feeling states. I think too often we cover up our feelings with words and explanations and abstract thoughts. The actual feeling is something else entirely.

Beginning the Process

A solid focused career and a life's work I could feel passionate about – that is what I wanted most when I began this process. I know I want to write; it was the getting started part that I struggled with. Once I got started I didn't have a clear idea of where I was going which made follow through nearly impossible. Endings were not a problem because I rarely got that far. Talking with Joe about the process I realized that my work was where I felt the strongest sense of frustration and it was the area I most wanted to improve. I realized right away that work is part of life and it is intertwined with love and relationships, self, home and play. You can't really separate it out, but it was still good to have a specific place to start. It was the most logical place to start too. I wanted to write about the process I was experiencing with Joe, and to write about it I would have to experience it. I set out on the journey with a sense of excitement and hope, and like any journey, the trials along the way were nothing I could foresee from the beginning.

Searching for Threads

When I began my life felt like disconnected fragments. I couldn't see the threads that held it all together and I couldn't see where I wanted to go. I wasn't living in the moment, I was living in fragments without a clear sense of my life. I could see a future full of possibilities but I didn't know how to make the possibilities into realities. I had already been earning an existence as a writer, it was definitely an existence rather than a living because I could barely live on what I made. What was missing, I realize now, was the ability to believe in myself and feel confident about my work and my place in the world.

Creating Form

The first feeling I mapped was fear of rejection. First I had to get the words right. "Fear of rejection" is an abstract phrase that could apply to just about anyone. It was not mine. What it really felt like was crumbling. I felt other people's moods and shifts so acutely that a slight dismissal or an offhand remark could cause me to collapse inside. To compensate I would look for a fault in the person, silently and cruelly judge them, and then retreat back into my own world. During the initial mapping stage I made the transition from the rather generic, possibly universal "fear of rejection" to the more personal "crumbling".

First, I acknowledged and embraced the emotion and I allowed all the reasons for its existence to fall away. It made me excruciatingly uncomfortable. It is a strange thing to really feel an emotion. I always tend to cover them with specific thoughts or I would turn away and find distraction. But now I had to just sit and feel it. As I did, I realized that giving the feeling form moved it from something vague to something tangible.

At first I didn't fully understanding how exactly an emotion or a feeling state was supposed to turn into an image. I had to immerse myself in the process to understand. Guided by Joe's questions I closed my eyes to try to see if the feeling had a shape and a form and a color. It did. A loosely collected set of yellow particles that collapsed and crumbled within me. "Yellow?" I thought, "Wouldn't grey or blue or black be more appropriate for this sinking feeling?" I sat with it. They were yellow. I shrugged. They really couldn't and wouldn't become any other color. As I sat with the feeling I felt the particles collapsing. As they collapsed I felt the familiar sinking feeling but this time it was different. The feeling existed on its own without a specific incident to attach it to. All I had was the feeling deep inside me. My core felt very heavy and I was intensely aware of the weight of gravity pulling me down into the chair. I emerged from the emotion feeling disoriented and shaky. I felt deflated and sad but I also felt a deep sense of understanding for myself. I drew the image. Drawing the image right after experiencing and mapping it solidified what I felt with a visual representation. As I went through each emotional state I often found that the drawing process allowed me to further develop the visual aspects of the feeling state. Seeing the image allowed me to objectify the emotion. It no longer felt frightening and illusive and overwhelming.

Once I identified the feeling, the words came through with striking clarity. "You shouldn't have put yourself out there, you should have kept it all closer". These were my words coming from a level of my conscious mind I had never heard before. Through life, being rather um…sensitive… I had constructed an instant awareness of the slightest shift in social acceptance, and I protected myself from further hurt by closing up, pulling back, surrounding my self with the protective wall. This may have protected me from a deeper feeling of social rejection, but it wasn't helping my social life, or my life as a freelance writer. It just wasn't helping anymore.

Shifting the Emotion

The experience of shifting the feeling left me stunned. It moved so quickly
and the feeling of relief and lightness was sweeping and overwhelming.
After identifying this first, intense emotion we shifted it. I began the
first shifting process by looking at the color. What color did it most
want to be? Yellow. The color stayed the same. I was disappointed. I
tried to make it a new color but it stayed stubbornly yellow. I moved
on. Particles swirling and sinking moved into a solid pillar in my center.
I felt it. It felt warm. Like the warmth of stone in the sun. It felt solid
under my hand. It felt good. Each element of the feeling was very clear.
I was surprised at the clarity of each part of the feeling. I tried making it
cooler but it didn't feel right. The temperature was very specific. Warmer
than body temperature but not hot. The color was specific. I tried making
it lighter, then darker. It would shift reluctantly and immediately I
would start to loose track of the good feeling. I brought it back to the
state where it felt best. I tried changing the shape. It wouldn't budge. I
allowed everything to return to its perfect state. A feeling of strength,
calm and confidence flooded over me. It felt right.

Physical Awareness

One of the most surprising, and intense parts of this process is the
physical feeling that accompanies the emotional states. It feels like a
real realignment is happening within, not only your mind and your
emotional state, but in your physical being as well. Shifting a strong
emotion was commonly accompanied by a feeling of tingling all through
my body, lightness and excitement.

The Surface Self and the Deep Self

During this process, I mapped two sets of surface-self parts and the
deep self. It's not always possible at first to know for sure if an emotion

is part of the deep self or one of the surface self sets. As I gained experience with the work, I began to feel the difference between the states. Surface-self parts were less intense than deep-self parts. Often moving a deep-self part left me feeling disoriented and off for a few days while moving a surface-self part left me feeling instantly better. After discovering a deep-self part, I often felt overwhelmingly sad or angry or frustrated. It varied depending on the nature of the feeling state. After shifting a deep-self part it would often take time to realign. The feeling of improvement took longer, but once achieved it felt solid and permanent. The first emotion I mapped and moved turned out to be a part of the deep self but at the time I was not even aware of the difference between deep self and surface self. Looking back, the intensity of the feelings as I mapped and moved "crumbling" to a feeling of solidity in my center or "core strength", indicates that it was a part of the deep self, but at the time I had no point of reference.

Isolated Outside

The next feeling I mapped was an emotion I called "isolated outside". I have always felt on the outside of things. Like a shadow observing but never invited to enter. I saw the whole world of social interactions as something I could never really be a part of. I felt comfortable interacting with one other person, but I always kept my distance emotionally and kept a very solid invisible wall around myself. In groups, I felt isolated as though everyone involved was a part of something I didn't have the ability to understand. "You're so quiet" is a comment I heard many times. I would smile sweetly and say something elusive and somehow people got the idea I was intelligent. I was happy to allow that perception when in reality felt lost and wary and lonely, and lacking in whatever it was everyone else seemed to have. I discovered that "Isolated Outside" is a part of self I developed in response to being so sensitive to people. A simple phrase that may or may not have been intended as a criticism or ridicule would just about destroy me. I kept an uninterested cool exterior image as a front to hide how fragile I felt.

I shifted "Isolated Outside" and I discovered a space around me that felt safe and that I influenced. It pulsed. It felt like a warm yellow light all around me. I saw it as a space where people could exist in my life. It was a space I held and it was a part of me but it was removed enough that what happened there could not destroy me. This was a huge relief. I look back at my self in this state and feel a deep sense of compassion, as though my self in that state were an undeveloped me, too young to understand but still kind of cute in its fumbling way.

Moving this part changed my interactions immediately. I began making friends quickly. People I had known on an acquaintance base for months or years got closer. The only thing that changed was me and all I did was shift my awareness of, and reaction to, other people. I created a space to let them in. I realize now that many people also feel shy or insecure or self-conscious at times. I am not the only one. This realization has transformed my interactions with people. I always felt judged by others because I was so harshly judging myself. Other people's reactions to me shifted. As I became more at ease in my self, people around me became more at ease in my presence. It has led to a wonderful unfolding in my social, professional, and personal relationships. This turned out to be another deep self-part.

Taking it all Apart

It's hard to clean up a jumbled closet without pulling everything out first. Things look worse before they look better. The deconstruction process was hard. We started identifying, feeling, and mapping emotions without shifting the first ones right away. Shifting I chose to do later. You can work either by mapping and shifting at the same time or by mapping everything and then shifting everything. Both ways work. I chose for the most part to tear it all apart before putting it back together. The deconstruction process left me feeling exhausted. I slept a lot. I felt run down. I got a cold that seemed to hang around for weeks. I felt like I was swimming though a dense fog. My mind felt wrapped in cobwebs and cotton. I slept and slept and slept. Old fears would grip me in stray moments leaving me in a state of panic. I felt in turns impatient, irritable and depressed. I was a wreck. My sense of self disappeared. I felt like a shell. Empty.

Finding the Threads

I read the seven volumes of Proust's A Remembrance of Things Past in four summer months when I was 20. I worked too, part time in a coffee shop and I spent all my free time reading. Often, I felt lost by his winding prose, his seemingly endless description, page after page after page of a hawthorn bush in bloom. I kept reading for the beauty of the prose and a dogged desire to get to the end of this monumental piece of literature. There is a moment at the end of the book when it all comes together, for the narrator, for the reader, for me. All the winding tangents blend as part of the whole. As I worked though the winding paths of my own emotions I often felt lost. A moment when I found a deep core feeling, and mapped it and shifted it I felt that it was all making sense. Though fleeting, that moment showed me a glimpse of what was becoming possible.

Experiencing the Wrong Way Intensifies the Right Way

Sometimes heading down the wrong path helps to clarify what the right path is. I had this experience mapping one of the feeling states. As I was imagining the color and shape it kept shifting, becoming more and more illusory. A feeling of mud became a path, supporting my feet, became a trail that lead out away from me. "A supporting path" I thought. And I began to create it as supporting path. It reminded me of a drawing I had seen as a child of a path bleached white by the moonlight leading over the hills. I began to describe this image I saw in my mind but it kept shifting. An unconscious part of my mind knew that this was not the true feeling state but an intellectual construct of my imagination. Still, part of me felt like I had already invested the time and I was reluctant to give up on it. I drew the image but it still didn't feel right. I had a sense of vague discomfort rather than the tingly feeling I had come to identify with shifting a feeling state. I said that perhaps I had allowed my intellect to intervene in the process. I felt embarrassed and guilty about wasting time with this tangent. We went back through the original state. I stripped my mind of every image and went into the feeling state. I even asked it "what do you most want to be" it felt foolish but as I asked I allowed my conscious mind to step aside in order to give the feeling room to become its most perfect state. As it shifted this time it felt right, solid and the physical feeling of pleasure accompanied its final shift.

Experiencing the reality of getting it wrong intensified my awareness of how powerful getting it right feels. Having traveled so far in the wrong direction once, I quickly learned to realize when my intellectual mind was creating the images. Sometimes I would start to see a pattern, like a waterfall or a pond and in my mind would start constructing images from there. Though often pretty and sometimes creative, they were only that. The images were far removed from the feeling states I was attempting to uncover and map. I learned to recognize these diversions early. Each time I had to return to the original feeling state, clear my mind completely, and allow the feeling to shift into its true form. I came to fully understand how a feeling can't become anything you want it to become. It has its perfect state, and it has the state it currently exists in. There is only one perfect state and you know when you get there.

Upheaval and Realignment

I felt this intense upheaval in myself as I went through this Feeling Path process. One of the tremendous qualities of this work is the rapidness through which you can move through feeling states. In traditional therapy, the blame and guilt may last years, or it may never be resolved. This whole process took less than three months. I thought about the work a lot in the beginning trying to see it objectively and track my process through I but at some point it stopped making sense. I finally stopped analyzing the process and just went with the ups and downs of the experience. As we started moving more and more of the feeling states I began to notice that states I had previously felt intensely I could no longer access. As I shifted some states, others naturally shifted or began to shift on their own. Each emotion is linked to other emotions so by going through the whole process, you are basically overhauling your entire emotional system. And it feels like a complete overhaul. Hard in the beginning, exhausting and overwhelming in the middle, but at the end you come out feeling kind of new and shiny, or at least you feel like you got rid of most of the useless crap.

Looking Back at the Process

It started to come together as we got to the end of the process but I really didn't see the whole shift until I had emerged on the other side. I can look back at myself in the midst of the process, and see the threads that tie it all together but at the time, it felt like a chaotic mess of upturned and scattered parts of emotions. I felt naked and exposed. Each part had an original state and its perfect state. As one part shifted it would leave other parts in chaos. Familiar ways of being suddenly felt unbalanced and ineffective. Each part I mapped and shifted was one point on the map of myself. Just the process of identifying each emotion is powerful and it gave me a deep sense of understanding. Once I shifted the emotions, I placed each one on the map. The new states make up my current self and the former states are a distant and vague memory. I say new states because it feels so new, but at the same time it feels like my most basic self stripped of all the layers of reactions, patterns and states of existence I had constructed over the course of my life.

Rebuilding

Still a fledgling in my new feeling state I am slowly beginning the process of recreating my life and my relationship to the world. I realize I don't need to be limited by old fears but they still show up rather regularly. I start to fall back into the patterns of my former state but as I do, I realize that that state no longer fits with who I am. It is disorienting at first. The old way doesn't really work anymore but a new ways aren't yet fully formed. I approach the process deliberately at times, and at times I just move aside and allow myself the freedom to react or act as it feels right in the moment. When I feel resistance or insecurity, I can look at it and move it to a feeling of confidence. I can also recognize when a negative feeling is telling me something important. Feelings are a guide. If something feels bad, its best to take another look and see if it is necessary in your life. Work you hate doing might not be the best thing to put your energy into and a relationship that constantly leaves you feeling bad might need to end.

As the weeks pass I realize increasingly that many of the ways I used to feel or react are simply gone. Once I went through the whole process, I felt rather raw and unformed. Now, slowly I am beginning to recreate myself as I always knew I could be, confident, happy, focused and self-aware without being self-conscious. As I find more energy to take care of my emotional self, I have more energy for other people. I have more energy to take care of my physical body, my career, my finances and my surroundings. I feel like I have been freed from a heavy burden that I carried for years though I had only limited awareness of it. It's not so much that I am a different person now, but rather I am the same person without all the issues.

Each area of my life has changed in some way. I find new opportunities to develop my business and my skills daily and I have the confidence to pursue the opportunities. I enjoy meeting new people professionally and socially. I enjoy participating in conversations and adding my voice to the world around me. Instead of destroying me, I find that criticism gives me the chance to clarify my thoughts and on a specific subject. The many little fears that used to limit me in the world have all but fallen away. When I do feel resistance or discomfort now, I take the time to look at the situation and at my reaction to it. I can use my emotional response to guide me towards rewarding work and experiences and away from useless, limiting or damaging situations. I enjoy starting new projects and solving problems in existing projects and this leads to that wonderful feeling of satisfaction when the job is done and I know it is the best work I can produce. I still hate the idea of public speaking, but I could probably do it without passing out. I just hope I don't have to find out anytime soon.

To write this I went back and read the transcripts from each session. I read my own words as Joe had transcribed them. All my fears and frustrations and hindrances were laid open. I thought about each feeling as I read. I started checking them off. Many I realized were gone, or at least they were a dim memory. I was aware of how different I felt but it took reading my own words to realize how far I had come. The rebuilding is an ongoing process. It is exciting and challenging. Life feels fresher, newer and the possibilities seem more possible and more numerous. I can see the threads of my life up to this point, and I see how I can shape my future at every step along the way.

Back to Joe: Comments

The big work that Olivia did is really just the beginning of her journey. Releasing the old, reactive patterns has freed up the feeling paths of her Deep Self and a couple of Surface Selves. Now, they are able to do the work of supporting her life, guiding her decisions, bringing that experience of wholeness with presence to every day.

Having her Deep Self fully available doesn't mean life suddenly becomes easy. There are big transitions to be made. It's like turning a big cargo ship; she has momentum in a certain direction, has made choices up until now that have created certain real constraints in her life and deprived her of certain important developmental experiences. Now is the time of doing the work to discern and remove those constraints and make her way through those key experiences which will bring her up to date with the capacity for full-on life she now has available on the inside.

Now she is able to seek those experiences and make those new choices as herself, without the distortions created by feeling paths locked into reactive ways of being. Now she is able to make those choices with full access to her inner wisdom, able to feel on the inside the possible consequences of various options and choose the actions and commitments which lead her toward her optimum joy.

Along the way, despite the ups and downs of reconfiguring the externals of her life, despite the not-knowing of being a beginner all over again in certain contexts, despite the vulnerability of a fresh new relationship with her own authenticity, she has available as a foundation this experience of wholeness with presence. In this wholeness with presence, she gets to experience the awesome richness of her inner life and the wondrous variety of influences and relationships available all around her. She gets to make her new choices from a smorgasbord of options and creatively craft her new life as an artist working with a full palette of color.

Gratitude

I've come to the end of this book, and I find myself overwhelmed with gratitude. It's done. All the things that were in the way are now gone, and all the influences that have supported me can now come to fruition.

Thirty-two years ago I was planning to be a scientist and surgeon researching the brain and consciousness. From where I stand today, I don't believe I could have made a more significant contribution had I continued down that road. This work fulfills the spirit of my original quest beyond what I could have imagined. My mission to understand more clearly what makes us who we are is being well-served through the fruition of The Feeling Path. For that I am most grateful.

As I look back over the journey from there to here, many moments seem important, all of them somehow, and with the moments, the people who shared or influenced them. So many moments, so many people swim through my head, I am having difficulty sorting through them just now. But I must write a bit more to finish the manuscript and send it off. I promise in the complete First Edition I will expand this section to give credit to those who have carried me all this way.

For now, thank you to everyone who has travelled even a short while on this journey with me. And a special thank you to those who have travelled a longer distance, especially my family. We've had our troubles, but I have felt your support in recent years and for that I've been grateful. I hope you have felt mine.

Cautions

I have shared perspectives, methods, stories and discoveries in this book which fall outside of conventional standards of expertise. Some of these make strong suggestions about an approach to personal suffering which runs counter to current standards of care in the mental health system. Some of the implications of this book deal specifically with the appropriate role of psychoactive medication in the treatment of suffering.

If you are currently using medication to manage a psychological condition, I advise you to rely on your own wisdom and the input of others you trust in order to determine your best path forward. Many medications in use today can be extremely dangerous if not used properly. Improper use can include the manner of tapering or cessation of use. Never make adjustments to your medications without the guidance and close involvement of a competent medical practitioner.

Not all experiences of emotional suffering are caused by the dynamics outlined in this book. Some have strong influences which are biological and thus fall outside the scope of The Feeling Path to address. Please be sure to avail yourself of appropriate medical advice when seeking assistance for any mental or emotional condition.

One last thing. I have explicitly suggested that you freely engage in Feeling Path Mapping with friends and family. However, there is one common circumstance which should be avoided. Please do not facilitate this work with one another when the issue being addressed involves you both. It may be OK to help your partner work through an issue at his or her job, but if the issue is something arising between the two of you, you will run into problems.

The reason for this is that any issue between two people is held equally by both people. Each partner is holding within themselves a reactive configuration of states which triggers, amplifies, and complements the other. When trying to work on this issue, both people will be trapped in the illusions and reactions of the pattern. In most cases, even the clear structure of the mapping process will not be sufficient protection from falling into the pattern together. In these cases, both of you please find another person outside your relationship to work with. Clear the pattern, then bring your attention back to one another to mend your connection after each of you is clear.

And if just one of you is wanting to do the work to clear the pattern you share, please do it! You don't actually need the other person to do anything, to shift a pattern which might hold you both prisoner at the moment. When you release the pattern within yourself, you will find yourself naturally disengaging from the pattern between you. Your partner may escalate his or her attempts to engage you in the old way, but eventually those efforts will fall to the side.

A Special Request: Join Me

For reasons I've described, I haven't been all that successful in putting this work out there to this point. I'd like to ask for your help in remedying that now.

- Who do you know, who would love to learn about The Feeling Path? Can you introduce them to this book and recommend they read it? Thank you!

- Who do you know, whose mission might be served by this work? Can you introduce us, and recommend they talk with me? Thank you!

- Who do you know, who might want to publish and/or promote the first edition of this book? Can you introduce us, and recommend this opportunity to them? Thank you!

- What group or organization might appreciate a talk on these topics, a training in the techniques, or facilitation to reach the group's biggest goals? Can you hook us up? Thank you!

Really, anything you can do to help me get the word out there, send me clients who would benefit from working with me, hook me up with opportunities and key people, anything at all... I would appreciate it immensely. And please consider offering me the privilege of facilitating your own explorations. I welcome any opportunity to share this work with you directly.

Finally, I would like to invite you to participate with me and others in further exploring these discoveries and how to apply them. We need one another to bring the wisdom of the feeling mind into our collective lives. I am creating a special kind of learning and collaboration community with a home base online but with activities that go beyond simple email or forums. For one thing, we'll be meeting by phone, participating through advanced teleconferencing technology in fully interactive explorations of the work. We will also very likely set up other avenues for engagement, including gathering for workshops and conferences as our community grows. I intend to support members in taking on leadership roles, pursuing the work in directions that serve and excite them personally and professionally.

The home base for this community is at FeelingPath.com, and I intend to grow it organically as people get involved and we discover exactly what we need. Please come join us!

Learn more at FeelingPath.com

Like at Facebook.com/FeelingPath

Follow at Twitter.com/FeelingPath

Made in the USA
Lexington, KY
20 October 2011